Niddrie
OF THE
North-West

Niddrie
OF THE North-West

MEMOIRS
OF A PIONEER
CANADIAN
MISSIONARY

John W. Niddrie

John W. Chalmers and
John J. Chalmers, editors

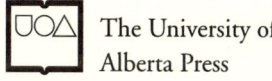
The University of Alberta Press

Published by
The University of Alberta Press
Ring House 2
Edmonton, Alberta T6G 2E1

Copyright © The University of Alberta Press 2000
Printed in Canada 5 4 3 2 1

Canadian Cataloguing in Publication Data

Niddrie, John W., 1863–1940.
    Niddrie of the North-West

    ISBN 0-88864-341-1

    1. Niddrie, John W., 1863-1940. 2. Missionaries—Northwest, Canadian—Biography. 3. Wesleyan Methodist Church—Missions—Northwest, Canadian. 4. Indians of North America—Missions—Northwest, Canadian. I. Chalmers, John W., 1910-1998. II. Chalmers, John J., 1939–
III. Title.
BV2813.N52A3 2000   266'.71712   C00–910649–9

All rights reserved.
No part of this publication may be reproduced, stored in a retrieval system, or transmitted in any form or by any means, electronic, mechanical, photocopying, recording, or otherwise, without the prior permission of the copyright owner.

Book design and layout by Carol Dragich.
Printed and bound by Hignell Book Printing Ltd., Winnipeg, Manitoba.
∞ Printed on acid-free paper.

The University of Alberta Press gratefully acknowledges the support received for its program from the Canada Council for the Arts. The Press also acknowledges the financial support of the Government of Canada through the Book Publishing Industry Development Program for its publishing activities. In addition, the Press acknowledges the contribution of the Alberta Historical Resources Foundation to this project.

FOR MY PARENTS,
JACK AND DOROTHY
CHALMERS
—J.J.C.

—AND—

TO THE MEMORY OF
JOHN W. NIDDRIE
AND
ANNIE NIDDRIE
—J.W.C.

CONTENTS

Preface	ix
Acknowledgements	xiii
Introduction	xv
Chapter 1 Kirk to Chapel, 1863–1885	3
Chapter 2 Immigrant, 1885	15
Chapter 3 Morley, 1889–1910	31
Chapter 4 Delayed Vacation, 1894	39
Chapter 5 Nature Interlude, 1896	49
Chapter 6 Men of Morley, 1890–1910	57
Chapter 7 Oxford House, 1910–1915	67
Chapter 8 Island Lake, 1915–1920	83
Chapter 9 Berens River, 1920–1938	93
Chapter 10 Annie Niddrie: The Caregiver, 1927–1938	107
Chapter 11 The Letters of John W. Niddrie	139
Postscript	213
Notes	215
About the Editors	219

PREFACE

LIKE FELLOW MISSIONARY JOHN MCDOUGALL, JOHN W. NIDDRIE ENTERED the Christian ministry by the back door, so to speak. Most nineteenth-century Wesleyan missionaries began their church careers more or less as jacks-of-all-trades, fetching and carrying at others' bidding, and serving as apprentices while learning their profession. Their education was usually limited to the secondary level, if that. Theological preparation was undertaken not in seminaries but *viva voce* from their sponsors. Many were not ordained until approaching or reaching middle age. Such a man was John W. Niddrie.

John's mother, Jane Kirkley, was probably born some time between 1810 and 1820. She married a man named Armstrong on an unknown date and in 1845 bore him a daughter, Elizabeth. By 1848, Jane must have been a widow, for on 6 July of that year she married William Henry Niddrie. Her groom had been baptized on 15 December 1814 at the High Fell Church in Durham, England.

McDougall Memorial United Church at Morley, set in the Alberta foothills and located next to the Bow River. A commemorative marker is placed next to Highway 1A, which runs past the church.

The Niddries and at least some of their offspring—there were seven young Niddries in addition to Elizabeth Armstrong—sailed to Canada in 1876. Within weeks, Jane's husband died of smallpox; his body is buried in an unmarked grave in Guelph, Ontario. The rest of the family immediately returned to the Old Country. But in May 1885, Jane returned to Canada, settling in Winnipeg with daughter Maria and sons William and John.

William Niddrie emigrated with his wife, *née* Hannah Dunning. By 1890 they had three sons: William, John G., and Fred. Maria soon married a man named Cornelius deWinter, whom she had met en route to Canada. In 1885, Jane's son John W. headed west to help complete the Canadian Pacific Railway, but he soon returned to Winnipeg, where his brother William had purchased a dairy.

In 1889, John W. moved to Morley, NWT (today Morley, Alberta) to join the McDougall Mission. The next year, William and his family followed him to Morley to live as homesteaders. William and Hannah had two daughters born to them at Morley: Annie and Fanny. Jane, now a grandmother, had lived with William and family in Winnipeg; after she moved with them to Morley in 1890, she stayed with John W., except when he was absent for lengthy periods.

John W. Niddrie never married and his memoirs tell us little of his domestic life. He lived with his widowed mother from 1890 until her death in 1895. Thereafter, for some years, he lived virtually as a member of the John McDougall family until 1910, when he left Morley to become a missionary in northern Manitoba.

For a year, two nieces from Winnipeg kept house for him at Oxford House. At Berens River in 1927, he was joined by still another niece, Annie Niddrie, who looked after him until he died in 1940. It is from her accounts that we learn much about Niddrie the man and the circumstances in which he and she lived in Berens River.

It may seem inappropriate that, in a work devoted mainly to the life of a Protestant missionary, an entire chapter is devoted to another family member. Annie Niddrie was John's caregiver who supported him in his work for a dozen years and cared for others at Berens River for another twenty years after his death. Yet while Niddrie's memoirs never once mention her name, Annie's own memoir is included to remedy that omission.

There is still another reason why her memoirs are included. John Niddrie appears to us only as an adult, his personality, character, biases and prejudices fully formed, his hopes and ambitions shaped in childhood and fixed for life, his skills brought to their highest level. But Annie's first-hand records enable us to recreate a familial environment of men, women, and children who worked hard, played occasionally, and loved one another. They always cooperated, quarrelled seldom or never, gave generously where generosity was needed, and remembered their duty to the Lord.

—J.W.C.

ACKNOWLEDGEMENTS

THIS BOOK WOULD NOT EXIST WERE IT NOT FOR THE WORK OF MANY others. First, there would be no manuscript at all if John W. Niddrie and Annie Niddrie had not written their memoirs. For their efforts, all readers can be grateful. Nor would there be a book if my father, John W. Chalmers, had not recognized the value of the Niddrie papers and organized them for publication.

Several other individuals deserve recognition. I am grateful to Harry Everett for permission to include his contribution about Annie Niddrie. Rev. Dr. Stephen Wilk of Calgary, an enthusiastic historian, supported this project from the very beginning. The University of Alberta Press also recognized the value of taking this work to print, as did their peer reviewers. The support of another historian, Rev. Dr. Gerald Hutchinson, and of Dr. Merrill Distad of the University of Alberta were vital to the completion of this project. Dr. Robert MacDonald of the University of Calgary and Dr. Jennifer Brown of the University of Winnipeg also endorsed this work. Thanks are due also to Rev. Sanday Scott of Berens River for his support and for arranging visits with those who knew both John and Annie Niddrie.

There are others too numerous to mention, but you know who you are. The staff of several archive collections assisted in locating and providing material during the research stage. To many relatives, near and distant, some of whom I have yet to meet, I wish to express my gratitude. Your support in providing material for the book and contributions to the Niddrie Memorial Fund have been instrumental in seeing this project through. Welcome financial support for publication was also provided by the Alberta Historical Resources Foundation.

In June 1999, when I thought the project of the Niddrie memoirs was nearly complete, I began to come upon additional material that took me through a search of ten widely scattered archive collections and beyond. The result was an increase in the book by some sixty percent, including all the correspondence, related materials, and most of the photographs. I am particularly grateful to the Glenbow Archives in Calgary, which is the source of all the letters by and to John W. Niddrie that appear in Chapter 11.

—J.J.C.

INTRODUCTION
THE MAN AND THE MANUSCRIPT

THE MAN

ALL PIONEERS WERE VERSATILE—OR, AT LEAST, THE SUCCESSFUL ONES WERE, whether they followed the plough or, as was the case with western Canada's nineteenth-century Wesleyan missionaries, laboured for a spiritual harvest. Perhaps more than their Anglican and Roman Catholic brothers in God, these early Methodist preachers shared a common background with the West's homesteaders. Like them, they usually came from fairly humble homes; like them also, their education, sound as far as it went, was limited. They counted few seminary or university alumni among their number.

Because they did not graduate from normal schools and were often not ordained until well on in their careers, they were generalists rather than specialists. They taught school and they preached sermons. When occasion demanded,

John W. Niddrie, centre with cap and moustache, among natives of Manitoba, likely at Berens River, ca. 1930s.

they turned their hands to farming, carpentering, furniture-making, fishing, medical and veterinary practice, and business administration. And before the term was ever invented, they were social workers. Such a one was Niddrie of the North-West, who crossed the Territories in 1885, returned to them—specifically, to Morley, NWT—four years later, and whose address became Oxford House, NWT in 1910.

John W. Niddrie was born on September 24, 1863, at the wee farm known as Ballachuan, sixteen miles from the Scottish highland village of Oban. His parents were William and Jane Niddrie. John was the last child in a large family of four brothers and three sisters, as well as a half-sister by his mother's first husband.

The interval between the oldest Niddrie, William, and the youngest, John, amounted to twelve years. According to the latter, his home was permeated with the spirit of stern Calvinism. He writes of his father "sitting in the Precentor's seat in the Old Kirk." John's nephew and namesake, John G. Niddrie, however, cites both his father William and his uncle Robert, John W.'s brothers, to illustrate another (and not necessarily contradictory) aspect of the old patriarch's character:

> George was the largest of the Niddrie boys, and was of prodigious strength well before he was twenty. That is why he was always delegated to go to the village inn on Saturday night when the need arose, and carry home his father on his back, inebriated from his associations of the evening with thirsty friends. Uncle John once brushed off grandpa's weakness by remarking that his father was unduly fond of good company. My Uncle Robert once told the same story of grandpa's weakness for liquor.

As a young man, John W. Niddrie must have cut a wide swath among the ladies, both white and Indian, whom he encountered. He was slim, over six feet tall, and his handsome visage was adorned with a most beguiling moustache. Yet he never married and apparently had little interest in women, for he rarely mentions them by name in his memoirs, and then only cursorily.

As a true Methodist, he eschewed liquor and tobacco. However, like many another celibate clergyman, he had one weakness: an inordinate fondness for food. By the time he retired at the age of seventy-five, his waist measured at least sixty inches and he weighed over three hundred pounds. Probably not coincidentally, by this time he was loathe to have his picture taken.

Family tradition has it that when Uncle John was charged one fall with purchasing the community candy for Christmas, he did so. But by December 25 it had disappeared, all thirty pounds of it!

Yet if Niddrie had an insatiable appetite for food, especially sweets, he was also completely unselfish when it came to his Indians, as he called them. Anything he had was theirs for the asking: food, fuel, even the coat off his back. He mentions the fact that two nieces accompanied him north in 1910, returning to Winnipeg the following summer. He does not explain that one reason for their departure was that they had nothing to eat but fish for some months because their uncle had given all the other provisions to his flock.

Niddrie was a man of vastly honourable intentions, but his generosity sometimes got in the way of his integrity. When his niece Annie went to make a home for him in Berens River, he promised her suitable monetary rewards and other perquisites. Instead, she got a bare living and an opportunity of service which continued for years after her uncle's death.

John Niddrie was wholly a product of his times and his environment. Despite his love for the Indian people, he regarded their culture as mere paganism, to be replaced by the white man's civilization. The only elements of their culture which he considered worth saving were those of value in the white man's world: their skills as woodsmen, trappers, voyageurs, and their artifacts such as moccasins, canoes, snowshoes, and log cabins.

An unswerving advocate of British institutions, he demonstrated an attitude towards Louis Riel that seems extreme for one who followed Jesus Christ, the ultimate exponent of love. In many papers not used in this work, he reflected contemporary bias. For example:

> The North-West Rebellion did not originate with the Indians. The arch traitor Louis Riel was the real instigator, with his nefarious plotting and planning, and managed to draw the poor unsuspecting Indian into trouble… He met with his just desserts and ended his life at the end of a rope… We have no use for traitors and dissemblers.

As a true Methodist, Niddrie viewed the Roman Catholic Church with suspicion and hostility. For example, he called one paper (badly fire-damaged and not used in this synthesis) "Are Christians right in rejecting the Roman Catholic doctrine?" Two of his subheadings include "The Absurd Doctrine of the Mass" and "The Idolatrous Eucharist Parade." Nor was his antipathy limited to Roman Catholic doctrine and dogma: he also regarded many of the priests as devious and unscrupulous.

In most respects, his attitude towards the education of Indians was conventional; he believed they should be prepared to enter the white man's world. In one respect he was ahead of his time. After many years as administrator of a residential school, he had grave doubts as to the efficacy of such institutions as compared with day schools. It apparently did not occur to him, however, that Indian children should be educated off the reserve and in public schools.

John Niddrie was a Highlander; he never forgot the hills of home, although he probably saw them for the last time in 1881, and certainly not later than 1885. Perhaps he loved the Alberta foothills so much because they reminded him of the Scotland where he was born and raised. At the same time, he was completely Canadian. His vocabulary and idiom were wholly indigenous to his adopted country. Fall, not autumn, followed summer; a stand of poplars was a bluff, not a grove. Any watercourse smaller than a river was usually not a stream, but a creek.

Indeed, he was no mean linguist. Although his mother tongue was Gaelic, he mastered English early, and when he lived at Morley, he became adequately fluent in the Assiniboine language of the Stoney Indians. At the age of forty-seven, he began the study of Cree, and in a surprisingly short time he was preaching as well as conversing in that tongue; he also mastered the syllabics by which Rev. James Evans had reduced it to written form.

How good a preacher was Uncle John? He never mentions having delivered an unsatisfactory sermon; as a true Scot he had no bad opinion of himself and perhaps he was as good as he believed himself to be. Family opinion would seem to concur with this assessment. Nephew John G. Niddrie wrote of one service which Uncle John conducted:

> On a certain Sunday afternoon in early fall of the mid or late 1890s, Uncle John was out in the district about ten miles south of our place preaching in a little log school house. He subject was the story of The Prodigal Son. The church was packed; and on the old

log stove in the middle of the floor sat Ed Hainstock, a man who was to work for us the following summer. As Uncle John proceeded with his subject, a favourite of his, Ed sat there on the stove, a sensitive and tender hearted man as he was, and cried throughout most of the service, and kept mopping up the tears with his old-fashioned red cowboy handkerchief. Uncle John must have been a wonderful preacher.

THE MANUSCRIPT

Between his retirement and his death, John W. Niddrie wrote the memoirs and articles from which this work is derived. In no sense did he attempt to write an autobiography. Frequently he prepared two accounts of the same events, each containing incidents omitted from the other. One document may telescope the passage of several years into a few pages; another expands into many a sequence of events scarcely mentioned or entirely omitted in the first.

He left numerous stories of his work during the decade spent at Oxford House and Island Lake, but few accounts of his professional life before or after that period. From his papers we gain a vivid impression of his activities as a preacher, but he gives us little information about his duties as an educator, despite his many years in teaching and educational administration.

John Niddrie was born a Victorian, educated a Victorian and wrote as a Victorian. His memoirs are replete with long, convoluted sentences, digressions consisting of moralizings and other editorial comment directed at his "dear readers," as well as clichés, ornate and pretentious figures of speech, verbosity, and the editorial "we."

In addition, he had his own idiosyncrasies. He was never addressed; he was always "accosted." His ultimate accolade was "splendid." Nothing ever happened before something else; it occurred "ere" the next event. People weren't busy in the mornings; invariably they were "astir." He lived "amongst" the Indians, never among them.

John W. Niddrie, studio portrait by W.E. Wing Studio, Calgary, ca. 1905.

His titles for the different documents recall the best efforts of nineteenth-century explorers and other travellers, such as "Lakes, Rivers, Rapids, and Portages" or "A Canoe Trip Amongst the Dusky Sons of the Forest in the Land of the North Wind." Another selection was headed "Under the Light of Western Stars," yet another "Around the Camp Fire in Foothills of the Rocky Mountains."

Sentence fragments, usually participial or gerundial phrases, abound in his work. His favourite position for adverbial modifiers, especially if they are long phrases or clauses, is between the auxiliary verb and the completing participle. Verbs do not always agree with their subjects, nor pronouns with their antecedents, nor did the writer believe that one should not change tenses in mid-sentence.

His punctuation is chaotic. His capitalization is almost equally so, although in some ways it is curiously consistent. For example, he always spells "Indian" and "Christian" with lower-case initial letters. Occasionally his spelling is highly personal. Legibility of the documents is low because the typing is all single-spaced with minimal margins and all of the material has suffered damage, occasionally extensive, from fire.

To produce a readable document, I have had to exercise considerable freedom of judgement. I have made an effort to arrange the narrative elements of the Niddrie papers into a sequential chronicle of his life from his birth to his retirement. To do so has meant extensive reorganization of the material, with pages from one document being preceded, followed and interspersed by paragraphs, and even sentences, from another.

Digressions have frequently been deleted, repetitions excised, sentence fragments incorporated or made into complete sentences, and other sentences restructured in the interest of clarity and readability. Yet, since the style is the man, such changes have been made in moderation; essentially the chapters that follow are in the words of the author and not the editor. I hope that although the voice is that of Jacob, the hands are not those of Esau.

But the result cannot be considered an autobiography: the final product is too fragmentary, too incomplete. Just the same, I hope it is a portrait, albeit partial, of John W. Niddrie—his interests and aspirations, his beliefs and prejudices, his lifestyle. It is also perhaps a picture of a type of man exemplified by James Evans, George and John McDougall, Robert Rundle, and many others: the Wesleyan missionary of an earlier age, who devoted his life to the spread of Christianity among the Indians of western Canada.

—J.W.C.

Niddrie
OF THE
North-West

CHAPTER I
KIRK TO CHAPEL, 1863–1885

Our paternal home was away across the blue waters of the Atlantic, amongst the heather hills of the Highlands of Scotland. Sixteen miles from the little tourist town of Oban, at a small farm locally known as Ballachuan, I first saw the light, on September 24, 1863. Very vivid are the memories of early youth; for example, our father sitting in the Precentor's seat in the Old Kirk, "lifting the tunes," and leading the psalmody, for it was considered at that time sacrilegious to use an organ or other instrument of music in the kirk, and it was denominated "a kist of whustles." In the days of which I write, men and women were not afraid of cracking their faces, but threw back their heads, opened their mouths, and sang from their hearts. The warning of the prophet Amos was not needed in their case—Woe unto them that are at ease in Zion—for they were both alive and awake to all the possibilities God gave them, both of doing and getting good. Very seldom indeed were they absent from Divine Service, even if some of them had to walk six or seven miles and change their socks, because of wet feet, before the service began. After supper on the Lord's Day evening, "the books were taken" and for an hour or more the family in a half circle stood up to read verse about consecutively, our father seated at the head of the table directing the reading. In those old days and even amongst the poor people of Scotland, all were grounded in the Scriptures.

Jane Niddrie, centre, with son William, right, and his wife Hannah, left, who came to Canada with John W. Niddrie and Jane's daughter, Maria, settling in Winnipeg. William and Hannah's three sons left to right, Fred, John and William, were born in Winnipeg. This photo was taken in 1890, the year Fred was born. Studio portrait, Steele & Wing's, Winnipeg.

When I try to describe my mother, I find it difficult to find adjectives and terms to express sufficiently my appreciation of her noble, generous, saintly womanhood. Dear are the memories of our angel mother bending over and teaching us that greatest of all prayers, the prayer lisped by so many childish lips: "Now I lay me down to sleep." I shall never forget those early memories. The tucking away in bed, the goodnight kiss when the great something we call a mother's love reached out and with its fingers clasped the youthful beating heart in an embrace so strong and secure that through all the following years it has never been rent asunder. The influence of a good mother follows man from the cradle to the grave and is a great factor in the formation of character.

Long ago that quiet living voice has been hushed amid the silence of the grave, and the gentle Holy Spirit called away to the Father's Home of Many Mansions. Our mother left us on a beautiful spring Sabbath afternoon in the Far West on May 19, 1895. We laid her body away to rest on the sunny slope of the hillside, where the sun shines and the birds sing in the nearby trees, with the grass and wild flowers and forget-me-nots playing hide-and-seek over her last resting place. The giant mountain pine trees stand sentinel over her rest.

William Henry Niddrie, father of John W. Niddrie, came to Canada with his wife, Jane, and children in 1876, but died of smallpox shortly afterwards. Jane returned to Scotland with their children but later came back to Canada with John W. and some family. Other children remained behind in Scotland and England.

These are backed in turn by a range of imperial mountains with their peaks towering heavenwards and their feet thrusting into the pines.

The first seven years of my life might be said to have been spent in the bounds of the family circle, my brothers and sisters being my only playfellows. When I had almost reached my seventh year, our parents decided to leave the old home and move to the Island of Mull. Why today linger over the breaking up of the dear home ties which caused us so much grief, children as two of us were? Why linger over the long journey of sixteen miles to the town of Oban, to catch the sailing of the old *S.S. Clansman* to transport us to the Island of Mull?

Mull is the third largest island lying off the west coast of Scotland. It has a sinuous coastline of approximately three hundred miles, and including Iona, Gometra and Ulva, extends to three hundred and fifty-one square miles. Its

Maria (Niddrie) deWinter, sister of John Niddrie, who came with her brothers and mother to Canada in 1885.

greatest length is thirty miles; its breadth, twenty-nine miles. The islands of Iona and Mull, divided by a narrow channel, three-quarters of a mile in width, are the two most historical islands on the west coast of Scotland. Here nature has been lavish in her charms, as witness the beautiful heathery hills and the glens with the rugged coastline upon which, near our home, broke the blue waves of Loch-na-kiel.

At that time, Gaelic was the language of the people; very little English was used. I still retain a great love for the language of my youth, but, ah me! I fear I have sadly deteriorated along this line.

I spent six happy years on the Island of Mull, formed many endearing friendships that have remained through all the years, the memories of which have often been green spots in my life. There is something that binds the Highlander to his native heath. Distance may intervene and years may roll by, but the memories of youth do not become obliterated. The days on the farm, the school days, the holidays in turn succeeded each other, fraught with the joys and pleasures of boyhood. There was so much beauty in the immediate physical features of my environment that it seemed to call out the best in my boyish heart, and time thus seemed to fly with speedy wings.

It was some time in the early days of the month of May 1876 that we again boarded the old *S.S. Clansman*, southward bound to the city of Glasgow. In due time we reached this metropolitan city, which seemed like a beehive of human industry. Here we remained a few days, then boarded the *S.S. Phoenician*, Allan Line. Our tickets read, "Quebec, Canada." Those were not the days of influx in immigration, and the passenger list was somewhat slim. With fifteen days from the point of sailing to Quebec, steam navigation had not at that date reached its present status of expediency. However, we met with every courtesy and kindness and, strange as it may seem, felt a little sad when the time came for us to leave the ship. Landing at Lévis, opposite Quebec, we remained the greater part of the day. We then boarded the Grand Trunk Railway for Guelph.

Proceeding inland, we reached Guelph, in Wellington County, having made one break in the rail journey at the now-great city of Toronto. This city at that date was a modest enough one, as it had not then reached its present-day proportions. Guelph was at that time a beautiful and prosperous farming district, and it was with this object in view our father had turned in this direction.

But although man proposes, God disposes. It may have been a week or ten days after our arrival that our father was stricken down with a complication of smallpox and heart disease. The former was no doubt contracted on board the steamer on the way across the ocean, as sanitary measures were not then actively enforced. Why today linger on this sad event which was such a heavy blow to our mother? Two weeks later, one of my brothers was taken to the hospital with a severe attack of smallpox. There he remained six or eight weeks between life and death, and all this time nursed by our faithful mother, in her anxiety for her son's recovery, almost made the supreme sacrifice of her own life. Later—it must have been on doctor's orders—and on account of the critical state of her health, we made preparations to return to the Old Land. Again we were whirled off to Quebec. This must have been early in the month of September. Upon reaching the seaboard, we found the *S.S. Canadian* (Allan Line) just about ready to sail, and lost no time in securing passages in same to Glasgow, Scotland.

We had been out but six or seven days when we encountered a tremendous gale, perhaps an equinoctial gale. For two or more days we were almost helpless, now riding the waves and again in the trough of the sea. The grave conduct of Captain Neil McLean and his officers convinced us that matters were quite serious. However, after vicissitudes of various characters (one being stuck on a submerged rock on the coast of Ireland), we reached the port of Glasgow by a Belfast boat, and were glad to be once more on *terra firma*. Here we met a brother who had remained in the Highlands, and after a day or two we steamed northward to the town of Oban.

Here again came my opportunity for further education, for I was enrolled as a pupil in St. John's Academy. Under the influence of a first-class Christian gentleman, the Principal, I got a grasp and a grip of things. For the next three years I remained in Scotland, part of the time in Tobermory, Mull. Tobermory was then merely a fishing village, and seat of the judicial court for the Island of Mull, with a population of perhaps twelve hundred souls. The beautiful sheltered harbour held great facilities and inducements to yachting parties. During the summer months there was a dual daily passenger steamboat service, with a freight service twice a week. Here I spent nearly two years in the employment of Mr. John Fletcher, general merchant, a man of indefatigable energy and unquestionable honour.

I later followed my family, who in the meantime had gone south to England. From the rugged, beautiful hills of the Highlands of Scotland to the low-lying park-like country of Cheshire, England, together with its language, habits, etc. was a great change for me, and at first I longed for a glimpse of the hills and heather. I remained in Cheshire about seven years and formed many friendships.

It was here and just after passing my eighteenth birthday that I was converted to God and began a new life in Christ Jesus. I was at once put to work as a Sunday School teacher. Many good Christian men were associated with the Wesleyan Methodist Church at Davenham, Cheshire, and I certainly enjoyed their fellowship. One notable feature—and it is to be commended—of those days and those Christian movements was that just as soon as a man was soundly converted to God, not the church, he was at once put into some kind of Christian work: teaching in the Sunday School, conducting prayer services, or, if he showed any talent, he was sent forth as an Exhorter. This is one of the greatest blessings to a young convert: to keep him employed in good, healthy Christian work. Such action was fostered and promoted by those good old Methodists.

Soon, or to be more explicit, some eight or nine months after surrendering my life to God, I was importuned by a good Christian brother, long gone to the Home of Many Mansions, to go out to conduct a public service. The appointment called for two services. There were two of us young men who fraternized those days who undertook this mission. Very well indeed do I remember that Lord's Day afternoon as we wended our way across the fields by the old country style road or foot-path. Ever and anon we halted in some quiet spot and supplicated the throne of grace for the help we so much stood in need of.

Finally we reached the little brick church. My good friend decided in favour of the afternoon service, leaving me to hold forth in the evening. The first service opened well. The singing was hearty, the prayer was earnest, and the congregation fell into an earnest attitude. Next, my friend announced his text, which was, "Yet forty days and Ninevah shall be overthrown." He proceeded famously for about ten minutes, and then came to a dead stop. Those were very anxious moments for me, as I had but one sermon and expected to deliver it that evening. However, after a halt of about ten or fifteen seconds, he managed to secure the threads of his points and went on to finish in splendid style.

The good people kindly invited us to tea. My friend accepted, but I asked to be excused as I wished to spend as much time as possible alone with God. Retracing my way across the fields, I sought a quiet spot where my meditations and prayers would be undisturbed. The time seemed incredibly short until I had to appear in the pulpit, and passed with a bound. At 6:30 P.M. the little church was crowded, quite beyond reasonable capacity. In some way, news had got abroad that two boys were preaching that day in the Wesleyan Church at Wharton Works, and the people who had missed the afternoon service looked upon the evening service as something sensational, or rather as an innovation. I gave out the opening hymn:

> When gathering clouds around I view,
> And friends are few, etc.

Even the slightest move was watched by the waiting congregation. However, all went forward decently and in order. After prayer and the singing of another hymn, I gave out the text: "What must I do to be saved: Believe in the Lord Jesus Christ and thou shalt be saved and thine house." As a literary production, that sermon was not much, but the spirit of God took hold of the people. Personally, I seemed to lose sight of the congregation. My eyes were focussed on the crucified Christ, and so remained to the end.

As was customary those days, I announced a prayer meeting following the service, at the same time inviting any who might feel dissatisfied with their state of mind to remain, and we would try to assist them in any way possible. One young man, a dear friend, that night surrendered his life to Christ, and through all the years has remained faithful to that decision. I left the church that night with a greater and deeper joy singing in my heart, for I had found the work God had for me, and henceforth my duty was plain before me.

I might write much of good friends among the young men of that day. I can never forget an experience I had about three weeks after I first surrendered my life to God, about six months before the service alluded to above. It was the custom of two or three of us boys to meet every night during the winter evenings and, seeking some quiet secluded spot, to hold an informal prayer meeting amongst ourselves. On this evening in question we had as usual met for this purpose. It was a dark, cloudy evening, threatening rain. We knelt under the spreading branches of a big elm tree. My friend led off at once in prayer, and I followed. It was while earnestly seeking for a clearer assurance of our acceptance as a child of God that the heavens seemed to open. The glory was revealed, and a double assurance given us of the New Birth.

> The opening heavens around me shine
> With beams of sacred bliss
> When Jesus shows His mercy mine,
> And whispers I am His.

Much might be written of the following four or nearly so years on the Northwich Circuit. This was a county, one with but three small towns of about ten or twelve thousand inhabitants each, and a number of substantial villages. Our circuit consisted of twenty-eight teaching appointments supplied by a staff of four ordained ministers and about seventy-two local preachers. Many of the latter were young men, some of them wonderfully gifted as public speakers. The tide of spiritual life was high. Those were the days of the old-fashioned Methodists revivals, and few evenings passed without men and women surrendering themselves to Christ, thus swelling the numbers of the Church Militant.

We were allowed one year of preparatory work. At the close of this year we had to preach a trial sermon, appear for our examinations, and qualify for what was known as "Accredited Preachers." I did not find the former of these difficult, but the latter was exceedingly stiff. I laboured hard that year: Field's *Theology, Methodist Catechism No. 6,* William's *Theology,* the first fifty-two of Wesley's sermons: their trend and main divisions, and a number of other books. My academic standing wonderfully assisted me. Possessed of a fairly good memory and by persistent application to my studies, when the year passed and I appeared for my examination, the Committee decided that I had passed with honours. Not so my friend, for he had not taken the work seriously enough and had to be held over for a second trial, which proved successful. Our Chairman and Superintendent of the Examining Committee was a splendid Christian gentleman who believed in making young men qualify and was very strict.

Had our quarterly appointments been equally divided, there would not have been more than three or four Sundays in each quarter in which we would have been engaged. However, more than half of the elder preachers never did much in conducting public services. The fewest appointments I had was ten out of the thirteen Sundays. That was my first quarter, and later I was fully employed every Sunday, sometimes with three services on the one Lord's Day, and perhaps a Sunday School address sandwiched in between. What we lacked in quality we supplied in quantity. One might wear out on that circuit, but rust out? Never.

One Saturday evening I was busy in the garden, for I was still blessed with a mother's kindness and care. Someone—I fail to remember who—approached and handed me a note. I at once recognized our Superintendent's handwriting and, hastily tearing it open, read:

Dear Brother Niddrie:

Please go to Holmes Chapel tomorrow morning, as I see you are free, and Brother Mason is sick and cannot go. You could take the morning service at that point, then walk across country to Bradshaw Brook for your afternoon and evening service.

F. Haines,
Superintendent

I might state here that I had but for a short time been preaching, and had never visited Holmes Chapel. Also, the appointed preacher designated as "Brother Mason," who had taken sick, was one of the best local preachers we had, and also an aged man. I at once felt the disparity between his ability and what must be my humble effort. Amongst all of the seventy-two local preachers, mostly young men, no one could efficiently stand in Brother Mason's shoes at a Sunday service.

However, my newly made vows were still upon me, and refusal, I felt, was an utter impossibility. Early the following morning I was astir. It was one of those beautiful spring mornings. The distance was about eight miles. The roads were, as all English ones are, in good condition. I felt little inconvenience regarding the distance; indeed, I was too busy in thinking my sermon over as I walked along to heed much else. Finally reaching Crannage Bank, I approached the church. The hour was yet early. The caretaker had been at his work and finished and had no doubt gone home to breakfast.

Entering, I noticed what I conjectured were the choir seats, although an organ or any other musical instrument was conspicuous by its absence. Leaving on the corner of the choir seat a small square of paper on which I had written the numbers of the hymns to be used, I mounted the steps to the high old-fashioned pulpit. Kneeling down, I poured out my heart to God in prayer for assistance. Rising from my knees, I next took a survey of the interior of the building. I found all along one side there ran a high box gallery, upon the face of which, and just opposite the pulpit, was an old-fashioned eight-day clock, ticking away the time all too quickly for me and bringing the hour of service nearer every moment.

Seating myself, I kept concealed as much as possible from the now-gathering congregation. I waited in anxiety and fear. All went well until the body of the church filled up, and the people began to gather in the gallery. I could not manage to conceal myself from these, who cast wondering glances at me. Watching the clock narrowly, I remained seated until five minutes after time. Not daring to dally any longer, I stood up. The people in the body of the church seemed to receive a shock, or as one good old Christian man afterwards declared, "Instead of the hoary head of old Tommy Mason, that poor boy stood up."

Perhaps that was one of the most eventful and far-reaching services I ever conducted, for surely the presence of The Lord was with us. Instead of an organ they had a well-trained orchestra, consisting of a bass viol, a violin, a clarinet and a flute. Two young ladies who knew how to sing accompanied them, while a boy of about fifteen sang alto splendidly. Before we finished the first hymn, all of my fears were gone, and from that time on to the close of the service I was at my best. Never shall I forget that Sunday morning and never again do I expect to hear such music until I reach the Holy City and join in singing the New Song. There was a crowded and very expectant congregation, as they had expected Brother Mason. However, everything passed off splendidly.

Two weeks later, I passed through that town on my way to a village farther on, about four miles distant, to conduct two services. Upon this occasion I dropped the preacher for the Holmes Chapel at a certain point, promising to call for him at 9:00 P.M. on our way back. I might right here state that the rule of the Society was when two or more preachers went in any one direction to conduct services, a conveyance was allowed and paid by monthly subscriptions. The man going to the farthest point retained control of the conveyance and picked up his colleagues at each lane end. Returning that evening and reaching the designated house, I hailed the house.

An old gray-headed, gray-bearded man, leaning heavily upon his staff came out in answer to my hail. He assured me that Brother H. would be with me in a few minutes and accosted me thus. "Is this the young man who preached to us here two weeks ago at the morning service about the death of Aaron?" I had to reply in the affirmative. "Oh, then," said the old gentleman, "I wish to shake your hand." Taking my hand in both of his, he called down upon me and my work the blessings of heaven right there on the road. The whole scene is before me today: the dark night, the buggy lamps, the old man with his gray hair waving in the night wind, and his earnest, unaffected gaze upon me. Many years ago this aged pilgrim heard the voice of Our Father calling him, and crossed the great frontier into the beyond, and is now before the throne of God, but his influence still abides and will continue beyond the eternal stars.

Many of the young men who were contemporaries were gifted speakers and real biblical students. Any man with any high flown unorthodox opinions was soon relegated to his proper status or thrown out. It was Christ and the Bible, or nothing. Amongst the young men, some were recommended and later accepted into the ministry after qualifying. As a Local Preacher, we were allowed one year "on trial," after which a trial sermon was required, to be reported on later by the Superintendent and other ministerial brethren. Then at the following Quarterly Meeting, an oral examination followed. This examination was not lacking in the elements of close questioning and one had to have all kinds of biblical proofs at his finger ends. It lasted one hour and a half, and after the examiners were done, any one of the thirty preachers was allowed questions regarding the first fifty-two of Wesley's sermons. Four years and three months preaching and travelling amongst these people of God cemented many bonds of Christian brotherhood and filled our time to capacity. Each quarter soon passed. The fact of having twenty-eight places on the Preachers' Plan in the circuit, and to be attended to by mostly young men with three ordained ministers was quite novel. We were being constantly moved about from place to place and appeared as new faces in the different pulpits. We seemed to have more than our share of the work, for which we today bless God. We shall never forget the happiness of life and joy of heart we experienced as we went from place to place.

The years seemed to pass away all too swiftly and carry me with them. When one is engaged in congenial labour—labour for the Lord—time never hangs heavily on his hands. The paths of duty and privilege of today are the markings of new paths for the morrow. There is no standstill on the journey of life.

CHAPTER 2
IMMIGRANT, 1885

O<small>N APRIL 15, 1885, AT HARTFORD AND GREENBANK STATION EN ROUTE FOR</small> Lima Street Station, Liverpool, with a lump in our throats and a pain in our hearts, we grasped the hands of those we had so learned to love. Reaching Liverpool, we remained one night with a sister. On the following day, April 16, we boarded the good ship *Sarmation* at Alexander Dock: mother, sister and myself. Our tickets this time read, "Winnipeg, Manitoba, via Québec." Those were the days of rush of emigration and the *Sarmation* was crowded even beyond capacity. Many people were leaving their native land and emigrating to find homes under western skies. Five hundred passengers all told would be a close estimate upon this occasion. In any case, two hundred and four of us slept in hammocks in one room. Many of these were "assisted" and "steerage" passengers, with about one hundred of German extraction.

Next afternoon we anchored off Moville in the north of Ireland. Here the tender brought out a number of passengers, fine looking fellows. These north-of-Ireland men were both respectable and thrifty, and would soon assimilate in a new country and become excellent citizens.

Finally, the ringing of the last bell warned us all that time was up, the anchor was weighed, and we were underway. Long I remained on deck that night, watching the fast-receding shore of the Old Land. Finally, taking a last look at what had become like a dark cloud, I went below. Here I found many of our Irish emigrants in tears, because of the severing of home ties. How shall

I describe that first night on board? Some whistling, some singing, some talking, and many others in a sorrowful mood. The weather during the first two or three days was beautifully fine, thus giving me an opportunity to get acquainted with a number of my fellow passengers, amongst whom were many young men of genial spirit and sterling quality. Three days out, our ship began to rock and pitch, and for some days subsequent we were "of all men most miserable." Here at this time I noted that, notwithstanding the boasting of many during the first two days as to their seaworthiness, they now became just as fallible as the rest of us, that is, when the testing time came. On account of the large passenger list we were very much crowded in our hammocks.

It was during this time that an infant belonging to a German family died and was committed to the deep. Being unable to go on deck, I did not witness the funeral, but was later informed by one who witnessed it that the poor frantic mother had to be restrained from jumping overboard when the body was lowered down the ship's side. Our voyage upon this occasion was not a rough one, although we tossed and rocked about some on account of a high side wind. After the siege of seasickness had worn off, I enjoyed the remainder of the voyage very much, although as we proceeded onward, on the upper deck one was always more comfortable under an overcoat.

The temperature became much colder as we progressed, this no doubt on account of so much floating ice. On account of these conditions, the captain became doubtful of effecting a landing at Québec. Consequently, changing our course, we landed at Halifax. It was on the eleventh day out that we steamed into this beautiful, historic harbour. Here for a time, after we landed, confusion reigned extreme as each one—and it really seemed all at once—ran around jostling each other in his efforts to secure his baggage and have it passed by the Customs Inspector. Remembering that the list of passengers totalled about five hundred, one can perhaps readily conceive of the task devolving on each individual in his earnest attempts to secure his own. Having succeeded in this, then it was on to the office of the steamship company and offices of the Intercolonial Railway to secure tickets for the overland journey westward.

Leaving Halifax about 1:00 A.M., the journey was begun. Later, as the daylight came upon us, we were able to behold the beautiful scenery through which we passed. We were a jovial company and had by this time become well acquainted, an ocean voyage being eminently conducive to this. Reaching Québec, we were met by an Allan Line agent, who informed us that the railroad around the head of Lake Superior was not completed and that the lakes were not yet open for navigation on account of the backwardness of the season. Therefore he proceeded to issue us transfers by way of Windsor, Detroit, Chicago, St. Paul and Minneapolis. This made a seven-day journey overland by train, but I want in all honesty to the Allan Line Company to state that they did their utmost to land us at our destination free of additional cost to us.

Main Street, Winnipeg, south from William, ca. 1885. When the Niddries arrived at Winnipeg in 1885, it was already a busy and impressive city. Within five years, the Niddries would move to Morley, on the prairies near the foothills, merely a frontier dot on the map compared to the metropolis of Winnipeg.

There were some magnificent stone block buildings in Detroit, also at St. Paul. At this latter city I received rather a shock because of the lack of Sabbath Day observances. I certainly would never have thought it the seventh day from outward appearances, as building, business, etc. were going on with great vigour. Here our train lay over from 8:00 A.M. till 7:00 P.M. We were thankful for the rest, for a seven-day train journey becomes both tiresome and monotonous. Leaving St. Paul on Sunday evening, we reached Winnipeg on Monday evening, May 4TH, at six o'clock, and for the time being our travelling was at an end. Well do I remember the snow storm that visited the City of Winnipeg on May 7 of that year. We concluded that surely we had reached the land of snow and ice.

Winnipeg in 1885 was quite insignificant compared to its present-day extensive proportions. The population may have been about twenty-two thousand. The city was then suffering from the financial stagnancy consequent upon the spasmodic building boom of 1883. That year of our arrival was also the year of the Riel Rebellion in the North-West, and much anxiety was felt as to the outcome of the same. The course of events was closely followed every day and commented upon. While the toll of human life at the Rebellion was not heavy, it caused a great deal of unrest. I have in subsequent years often felt grieved to hear the Indians blamed—and unjustly, too—for this trouble, but the rebellion did not originate with them.

It is really sad to think that the poor Indians became the dupes of unprincipled half-breeds and were even against their own will (some of them) led into this trouble. One can only regret that justice did not overtake the guilty ones years prior, at the time of the first Red River Rebellion, when the loyal Scott was so foully done to death by a capricious tyrant, for he was ruthlessly butchered. The arch-rebel traitor Louis Riel was the real instigator; with his nefarious plotting and planning he managed to draw the poor unsuspecting Indian into the trouble, thus fanning the smoldering fire into a great blaze. He met with his just deserts and ended his life at the end of a rope in the Mounted Police barracks in Regina in the late fall of 1885.

I was much impressed with many of the features of the new country to which we had come, such as the long unbroken stretches of prairie, sparsely settled, all around us, offering inducements to the incoming settler, and the daily arrival and departure of fresh immigrants. The streets in and around the city were not at that time in their present-day efficient condition. Main Street was block-paved from the C.P.R. station south to the City Hall. Farther south, virgin mud prevailed. The old horse streetcars pounded along Main Street, up Portage Avenue, and down Kennedy Street. The flashy eastern buggy and the old Red River cart stood side by side.

The city was then in the throes of a serious stagnancy. This was consequent upon two factors. First, it was suffering from the results of a spasmodic building boom of 1883, which had been out of all proportion of sense and reason. Secondly, matters in the Far West connected with the North-West or Riel Rebellion and its possible outcome caused men of capital to move very cautiously. During my first eight weeks in this country it seemed impossible to secure one day's work. As one old-timer declared, "You could not get a job for love or money." In vain I endeavoured to secure employment. One day, walking along Main Street, I passed the office of the C.H. Wallow Company, ticket agents on Main Street at that time. Noticing an advertisement in the window to the effect that, "Men are wanted for the Railroad Camps Construction Department in the Rocky Mountains," I entered to make enquiries.

"Can you work?" I was interrogated.

"Oh, a little," was my reply.

"Well, then," answered the man at the desk, "if you pay us three dollars, we shall issue you a pass to the mountains to those camps in need of men."

"Which would be all right so far as you are concerned," I replied, "but how am I to get back to Winnipeg in the late fall or early winter?"

"Oh, do not allow that to give you any anxiety, for you will be granted a free pass back when the work closes in the late fall."

Securing the said pass and having importuned a young man then staying at our home (a man who had crossed the Atlantic with us) to accompany me, I gained his consent. Behold us then on the morning of July 6 on board the west-bound train at the then-insignificant station at Winnipeg. There may have been eighty men on said train travelling to the same destination, and with the same object in view.

The journey across the prairie was to us, fresh from the mother country, an eye-opener. Limitless stretches, it seemed to us, awaited incoming settlers, homes for tens of thousands yet to come, hundreds of acres of land with immense possibilities on every hand. How widely different from the Old Country with its crowded over-plus of inhabitants, struggling and pushing to gain a livelihood in the country which we had left! Portage La Prairie, Brandon, Moose Jaw, Broadview, Qu'Appelle, Medicine Hat, so the little towns and sidings ran, but after Brandon the homes of the settlers were few and far between. The trend of oncoming settlement had not as yet turned this way.

At Swift Current, Saskatchewan, I came for the first time in contact with a number of painted, feathered, and blanketed Indians. They boarded the train, endeavouring to sell bead work, moccasins, polished buffalo horns, etc. Notwithstanding the terrible stories told us on the train regarding their inhumanity, I must say they seemed peaceful enough, although a few weeks prior, rebellion and bloodshed had been going on not far to the northward. The Rebellion was now almost over, as a short time before Big Bear had surrendered to the Mounted Police. But the western country was still in a state of unrest, consequent upon the warlike Red Men.

We reached Calgary about two o'clock in the afternoon of Wednesday, July 8. It was at this time denominated in the parlance of the country, a "cow town." There may have been between five and six hundred inhabitants, but at that time a floating population, as many of those were freighters and teamsters. Calgary, as it appeared to me at that time, was beautifully situated on the banks and at the confluence of the Bow and Elbow Rivers. As one had written, it was slumbering in metropolitan dreams and ambitious aspirations of the future, which have surely eventuated, for today it has become a great business centre of commercial enterprise and may be truly be styled "The City of the Hills."

Calgary, at the time of which we write, was in its embryonic state. Everything connected with this frontier village was in a pioneer and primitive condition. Police barracks, three or four trading stores, one or two saloons, with the complement of a few gambling dens, a few shanty-roofed dwellings, and you have it all.

Those were the days of the prospector, miner and cowboy regime. Much of the land where the city of Calgary now stands was unoccupied. Along the river banks, among the willow scrub might be found a few mud-roofed shacks, the dwelling of some of the more adventurous of the "squaw men" and their families.

Then latterly, ere reaching the immediate environs of this western town, we had found the face of nature changed and had got amongst the rolling hills, which, however, had not yet gained any high altitude, but which seemed, as we progressed westward, to become more rugged. Very soon we entered the glorious foothills, and the face of nature presented a new and more fascinating appearance. These glorious foothills of the Rockies: how shall I describe them? Even if it is claimed that hills and valleys appeal to the Highlander, I am fully convinced that I can never do justice to the hills and valleys we now rushed through as the iron horse plunged forward. Steadily climbing we turned the bend at Radnor, and for the first time the giant form of the Rockies at close range burst upon my vision. Away to the westward about twenty miles I beheld the snow-clad peaks towering heavenward.

Soon after we had left Calgary we began to climb the steep grade between us and the Rockies. The rolling rounded hills through which we had been passing for nearly one hundred miles now began to merge into more precipitous hills, which in turn gave way to timber-crowned ridges, ever growing higher and higher as we proceeded westward. Almost exactly nine hundred miles west of Winnipeg, we reached the historic spot known today as Morley, lying among the foothills, and at an altitude of 4,078 feet, on the direct route of the Canadian Pacific Railway on its way to the western terminus.

Prior to the 1870s, very little was known of this beauty spot. True, it was frequently visited by nomadic bands of Indians who named it *Mun-u-chaban*, signifying the place from which wood is taken for the manufacture of bows and arrows, which at that time were extensively used in tribal war and in buffalo hunting. The Douglas fir tree supplied the wood for bows as it was tough and fibrous, while the saskatoon bushes supplied the wood for the best arrows.

It must be remembered that a hundred years ago, the whole of this western country was in the throes of tribal war, and conditions were distinctly different from those of the present day. The Red Men were constantly in quest of scalps and often those beautiful hills and valleys echoed the revolting war whoop.

During the months of June and July, the foothills are seen at their best. The beautiful rounded grassy hills in many places variegated with the western wild rose bush gives the hilltops and sides a beauty all their own. As one would ride along on horseback, the chief mode of travel, the aroma would strike the face, inflate the lungs, and create an atmosphere difficult to describe to those who have not enjoyed a like experience.

The first Methodist mission premises at Morley were away up in the foothills north of the Bow River. At that time it was unsafe to move out in the open on account of the warlike condition of the Blackfoot Indians who were constantly prowling about in search of scalps. Here in the fringe of time the work was begun and progressed most favourably for about two years. Later, after the advent of the North West Mounted Police, and also other favourable conditions, the church and mission house were moved to the banks of the Bow River, and near the creek which now forms the boundary between the north end of the Stoney Reserve and the white settlement.

Here the great work was carried on. Still later, after the incoming of white settlement, two services were held each Sabbath day, one for Indian people and one for the white settlers, who in the meantime had come in. The old McDougall church still stands today, a mute witness to the great and good work of the bygone days. To us, the building is sacred as we think of the many Indian people who worshipped within its walls and are now gone on and have crossed the great frontier.

Climbing, climbing, climbing, we reached Canmore about 6:00 P.M. This place was a divisional point of the railroad, with a roundhouse and complement of about twelve men, turntable, repair shops, etc. It is one of the most beautiful sites we have seen in the Rockies for a mountain town. Approaching it, we passed the "Three Sisters," a profile so striking that it is easily distinguished, the highest peak reaching a height of 9,774 feet. In the same neighbourhood is a group of pillars known as hoodoos, some of them ten times as tall as a man and of sufficiently hard material to withstand the weathering that has played havoc with the surrounding bank. Years subsequent to the time of which I write, I was privileged to preach at Canmore and the scenes of former times described lay here all around, awakening memories of the past.

At that time Canmore had a population of about a hundred people, mostly men. Today it is a busy coal mining centre with a staff of over seven hundred men employed in the mines. Here our train had to lay over for the night on account of the unfinished condition of the road bed, the engineers preferring to have daylight for this part of the run.

It was still early and a misty haze hung over the mountains next morning when I heard the conductor's, "All aboard going west." At 3:00 A.M. our engine whistle blew "Brakes off," and we proceeded westwards. If at all possible, the beauty and grandeur seemed to be still greater. All in good time we reached Banff, which at that time consisted of but a railroad section house. This place at that time was insignificant enough. The mineral hot springs had not yet been discovered. Indeed it was that same fall that they were found.

Today it is a far-famed summer resort with its mammoth tourist hotels, medicinal hot springs and many other wonders of nature. Passing Silver City, where two years prior there had been a spasmodic silver rush which did not materialize, and which was now humdrum enough, there being only one family resident and that connected with the railroad company, we found the grade stiff and difficult of ascent.

Reaching Laggan, today known as Lake Louise, we were reinforced by two Mogul engines of one hundred and five tons each. With the three, we struggled and puffed and groaned up the steep ascent. Our locomotion was slow in the extreme and great care had to be exercised. Many of the boys alighted and walked behind the train. Gaining the summit of the Big Hill, as it was then known, we now beheld the first water flowing Pacific-wards. Here we noticed a small creek taking its rise in a small lake. Further on it crossed and recrossed the railway track. Presently we beheld it from the car window, leaping over giant boulders, again tumbling over cascades, disappearing in fissures and grottos of the rock, until in a cloud of spray and spume it disgorged itself around a sudden bend, then rushed out hundreds of feet below. This was our first view of the picturesque Kicking Horse River, so far famed for its beauty and glamour.

Ever since leaving Winnipeg we had been steadily climbing the slopes of the continent. Now at the Great Divide we had reached an altitude of 5,338 feet. This is the highest elevation reached by the railroad and at the same time is the boundary between Alberta on the one side and British Columbia on the other. This point is six miles west of Lake Louise and fourteen miles east of Field, and is the very backbone of the continent. It is marked by an arch spanning a stream under which the waters divide. The waters that flow to the eastward eventually reach Hudson Bay and the Atlantic, while those flowing westward eventually add their might to the Pacific by way of the Columbia River systems. Right at this point and on the left of the railroad track, is the granite shaft to perpetuate the memory of Sir James Hector, the discoverer of the Kicking Horse Pass, which permits the Canadian Pacific Railway to cross the Rockies. The Pass owes its name to an incident of exploration days in which a kicking horse lashed out and with both feet struck one of the explorers.

At the summit of the Big Hill, one of the Mogul engines had been detached, and with brakes on as tight as safe, we descended the other side of the hill with reversed lever on the engine. I am told that today this route has become obsolete. The Twin Spiral Tunnels have dispensed with this danger, and travel is more luxurious in consequence thereof. Any man making this trip today cannot help being impressed with the wonderful skill shown in the building of this section of this railroad and must feel that indeed it was the speculation of the age in railroading. The belting of this land from the Atlantic to the Pacific through the Kicking Horse Pass was a feat almost without parallel in railroad construction.

Passing Field and Ottertail Bridge, we reached Golden City in the afternoon. This must at that time have been an embryo city. One of its most notable features that day to me was the number of drunken miners, sure evidence that whiskey smugglers from across the United States boundary line had evaded the vigilance of the North West Mounted Police and, disappearing, had left this stamp of vice in their wake. This village consisted of about a dozen mud-roofed shacks. Standing out with more prominence than the rest, no doubt feeling its disparity, was a larger one, but of the same style of architecture. Straggling letters nailed on the wall facing the railroad track spelled out "Nip and Tuck Saloon." Here the most scanty meals, and cooked in the most primitive style, could be secured for the modest sum of seventy-five cents. Add to the afore-mentioned shacks a number of miners' tents together with the railroad siding, and you have the full extent of this embryo city. Visitors to the town today would fail to recognize it, for it has at present a mammoth gold crusher, smelter and branch railroad up the Windermere Valley.

The whistle of our engine had blown, the bell had clanged out its warning, and we were amusing ourselves reading the straggling, primitive letters on this emporium of accommodation when we received somewhat of a shock, for there issued from the door of the saloon two men of the North West Mounted Police in their usual soldierly bearing and neat uniform, hurrying towards our train, and alongside them, hobbling along in shackles, were two desperate-looking criminals securely handcuffed together. You may perhaps conceive of the shock we got at the sight of these. It has always given me a painful sensation to see men thus deprived of their liberty. Closely watching them, even in our ignorance, we could see these men were hardened criminals. We learned later they were notorious horse thieves and their hands were red with the blood of their fellow men crying out for vengeance.

Perhaps some day the citizens of western Canada will awaken to the debt they owe to the brave men of the North West Mounted Police who in the early days accomplished so much to preserve law and order. This was the first time I had come in contact with the men of this force as they sat only a few feet away. The elder of the two, and by his stripes the officer, might have been thirty-five years of age. He was tall, square shouldered and of splendid military physique, short brown hair, clean-shaven, save for a military moustache, and perfectly self-possessed. He had a way of looking at one with those keen blue eyes from beneath his sombrero which seemed to read one's thoughts. Courage and alertness were written on every line of his features, sun-browned as they were.

The other guardian of the country's morals was much younger, certainly not more than twenty-two years of age. He was fair-haired, blue-eyed, clear-skinned, handsomely built, and I should judge was from the Emerald Isle by the few words of his conversation. He was very wide awake and, as one of our passengers, an old Yankee, said, "Would be a tarnation hard man to get away from." However, in justice to them, let it be stated that they did not attempt to humiliate or in any way act harshly with their prisoners. That is inconsistent with their duties, for when one of the prisoners began swearing because of the chafing of the leg irons, he was cautioned by the fair-haired boy to be careful of his language, and assured that we would soon reach Donald, where his trouble would be attended to. Arriving at Donald, the first crossing of the Columbia River on the course of the Canadian Pacific Railway, the prisoners were removed from our car, tried that afternoon, and committed to the penitentiary for a long term of service.

At that time, Donald was at the extreme end of passenger traffic. From there westward for thirteen miles only construction trains travelled, carrying contractors' supplies to the real "jumping off place." We were warned by the station agent at Donald that if we wished and were willing to take the risk of our lives, we could proceed that far.

"Oh, yes, yes," interjected an old American railroader, "it will be better than hoofing it."

Of necessity, a good deal of business was transacted at this point, although houses were in the minority. There was a shanty-roofed shell of a building on the station platform which answered to Train Dispatcher's office, ticket office, and general freight department. Then there was the Selkirk House, a frame building the dimensions of which were about twenty-four by twenty feet. Farther back, near the edge of the bush, was the red light section, consisting of about eight or ten huge tents.

We now went about making the necessary preparations to spend the night, our first night in the open under the western skies. Upon this occasion we found that we formed part of a wild and motley group, mostly western Americans of the roughest type, largely from the Michigan lumber woods. From almost every belt hung a bowie knife and six-shooter, while the oaths and shameless profanity were sulphurous. Passing the night with as much comfort as consistent with circumstances, we awoke the next morning. Accommodation at the Selkirk House was of very indifferent quality, and indeed to me, seventy-five cents seemed a high price for a meal at that time. In any case, next morning found us creeping westward. This part of our journey was dangerous in the extreme, and on more than one occasion we feared the engine had jumped the track. Sometimes walking, sometimes riding, and again halting, we proceeded slowly, and as all things come to those who wait, we finally reached the extreme end of the steel, the "jumping-off place." It is a matter of deep regret to me today that I cannot locate this point exactly on the line of the C.P.R. However, be it understood that we were in the forest primeval of British Columbia.

We found here some half dozen tents, also two or three box cars which had been shunted off on an unfinished siding. Coupled with these were two boarding cars of large size, one of which I was afterwards informed, was what was termed at that date and at that place a hospital car. The other was occupied by the railroad doctor and a Roman priest named Father Fay. Part of this car was used as a medical dispensary, and the other part conjointly was used as sleeping and boarding service for these two men.

All the men employed on the Canadian Pacific Railway at this time in the Mountain section were charged one dollar and fifty cents per month for postal facilities, which was retained at the time the pay car arrived. In like manner, one dollar per month was retained as doctor's fee. In this latter case, many men paid the doctor's fee monthly. They seldom utilized his services and in fact would not know him were they to meet him. However, these were the rules at that time and at that place, and it would have been foolish to object.

It must have been between 7:00 and 8:00 A.M. when we left this place with our indispensable gunny sack carrying our all. The real difficulties of our journey now began. In some places it was easy to follow the course of the route, for what was termed in railway parlance the "right-of-way" was cut through the timber, while in other places we had to follow the blazes and figures on trees and in yet other places we found stakes driven into the ground and figured. It will be easily understood by this that the ground over which we travelled was very rough. Climbing over logs, again at other times circling rocks and wading rivers almost waist deep, we pushed on. We had just forded one such stream at the base of a steep hill and upon reaching the top found a bush restaurant named Brewster's Saloon. As we had now travelled until after midday, we decided to call a halt here and refresh the inner man. Upon entering this metropolitan house of entertainment, we were informed that dinner would be served to us at the rate of seventy-five cents each. Seating ourselves, we very patiently awaited culinary operations. Presently one mug of black coffee without either milk or sugar, two small baking powder buns, and two slices of grizzly bear steak were placed in front of each of us, which comprised the meal, served up in primitive fashion with tooth picks for dessert. Humping our swags, we pulled out from here about 2:00 P.M.

As we pushed westward, some of our men met with those who upon former occasions had been their employers on other railroad work; consequently, one by one they dropped off to work for these men. It was 8:00 P.M. when we alone (all the others had dropped off) reached McKenzie and Irvine Camp No. 1. Here we presented ourselves and our identification ticket, and were informed that their contract was about to be completed on this section and instructed us to proceed to Camp No. 2. Inasmuch as we had been travelling strenuously since early morning, we flatly refused to do so, fully assured in our own minds that we had covered at least forty miles. We were then informed that we could sleep at this camp that night and proceed to Camp No. 2 in the morning, and that in the meantime supper and breakfast and also sleeping accommodation would be given me. To say the least, the dining camp was in a most filthy state. However, I made an attempt at attacking supper, with more or less success. We were then shown across the creek to the sleeping tent, which was a large one and housed between thirty and forty men. Here we spent the night with more or less comfort, had breakfast next morning, and made Camp No. 2 about 8:30.

I did not remain long here, just long enough for my partner, who had been left behind at a way station, to make his appearance. If possible, the camp accommodation at Camp No. 2 was even more primitive and undesirable than at Camp No. 1. Food there was in abundance, but owing to the big crew of men to be fed, the cooks simply had not time to prepare the meals properly; consequently there was much good food wasted. We decided to return eastward, where we could obtain better jobs. Behold us then retreating on the ground over which we had travelled westward shortly before. That evening we made the end of the steel and, proceeding a distance of two or three miles, reached Sproat and Knowles' railroad tie camp. These men had a contract to cut and deliver at the track half a million ties, and also five thousand cords of wood. Coal had not made its appearance here yet, and the engines were wood-burners.

Many pleasing memories come to me today of the happenings of that summer amongst the pines in the forests of British Columbia: the busy chopping axe, the rasp of the crosscut saw, the evenings around the camp fire, the companionship of these men of higher thought and nobler manhood than those in the construction camps. The men in this camp were men of splendid physique, and veritable princes of axe men from Glengarry, Ontario. The quiet, peaceful Sabbath days were spent far from the busy haunts of men; the blue vault of heaven overhead, the rugged peaks under which we reverently worshipped, with the aroma of the sweet smelling pines all around us.

There are periods in the life of a man when to be alone with God means a great uplift to his nature. Such periods are highly essential to bring out all the best that is in him, to enable him to gather strength, "to fight manfully the battles of the Lord." Just at this time there was so much manifest in our immediate environment of the power and majesty of God on every hand, that one could not help feeling impressed. To me, it has many times seemed enigmatical how men created in the image and likeness of God, endowed with reason and capability, preserved by His kindness from day to day, and at the same time surrounded by so many evidences of His creative skill, should remain unmoved amongst so many evidences of His power.

We think of the busy little ants, carrying the earth atom by atom across the road or building their mounds, the industrious beaver damming the brook to flood the meadow, the horse in his fleetness covering miles of country. These all performing their tasks by instinct or command, and yet we have heard such remarks fall from the lips of careless men, "Let us take it easy, we are going through the world for the last time."

Our next move was back to The Gap at the entrance of the Rocky Mountains. It was upon this journey that we had a narrow escape from a grizzly bear. We had ascended about half way up the Big Hill and reached what was then known as the "Mud Tunnel." Being weary from a long day's tramp, we decided to spend the night in a small cabin of single-thickness rough boards. It may have been about midnight or perhaps a little after when we were awakened by a sniffing and scratching at the door. In fact, it was pushed nearly open. We were entirely without any weapons of defence. However, as the attack grew more vigorous and determined, we had to take some kind of action, which we did by lighting a fire in the stove and leaving the stove door open. This very effectually caused the bruin for the time being to disappear. Later and near morning he returned and we had to repeat our attempts at driving him away. It is well known that all wild animals have an extreme dread of fire. When we opened the door after daylight next morning (and you may be assured that we did so carefully), we had much evidence as to the intruder in the huge bear tracks round the cabin.

It was on a Tuesday nearing the end of July that we reached The Gap, five and four-tenths miles east of Canmore. Two men were most urgently needed on this section of the road, the complement of men employed at each section at that time being four. That is, a foreman and three men under his supervision. The foreman at this place at that time was George W., an Englishman with a wife and one little girl. He seemed to be very anxious that we remain with him. After some conversation as to the wages, accommodation, etc., we decided to at least try it for a time. We were new to the tasks set before us, but managed soon to assimilate. Our foreman was sociable, and Joe the Frenchman was both quiet and agreeable to get along with. Upon rare occasions he would break out when in a genial mood and entertain us with stories of his experience across the line or in the far east. Like most Canadian Frenchmen, he was an adept axe man. Having followed the railroad for twenty-seven years he was also an expert railroader. Many of his sayings still remain with me today.

For instance, upon one occasion we enquired, "Joe, how are your people in the east? Are both father and mother alive?" His reply was, "Oh, yes, they are fine. I saw a man last year who had seen them three years ago, and they were fine." Joe's measurements of time were by months and years. He was withal a good companion and not in any way offensive, if we omit his feelings some times when lining the track, when he had not very much respect for the third commandment. He and Alex and I had the bunkhouse to ourselves. Our foreman and family were next door neighbours.

Our facilities for receiving and transmitting mail were somewhat primitive. In mailing letters, we fastened them to a barrel hoop and upon the approach of a train caught the engineer's attention, who reached out his arm in passing and swept up the hoop bearing the mail. In receiving the mail we had no official Post Office and were dependent to a great extent on the courtesy of train men. Never did we know the engineer to miss or neglect our letters.

The fall of 1885 was a beautiful one, weeks and weeks of fine weather. The variegated leaves on the mountainsides and valleys, backed by a deep, dark green belt of spruce, lent continued and fascinating beauty to my surroundings. I have read many accounts of the beauty of the Rocky Mountains, but may safely say that no one has been able to express their real beauty. Meanwhile, during my stay in the mountains the Riel Rebellion had come to an end with the arrest of the Arch Traitor and the surrender of the Indian chiefs who had been led into it. There are no people under the sun who enjoy greater liberty, justice or protection than those living under the grand old Union Jack. Yet we have known men living under this flag and under this protection and justice, and they were not loyal citizens. These happened to be neither Indians nor half-breeds.

It was some time in the early days of the month of December that I left The Gap, eastward bound. I had enjoyed the summer immensely, perhaps on account of most splendid and vigorous health and steady work. I was sorry to depart, but had left members of my family in Winnipeg to whom I had to return. As I had completed my contract and remained until the work was done, I was entitled to a free pass back to Winnipeg. Reaching Calgary, I again met my friend Alex who had been my companion until recently. Boarding the east-bound train at Calgary, we whirled off en route to Winnipeg. At Medicine Hat we were held up for three days awaiting the pay car, which arrived in due time. While we remained here we made pedestrian tours each day in the country. Medicine Hat at that time was but an insignificant village. At the rear of the village and upon the hilltop to the south, we could see the dimensions of what had been the military fort and, yes, the rounded mounds of where some of the boys had been buried. Farther out, the prairie sod was littered with the bleached bones of buffalo, a sure sign that some time not very much prior, these hills and valleys had thundered to the tread of millions of these prairie monarchs. The country at this time was but sparsely settled. Rebellion and horse thieves were the chief factors in barring incoming settlement.

The weather was beautifully fine with frosts morning and evening and about one or two inches of snow with a clear sky overhead. Finally the pay car arrived and we began to think of getting off eastward. Proceeding eastward, we emerged into a lower temperature, so that by the time we reached Winnipeg the thermometer registered about twenty-two below zero, with over a foot of snow. Well do I remember the winter of '85–'86 in Winnipeg, our first. The weather all winter was extremely cold, and business and the labour market were still in a stagnant condition. The winter passed and spring came upon us in due time. It was highly amusing to see the pioneer west and the effete east endeavouring to adjust themselves, or so it seemed to me, as I beheld the Red River cart, the chariot of the plains, and the beautiful polished eastern buggy standing side by side, as if trying to fraternize.

For the next three or four years I remained in and around the city of Winnipeg, became acquainted and formed many friendships. The more than useless Rebellion being over and the war clouds completely dispelled, business and commerce began rapidly to improve, enterprise and industry once again coming to the front. Visiting this metropolitan western city today, one cannot help being impressed with its speedy and phenomenal growth and beauty, and yet not many years previously the old Red River cart squealed and screeched along the road from Upper to Lower Fort Garry, which had at the time of which I write, been converted into Main Street, and was graded, concreted and boulevarded. It is quite true that outside of the city limits the prairie sod was still in its virgin state, although here and there at considerable distances there may have been a few shanties, the beginning of settlement. However, these were confined largely to the banks of the Red and Assiniboine Rivers.

In later years and with incoming settlement the face of nature has pleasingly changed. The tide of immigration turned steadily westward; the homes of settlers—some of them—at first rather crude in construction, began to dot the prairie. The hum of human industry became apparent everywhere and the prairie began to blossom as the rose. In travelling across the plains in those days, one met with many diligent and resourceful people. Some of these had left their loved ones behind for a time and, preceding them, prepared homes in this new land to which they were brought at a later date. All honour to such men who had a vision and followed the gleam, and by industry and perseverance have hewn out for themselves and families homes in this new land. Succeeding generations owe much to the sturdy pioneer, although they are often tardy in acknowledging such debt.

CHAPTER 3
MORLEY, 1889–1910

I**T WAS NEAR THE END OF JULY 1889 THAT I FOR THE SECOND TIME LEFT** Winnipeg and steamed across the western plains. Upon this occasion Morley, on the line of the Canadian Pacific Railway, was my objective point, nine hundred miles westward from Winnipeg, and almost under the shadow of the Rocky Mountains.

Even in the four intervening years, that is, since my last journey across the plains, many changes had appeared upon the face of nature, and the prairies presented quite an altered appearance. The former unsettled state of the country, consequent upon the Riel Rebellion, had passed, and these western plains were now becoming dotted with the homes of incoming settlers. Now that Rebellion and bloodshed had been quelled, surely there were multiple inducements for such proceedings.

Miles and miles of unoccupied lands, acres and acres of virgin soil awaited the plough, a splendid country watered by springs, lakes, streams. Beautiful skies arched overhead, clear air surcharged with ozone. This was the heritage that had fallen to the white man at that time. A free grant of government land of one hundred and sixty acres, with an entry fee of ten dollars, to every young man of eighteen years of age and over, and at the end of three years, if homestead duties had been completed, a patent of the land to him and his heirs forever! These were the conditions prevailing at the date of which I write, in this western province. Needless to say, in the years subsequent, thousands availed themselves

Two Stoney Indian women at Morley, photographed by Mary Walsh ca. 1901. Miss Walsh was hired by John W. Niddrie in 1899 and returned to Morley for a second term as a teacher.

of the grand offer, and today rank as substantial citizens of this great commonwealth. In due time I reached my objective point and settled down to the tasks of life as they presented themselves to me.

Morley is named after the great English divine and eminent preacher and lecturer, the late Reverend William Morley Punshon, D.D., who visited Winnipeg (or rather Red River, so designated at that time) and who opened and presided over the first Methodist Conference west of the Great Lakes and held at that place in June, 1873. Prior to that date, very little indeed was known of the Morley district. It was called in the native tongue *Mun-u-chaban*, meaning the place from which wood was secured for bows and arrows. It was visited by roaming bands of Indians only, who secured from it the wood for the making of their bows and arrows so much used in hunting the buffalo and in tribal war. The wood of the fir or mountain pine, being the best and with the most elasticity, was used for their bows and the wood of the saskatoon bushes growing on the river banks made excellent arrows, thus supplying the instruments of warfare.

Perhaps a few words might not be inappropriate here regarding the physical features of Morley, nestled amongst the foothills of the Bow River Valley at a distance of fourteen or fifteen miles from the base of the mountains and with an extended range of vision eastwards. With an altitude of 4,200 feet in the valley, it ranks as one of the greatest beauty spots in Canada. During the months of June, July and August, it is seen at its best.

In some places the whole hillsides are of a beautiful pink colour with the blossoms of pink roses and other florals. These hilltops, in some cases three

Stoney Indian boys at Morley, with firewood; photographed by Mary Walsh, ca. 1901.

hundred feet above the valley level, and the real Bow River Valley with the river of this name flowing eastward like a silver ribbon, conjure up a picture not easily forgotten. Away to the westward the mountain peaks tower heavenward like fragments of a petrified eternity. Adjacent and to the northward there were other valleys which have no doubt been long appropriated by stock raisers, for this is exclusively a stock country.

The Mountain Stoney Indians, who were the most warlike tribe on the continent of America, and who are a branch of the great United States Sioux tribe, eventually settled down at Morley. They are a unique people, speaking a unique language and having unique habits of life. They have a great prestige behind them. In the days of tribal war they were never known to suffer defeat at the hands of their enemies, this no doubt owing to the fact that when attacked, they—Indian fashion—retreated behind timber and rocks. There they were able to pick off their enemies at will without any risk to themselves. There is nothing that a Plains Indian fears more than rocks and trees, as in their superstition every rock or tree conceals an enemy or evil spirit, which must be avoided by all means.

In later years and when I had got fully acquainted with the Stoney Indians, I found them high strung, fearless and arrogant in many cases, and sometimes not just peacefully inclined. I must, however, in all honesty state that I met many of them who were of sterling quality. Tact much more than talent was required to make a success of missionary effort amongst them. All through the Riel Rebellion they remained splendidly loyal to the Canadian government; indeed, so much so that three or four of them went out with our troops, acting

Stoney Indian girl pupils, Class IV Honour Roll at McDougall Orphanage, Morley, 1901; photographed by Mary Walsh.

as scouts, and did splendid work. It takes generations to uproot the customs, habits and traditions of an aboriginal people, and to instill amongst them loyalty to good government.

Yet here was a people not far removed from the extreme nomadic who manifested a great desire for peace and good will towards all men. I found they had a great reverence for the "Great Spirit" (meaning God), the Sabbath Day, and the House of God. When I met some of these "dusky sons of the hills" in the mountains in 1885, they would never think of travelling on the Lord's Day, or carrying a rifle in their hands. This convinced me at once that they were consistent with the profession they had made. It is true, and there is no denying it, that their concepts may have been a little misty, but according to their light and the teaching they were receiving, they endeavored to live up to the light they had.

There is one name which is, and will forever be inseparably connected with Morley. That is the Reverend John McDougall, D.D. He was instructed by the Methodist Conference, already mentioned and held at Red River, to open up a mission along the foothills of the Rockies amongst the warlike Blackfeet and their still more warlike hereditary foes, the Mountain Stoneys. Eventually Morley was decided upon as the site for the new mission. This was a most serious undertaking and required a man of brave, self-denying spirit, and one that was not easily intimidated, all of which qualities McDougall possessed in abundance, young as he was.

Late in the fall of 1873, or to be more precise, late in November of that year, the new missionary reached this point. Prior to this, only roving bands of

McDougall Institute (Indian Residential School) at Morley, ca. 1905.

Indians visited this spot; they may or may not have had a visit from some passing missionary. But even if such were the case, the visits must of necessity have been few and far between, perhaps largely on account of the migratory habits of the Indians. The whole of western Canada was at that time in the throes of tribal war. For thirty-three years or more, Dr. McDougall and his noble and devoted wife, Elizabeth, laboured with untiring energy for the uplift of these people.

When he first appeared amongst them, they were war-like in the extreme, and most nomadic. When he left them, they had made great strides towards Christianity and were worshippers of the true God. It was on August 1, 1890 that I went to Rev. John McDougall at the old Indian Mission at Morley, Alberta. For four years I sat at his table in his home and fraternized with his family. Many times indeed I sat by his side in his services in the old McDougall Indian Church at Morley.

Before incoming settlement, Mrs. McDougall had perforce to be left weeks and weeks alone, with only a bodyguard of the Stoney Indians. This consecrated lady passed through many a severe hardship that the outside people know nothing about. I have seen her walking across the hills to visit sick people, and carry them little knickknacks to coax their appetites. I have known her to stand beside the open grave and read the burial service in the absence of her husband. Surely hers has been a devoted life and she deserves the appreciation and respect of all.

Many times I accompanied Dr. McDougall across the Morley hills. Frequently arriving at Indian wigwams where the sick were, he would say, "You

McDougall Memorial United Church, Morley, August 1951, before restoration.

stay here, Niddrie, and hold my horse for a few moments." Stooping down, he would enter the camp. I was not familiar with the Cree language in those days, but could hear him say a few words, after which he would sing a verse, sometimes, "Nearer my God to thee" or "In the sweet bye and bye." I would hum it in the English language outside while they sang in Cree. Then followed a prayer and I hung my sombrero on the saddle horn and bareheaded waited patiently for the next "Amen." He would come out and we would proceed to the next camp.

At other times riding on the Reserve and passing the camps at eventide we would sit on our horses reverently and bareheaded while the old people concluded their evening worship. When I was teaching at the old No. 1 Day School on the north side, Dr. McDougall and his good wife would appear on Wednesday evening to hold the weekly prayer service. I have counted as many as ninety Indian people in attendance. As the meeting waxed warm we have heard as many as three old Indian ladies praying at once, and pounding the benches in true old Methodist style.

I taught under McDougall's superintendency in the Sunday School. Often have we ridden over the Morley Hills on the Reserve when he visited the sick. For four years more I taught at the old No. 1 Stoney School, where some of my happiest days were spent. After four years, on June 20, 1898, I was transferred and assumed principalship of the McDougall Institute for seven years. Here I experienced many of life's joys and sorrows. Added to the multifarious duties there was the responsibility of the children's health, which at times weighed heavily upon us. We noticed that somehow those who were most lovable and

McDougall Memorial United Church at Morley, post-restoration, as it appears today.

promising were the first to be called away. Subsequently I was again back at the Reserve School. In all this work I was more or less connected with Dr. McDougall and under his superintendency.

I always found him devoted, faithful, courteous and far-seeing. As a speaker of the Cree language, he was without a peer amongst the white men, and possessed the confidence of the Red Men from coast to coast. While as a diplomat between the Department of Indian Affairs at Ottawa and the Indians of the different reserves, he facilitated matters for the government. No wonder that widespread grief was felt at his passing. The Indian peoples of western Canada were in consequence thereof bereft of a good and faithful friend, the government of a loyal supporter, and his nearer friends of an able and far-seeing advisor. A cairn to perpetuate the memory of the McDougalls, father and son, has been erected directly on the Banff–Calgary highroad on the Morley Flat near the old McDougall Church, while little more than a stone's throw from the site of this lies the dust of Rev. George McDougall, father of the devoted missionary, John.

It was sometime about mid-winter, 1876, after Dr. John McDougall had opened the Morley mission, that Rev. George McDougall, at that time stationed at Edmonton, visited his son John at Bow River Valley. The larder of the missionary of those days was precarious and depended to a great extent upon the migration of the buffalo. Flour was generally a scarce commodity, as the steel of the railroad was not yet in use in this western country. Dr. John McDougall and his father, Rev. George, had left the little fort among the hills and gone out eastwards in the direction of where Calgary now stands in quest of buffalo, the meat of which was the staff of life to them. The weather was severe and about one and a half feet of snow lay on the ground. Erecting their buffalo skin lodge, they next morning sallied out in quest of buffalo. After a hard day's hunt they managed to secure six animals. Two of these were given to an Indian and his boy who had accompanied the party. Dressing and skinning the animals, they late in the evening started for camp. Proceeding until about two or three miles from camp, the father addressed his son, "John, I shall hurry to camp from here and have supper ready when you arrive. The camp is right under that star, is it not?", to which his son assented.

He rode off. The night was not exactly what might be termed a rough one. There was a light wind, and the stars shone overhead. That was the last seen of him by any of his family. About ten days later his frozen body was found under a winding sheet of snow. It was taken by kind hands to the Morley Indian Cemetery, where it was laid in the sure and certain hope of a glorious resurrection.

Twenty-eight years later I stood by the side of another grave in close proximity, and read the funeral service over the devoted wife of this man of God. Returning after the service was over, and as we drove down the hill, I heard David McDougall, another son of the deceased, to remark to his brother, "Well, John, this is just such a day as we laid our father's body away up here in the hill."

CHAPTER 4
DELAYED VACATION, 1894

ANNUITY PAYMENTS TO THE INDIANS WERE MADE IN 1894 ON AUGUST 26. Consequent thereupon, my school duties were for the time being over and my delayed holidays began. This was as per arrangement with the Department of Indian Affairs, i.e., that I should teach school during the summer months and enter upon my holidays at the departure of the Indians for their fall hunt. Behold me, then, putting into execution a project I had for some time been contemplating: that of paying a visit to my friends on the Big Red Deer River, a distance of between seventy and eighty miles to the northward from Morley.

For some time I had alternated between hope and fear, being doubtful and uncertain as to the route and distance. However, I finally decided to make the attempt, and went about making necessary preparations for the trip. More especially was I constrained to proceed, as information had reached me to the effect that they were suffering from lack of food supplies. I in the saddle and with an ordinary good pack horse could freight in to them at least two hundred or two hundred and fifty pounds, which would very materially relieve their need.

It was eight o'clock on Saturday morning, September 1, 1894, when I left the northeast end of the Stoney Indian Reserve, northward bound. One of our Indians had kindly promised to accompany me to what he designated as "The Forks of the Trail." I am free to confess that when we reached the indicated spot, if there were any trail at all, it was most indistinct, so much so that we failed to find it. Riding along over the hills that morning, the quiet was broken by nothing of more importance than the whirring of the wings of a flock of prairie chickens in their flight from us. In the still morning air the smoke hung like a heavy curtain around us, rendering it impossible to behold anything until we rode right upon it. Reaching the last home in the settlement, and calling to say "Good-bye," the lady of the house, who was baking, presented us with a loaf of fresh bread, which I thankfully accepted.

Striking northward, we skirted the Big Canyon. Climbing the western slope of the hill, we descended the opposite one and approached Ghost River. Splashing through the ford, belly deep on our horses, we climbed the northern bank and terraces. We then followed the depression in the hills leading on to what is today known as Bonanza Valley. Here the scenery became very picturesque: the grassy sloping hillsides with the narrow valley between, through which flowed a winding creek like a silver ribbon in the sunshine. The banks of the river, being water fed, were covered with a beautiful green fringe of grass. This grass, in a country where everything was brown and sere, presented a pleasant appearance.

In due time we reached the Little Red Deer River and here called a halt for a short time in order that both men and horses might eat and drink. This is one of nature's beauty spots: the high hills, the winding river hemmed in on all sides by the three-cornered flat, then away beyond this the beautiful rounded hills, tier upon tier, from the top of which—were it not for the smoke clouds—the grand old mountains would have been visible. Soon we were again in the saddle and pushing northwards. Climbing the very steep bank and following the timber-crowned ridge for about two miles, we descended the northern slope and reached Greasy Plains. Here my friend Jimmy was to leave me. This was what he had nominated "The Forks of the Trail."

To be perfectly candid, nothing resembling a trail could be found, that is, heading in the right direction. Jimmy would have been correct had he called it "The parting of the ways." It is perfectly true that ever and anon a perfect maze of buffalo trails was in evidence, proving that at some period not too far distant these hills and valleys had trembled to the tread of thousands of these mighty monarchs. All of these old trails, however, seemed to meet at right angles to our supposed route. As Jimmy had kept his part of the agreement faithfully, he took my hand in his and in the native language, pointing in a northerly direction remarked, "There is your direction, my brother, and may the Great Spirit guide you." Then, with an upward glance at the sun (the Indian measurement of time), he added, "I must hasten on my return journey, as our people camp at Pine Lake tonight."

Many times when travelling in the west in the early days, I have paused to admire the engineering skill of the buffalo. When approaching a soft spot or what I should pronounce a bad crossing, if I followed a buffalo trail, my difficulty was solved and I crossed safely. Their instinct always seemed to guide them in the right direction.

Wheeling his horse, Jimmy retraced his journey and I was left alone. It cannot be denied but that I, with my quite lonesome feeling, took up my route. Calling my dog, I splashed through the stream which at that point was about fifteen or twenty yards in width. Following the valley northward, I carefully scanned the ground in search of a buffalo trail to assist me in crossing a rather nasty, miry creek. Here again I had evidence of the fact I have just expressed, for I was soon across and on high ground. The distance was long, the way hard. The trail, if any at all, was very indistinct. As I approached the timber, I chose what I considered the most open space. My chief annoyance was the scrub bush, which made it difficult in the extreme to make any kind of reasonable speed. However, by pushing ahead and keeping at it, I reached the top of an exceedingly high hill. With considerable difficulty I managed to descend the north side. I had considerable difficulty in navigating my pack horse through the fallen and leaning trees without his being denuded of his load, which was a high and heavy one. Finding a crossing on the next miry creek, and reaching solid ground, I had to crowd the timber in order to escape being bogged. Finally I was brought up to a dead stop. A huge forest fire had destroyed not only timber, but had burned the ground to a depth of two or more feet; this was consequent upon the preceding hot and dry summers. This fire had so obliterated any semblance of an open route or even the faintest sign of a trail that it was perplexing in the extreme.

Dismounting and tying my horse to a tree root which in some way had escaped the ravages of the fire, I made a wide circle on foot and was fortunate in finding beyond the fire zone a creek. This I decided must be Fallen Timber Creek, a beautiful stream of clear cold water, spring fed and running through two small lakes or really large ponds. I was now cheered as I was to some extent assured that I had been travelling in the right direction. Following the serpentine course down for some two or three miles and having forded it five times, I turned from its course and crossed a high hill, descending into a narrow valley. At the base of this hill I found the first semblance of a trail through the bush. This was the first sign of a defined trail I had had since early morning when leaving home. For the next six or seven miles I rode through poplar bluffs. Eventually I emerged upon a large open flat. By this time the sun had swung low in the heavens, and I began to feel anxious as to my exact whereabouts. I hurried my weary horses along. For the last twenty-five miles or so I had seen very few signs of life—indeed, nothing except partridges or prairie chickens and rabbits, the latter being in abundance. However, on a trip such as this one, one longs for more than the companionship of a willing horse or a faithful dog. Indeed, the uncertainty of the whole outcome was somewhat of a strain on the nerves. By the time I had crossed the flat and suddenly dropping down the hill, behold! the Big Red Deer River flowed at my feet.

Two courses were now open to me. One was to push on and try to reach my friends; the other, to camp for the night and proceed in the morning. In the deepening twilight I endeavoured to ford the river. At this point it must have been fully a quarter of a mile in width. It consists of many channels and gravel bars. Fording a number of these, I came to the main channel. This I succeeded in fording about half way across. Owing to the treacherous river bottom and also the fact that I did not know the ford, I found it too dangerous to continue, and decided to return to an island I had noticed in the river bottom, which I had passed on a dry gravel bed, and await daylight for a further effort at crossing. Therefore, returning to this island, I found splendid grass for my horses, and an immense quantity of drift timber on the upstream end, which had been carried there when the river was in flood and was now perfectly dry.

Unpacking and unsaddling and tying out my horses to browse the splendid grass, I proceeded to make a night camp. The procedure in this case was simple enough; it consisted in setting fire to the immense wood pile ready to hand. Such fire could not escape as it was so far from the main shore with a number of channels of running water between. Rolling in my blankets with my feet to the fire, I sought a much-needed night's rest. For some unknown reason, sleep failed to visit my eyes. I lay there listening to my horses crop the grass a few feet away. My dog howled, the wind sighed through the treetops, in the distance the wolves howled, the river lapped the stones close by, but I lay awake. The hours passed away. The Aurora Borealis flashed and scintillated overhead, the moon set, and then, bye and bye, away up yonder—it seemed to me in the north, although it was really in the east—the beautiful daylight broke upon me.

I was soon astir and watering my horses. I changed the picket pins in order that they might have fresh pasture, then, seating myself, I meditated as to my best course of procedure. This was the Sabbath Day, and from earliest infancy I had been taught to revere the Lord's Day and keep it holy. Now in my dilemma I hesitated whether to remain here quietly in camp or proceed to my friends. Somewhere within twenty miles, perhaps more or less, they were camped and suffering through lack of supplies. I had food and in probability would be able to reach them that day. Long I pondered, weighing the matter over in my mind. Finally I decided to proceed.

Saddling up and loading my pack horse, I made a fresh attempt, this time a successful one, in fording the river. It was not without considerable risk, for the water was deep, and it was with thankfulness I reached the north bank. Lying stretched out before me was the flat known as Bearberry Plains. This flat might be between fifteen and twenty miles in length, and of irregular width owing to the serpentine course of the river. It would in any case average four to five miles in width. Never before in my experience did I see the prairie chickens in such numbers everywhere around me, and even among my horses' feet as they were that Sabbath morning. It may appear incredible, but when we take into consideration the fact that they had never been hunted or shot at, it may be easier to believe this. Scanning the ground narrowly for tracks of cattle or horses or any other animals, no signs whatever of such could be found. Primeval nature was everywhere around me.

The blessed stillness of the Sabbath morning was upon me as I guided my steeds through the long grass with many misgivings as to direction. One thing alone aided me. It was this: ere leaving home I had been told that after fording the Big Red Deer River I should make for the highest bald-headed hilltop, that at the base of such I would find a hay camp with men. Now, away beyond, through the smoke cloud I could see a range of hills. Just whether the highest was a bald one or not I could not at that distance tell. However, I made for it. Pushing across this big flat, I later came upon a wagon trail.

The evidence of human life seemed to put new life into me, and not only me but my steeds also. Galloping along for two or three miles, I came to a stake-and-rider fence. Hastily removing the top rail, I jumped my horses over and galloped them across a large field about one mile square. Reaching a willow-fringed creek, I succeeded in making a crossing, although not without a good ducking and narrow escape at drowning, for the water was deep. Emerging from the willows, I could see across the field at the foot of the hill a mud-roofed shack. My horses, seeing this, still more quickened their speed, making the ground seem to fly past me. Closely I watched for smoke or other signs of occupancy. None at all was visible. Riding up to the door, which I found slightly ajar, I shouted, "Hello!" Back came the answer, "Hello yourself and see how you like it!" In less time than it takes me to write, this Jack appeared before me in his sleeping dishabille, not even having stayed to dress. Our meeting was mutually happy. My first duty was to my horses, for they had carried me and my packs a long way. After attending them rightly, I proceeded to the shack to partake of Jack's hospitality, which was lacking neither in the elements of kindness nor quality.

During breakfast I delivered all the news from the outside. After dish washing was over, I signified to my friend Jack that I push ahead to my friends. Jack in his generosity signified his intention of accompanying me. It will be remembered that at that time a ride of twenty-five or thirty miles was little thought of in the Far West. I, however, protested at this kind offer of my friend to accompany me, but Jack was firm in his determination, and I was afterwards thankful that he had held to his wish. Riding off, we again reached the Big Red Deer River and proceeded to ford it back again to the east side. This time I was accompanied by a first-class guide and made the ford (quite a dangerous spot) in safety. Twisting and turning, we reached another large flat, at the far end of which we could behold the white-topped tent of my friends. It was Sunday morning, September 2, 1894, when after a hard and anxious journey in the saddle, we reached the camp of our friends on a large flat on the banks of the Big Red

Deer River, near what was known at that date as "The Big Springs." We were again among friends, and our journey for the time being was at an end.

We had that morning been alternating between conscience and necessity as to whether we should proceed on the Sabbath day or not in order to reach their camp. For we had from boyhood days been taught to refrain from anything like a desecration of the Lord's Day. But we must confess that knowledge had reached us regarding their shortage of food supplies, and that spurred us on.

However, after our arrival in camp, the despatch with which Mr. C. called into requisition all the various pots and pans and other cooking utensils, and the despatch with which he proceeded with his culinary operations convinced me that I had performed a Christian act in hastening to their relief. The culinary preparations for the mid-day meal completed, we gathered round the camp fire to partake of the much-needed victuals. It was one of those beautiful September days so frequent in Alberta. The smoke cloud which for weeks had darkened the air had lifted. A fresh wind blew up, while the gathering clouds predicted a thunderstorm.

The meal being finally over, and accompanied by a friend of those days, we climbed the bench, threaded the timber and ascended to the hilltop. Away across the valley and standing out in bold relief was Eagle Hill; the range of hills adjacent was completely timber-crowned. Between us and that range of hills was a valley through which meandered a creek like a silver ribbon, which disgorged itself in the Big Red Deer River. Far as the eye could reach there was neither sight nor sound of a human being or human habitation. From where we stood were poplar bluffs; yonder, belts of green spruce, and intersecting the splendid flats with luxurious grasses, as if fresh from the hands of the Creator God. In such an environment, one's thoughts are surely raised from nature to nature's God. If we, standing that beautiful Sunday afternoon gazing upon these wonderful sights, had been at all prophetic and laid my ear to earth, I might almost have heard the hum of in-coming settlement, for it seemed that no power on earth could prevent such. Certainly such land would not be allowed to remain long in its virgin state, and would soon be darkened by the black fingers of modern industry.

By this time, dark clouds began to gather overhead, the lightning flashed, the thunder roared and the gloom deepened, warning us to seek shelter somewhere from the gathering storm, the first such storm of that year. Such thunderstorms generally come up quickly in the west during the summer months. Making a rush for the nearest haystack, we succeeded in reaching it just in time and burrowed under its side ere the storm broke, thus securing a perfect shelter. After a short time the storm abated, allowing us to return to our friends, who had become anxious for us as we were dressed in summer garb. Later that night we retired to a well-earned night's rest. Next morning our friends moved camp across the hill and went on with their hay-making.

It may have been about the twentieth day of September or perhaps earlier that a fall snowstorm came upon us. The snow fell to a depth of nine or ten inches and seemed much deeper on account of the long grass. This was purely a local mountain storm, such being frequent in the far west near the base of mountains, after which weeks of beautiful fall weather succeed. Immediately after this storm it was decided that I, accompanied by my friend, make a journey to the then-little village of Olds for more supplies. It was shortly after our return from this journey that our horses, which had been running loose, stampeded in the night, no doubt due to a scare from some prowling wild animal, perhaps a bear.

The following morning it was found that all were gone with the exception of one saddle horse. The day was more or less spent in trying to discover their tracks. This proved a fruitless search. We concluded they had back-trailed to Morley and decided as soon as possible to follow and bring back the truants. With this object in view, one of our friends was despatched to borrow some horses for immediate use. That same evening he returned leading three horses, kindly loaned by our good friend Jack.

It was decided that evening that my friend and I should early next morning take up the trail to Morley. It proved one of those beautiful fall mornings such as are quite common in Alberta. My mount was at first a little wild, but not at all unmanageable. After a little patient effort he quieted down and we started off. It has always seemed to me since that there was something—what shall we call it, magnetic, or shall we say mesmeric—about that morning which we can not easily define. So many things conspired to make it so beautifully bright and cheering. Perhaps it may have been partly that we were both in such perfect health. Our diet for the last two or three weeks forbade anything like dyspepsia or any other bodily ailment and all the open-air exercise, then the beauty of the morning with willing steeds under us no doubt had their influence on our lives.

After a ride of about twenty-three miles or thereabout, as nearly as we could guess—for the surveyor's chain had not passed over much of this land as yet— and while passing the home of a settler, we found one of the truant horses tied up to the fence with the hobbles still on, and his legs badly chafed. This no doubt the poor animal had done in his efforts to keep up with the remainder of the band. This was on the banks of the Little Red Deer River. We removed the hobbles from the poor horse and left him to rest and pasture, while we continued our search. After we had travelled another twenty or twenty-five miles, we suddenly came upon the remainder of our horses. Being now within twenty-five or thirty miles of Morley, we decided to push on through. In subsequent years, I have often thought of that stretch across "the desert," so known at the time. It was incumbent upon us to make all possible speed in order to reach our destination ere darkness came down upon us. Even with our best effort it was quite late when we reached the home of our friend, after covering some seventy-five miles since seven o'clock that morning.

Here I remained two or three days, consequent upon the performing of various duties and the securing of additional supplies which I had determined to take out. This was my opportunity for such, as I had horses and could secure pack saddles. It was Saturday morning ere I managed to make a start on the return journey. Three horses were packed with needed supplies and the remainder allowed to run loose in the train. I had decided to return by the "bush road"—for convenience we call it a road, although it was in many places nothing more than the clearest and most open part through the scrub bush. It was particularly rough riding and hard on the horses, but had the merit of shortening distance considerably. Upon such a journey the preparing and getting away are quite a formidable matter. It was well in the day ere I got started and turned my horses' heads northwards. I camped that night at Little Red Deer River. I here found a beautiful camping ground with the four requisites: pasture for four steeds, water in abundance, dry campfire wood and a level spot on which to roll out blankets and sleep. The night was somewhat cool and had the tang of early fall in it, with a slight frost. Had I made more elaborate preparations, I might have been more comfortable, but I was short on blankets. The night, however, passed, and the Sabbath morning dawned upon us.

I fear right here that my readers will begin to think me an habitual Sabbath breaker, but I hasten to assure them that this was not the case. When in the wilds, many things crop up over which one has no control. Stern necessity compelled me to proceed, and I did so as reverently as was consistent with the circumstances. Again it took me considerable time to get properly packed up, as some of the horses were not accustomed to this mode of transport. It was a beautiful still fall Sabbath morning, and we made good speed after getting started. Climbing the very steep hill and following the narrow timber covered ridge, we eventually descended and came to Greasy Plains. Following the open ground as much as possible, we again entered the timber and reached the top of a very high hill. Descending the almost perpendicular hill, we entered a long swale. Crowding the timber as closely as possible on account of the soft ground, we hurried along with what speed was consistent with the nature of the ground. Near the middle of the day we duly called a halt at Fallen Timber Creek, a beautiful stream of clear limpid water which proved serpentine in its course, for we forded it five times. Here I remained to lunch. Owing to the amount of work, I decided not to "off saddle," but just to slacken the saddle girths and allow the horses to browse. Again, the charm and beauty of the camp appealed to me as I rested for a little while.

Again I pushed forward. Passing through more timber we descended into a long, narrow valley. Following this some distance we entered the poplar bluffs and travelled eight or ten miles. The horses gave considerable trouble through the scare of a bear, and it took some little time to get them again under control. Reaching the Big Red Deer River, we made the ford with little trouble, being now, to some extent at least, acquainted with the treacherous river bottom. Crossing the big flat, in Jack's absence and as per agreement, I left the horse I rode, at the same time thankful for Jack's kind generosity. I had not seen one soul since leaving home the day previous.

It was late in the evening ere I reached my friend's camp; indeed, it is somewhat doubtful whether or not I should have found the same, as they had moved. Were it not for the fact that they had kept a brisk fire burning, I might have passed it in the dark. We were glad to be once more a united party in camp, and I was soon engaged in delivering every item of news I had heard out in civilization, which I thought might be of interest to them.

The next three weeks passed away very pleasantly. My time was largely taken up in aiding my friends in erecting winter quarters—felling and hauling logs, erecting buildings—and occasionally range riding after stock kept us constantly on the move. That was a beautiful fall. After the snowstorm we had weeks and weeks of fine clear weather. Nearing the end of October, I was reminded that my holidays were about over, and that I must soon return to my school work under the shadow of the Rockies. On the morning of October 29TH, with my two horses saddled, I said good-bye to my friends whose hospitality I had so much enjoyed, and turning my horses' heads homeward, I rode off.

It was a beautiful still morning, with the promise of a fine day, not too hot. I was busy with my thoughts that morning as I began my seventy-six mile trip. Riding at a steady jog trot, I stopped later at the Big Springs to lunch. Starting out again, I reached Dog Pound Creek in good time in the afternoon. Here again I remained a few minutes to allow my horses to drink and snatch a few mouthfuls of grass. Climbing the steep hills, I crossed "the desert." The sun was swinging westward as I descended into Grand Valley. Leaving the regular roadway, I turned a little north, and passing the Mount Royal Ranch, crossed the Ghost River and reached Morley that evening.

Arrived at home, my duties were simple enough and easily performed: vegetables to be housed and made frost proof, timber to be hauled and cut into stove-wood lengths, and a few other minor duties, all of which were soon completed. The weather continued beautifully fine until New Year's. Indeed that was the finest fall I experienced in the Far West in twenty-one years. As the Indian people came trooping in from their fall hunting camps, our school duties again began and a great joy came to us in the performance of life's tasks. This was the happiest time of my life on this side of the Atlantic.

CHAPTER 5
NATURE INTERLUDE, 1896

H ERE IS A CHAIN OF PEAKS TOWERING THOUSANDS OF FEET IN HEIGHT, AND in many places snow-mantled, extending from the Arctic Circle to the northern boundary of Mexico or nearly so, a distance of approximately three thousand miles. For hours at a time, seated upon some hilltop near our home at Morley on the main line of the Canadian Pacific Railway to its western terminus, I have gazed entranced upon these mighty monarchs with their peaks which seemed to me to pierce the ethereal blue of heaven and their feet thrust into the pines. Again, again, and again have I gazed spellbound upon the different shades of light and shadow as they chased each other across their wrinkled faces upon which the hand of time had written so many different happenings. From my outlook they presented no even chain of serrated peaks, but the eye seemed to rest upon a jagged wall which held the beholder under the spell of its enchantment, this to be broken only by the shrill screeching of the siren as the railroad engine rushed westward towards The Gap.

The rounded grassy hills, the timber-crowned ridges, the sloping, curving valleys through which there meanders in almost every case a mountain stream: all of these beauties present to the human eye scenes not easily forgotten. Like the giant Rockies, the foothills run north and south along their base. Fifty or sixty years ago, this hill country had not as yet come under the subduing hand of man, but was in its primeval state and seemed fresh from the hands of the Great Creator. Today the black fingers of modern industry have materially changed the face of nature in those parts. In the early days it was my privilege to cover great distances in the saddle in this western country. Generally speaking, the nature of the hills and valleys at that time, devoid of anything like roads, forbade all wheeled travel. All of this had to be accomplished in the saddle. Upon the hilltops and sides, spruce, jackpine, and Douglas fir predominated, with here and there a sprinkling of silver birch, that is, in the line of timber. At a lower altitude and farther away from the mountains, bluffs of beautiful white poplar could be found. To witness these hills at their best, one should visit them in the months of June and July. At that time the aroma of the wild rose bush with its abundant pink blossoms covers the hillsides. There is also an abundant variety of wild flowers which clothe the hills with their rainbow colours, all of this buttressed by a range of imperial giant mountains which is not only charming but inspiring to the beholder, that is, provided always that he has any artistic feeling at all in his make-up.

The foothills have a style of beauty all their own. Here timber-crowned, yonder grassy-knolled, and again pyramid-shaped: it is this diversity that makes them so strikingly charming. In the days of which I write, many rough, rugged spots could be found where the foot of the white man had never left its imprint. Then at a lower altitude and in the sloping valleys, old buffalo trails cross and recross and intersect in all directions.

The buffalo bunch grass predominates in the foothills. This is a species of grass possessed of great nutriment and eminently adapted for the stock-raising industry. It does not seem to extend far beyond the foothill country. In the old days this industry was very extensive, and a great revenue was derived from the sale of beef cattle. Those days might be denominated "the cowboy regime." However, this has largely passed away on account of the incoming settlement. Today, many men are engaged in what is known as mixed farming, but proximity to the mountains and the night frosts consequent thereon have seriously interfered. Many men of honest enterprise have engaged in this effort, but climatic conditions are against them as the foothill country is not an agricultural district.

Travelling northward along the base of the mountains from Morley, one has to cross many streams, all of which seem to run eastward, or away from the mountains. The first stream on this route is the south fork of Ghost River. This stream takes its rise near the base of Mount Pechée and a few miles almost directly north of Canmore. It is mountain fed, and especially after its junction with the north fork near Starvation Hills becomes dangerous at flood tide. Indeed, I have known cowboys held up on the western side of this swollen stream for nine days awaiting abatement of its waters ere they could make a return crossing and reach their home. I myself have run no small risk in crossing this river on horseback. However, today this has all been facilitated by the building of many bridges.

The north fork of Ghost River is considerably smaller and does not present so many dangers to the traveller. However, none of these mountain streams is to be trifled with when in flood. I know of many sad happenings because of lack of carefulness and good judgement. This stream is very little larger than a good-sized creek, and its rise is consequent upon the rainfall in the upper country.

We next approach Little Red Deer River. This is a beautiful stream and, while normally not of any exceeding size, it is a long river and is twice reinforced by tributaries ere it disgorges itself into the Big Red Deer many miles eastwards. Its tributaries are Grease Creek and Dog Pound Creek. I presume that the name "Grease Creek" is owing to the fact that this stream runs across Greasy Plains, a tract of rough land some eight or ten thousand acres in extent.

The next river on this course is Fallen Timber Creek, or in the Indian language, Thickwood River. This is a beautiful stream of clear limpid water and seems to take its rise in two small lakes which in turn are mountain fed, as they flow from that direction. Fallen Timber Creek is very serpentine in its course. I have crossed it five times in a distance of two miles on the old Morley–Bearberry Plain bridle trail. This river is also a tributary to the Big Red Deer River. I remember some beautiful tall poplar bluffs on the course of this river, interspersed with some mammoth flats where the luxuriant grass scraped my knees as I rode along on horseback. No doubt these flats have long ago been appropriated by the incoming settler and made to blossom like the rose.

Turning again to our original direction, we approach the banks of the Big Red Deer River. In flood, this is the most turbulent stream of any I have enumerated. Seated upon horseback on the banks, I have seen great trees which have been torn from the banks higher up sweep past with frightful velocity. Then again, the waters spread out, when in flood, over the various channels for nearly a quarter of a mile, while many of the islands visible at low water are completely submerged. This stream is glacier fed, and at certain seasons of the year proved a formidable barrier to travellers. A number of bridges, built at various points and at different times, have succumbed to the rushing, foaming current. Far up in the hills I have known of Indian men to have many dangerous experiences in attempting to ford this stream while in flood and on horseback. The river drains miles and miles of foothill country, then sweeps majestically across some great prairie land ere emptying itself into the south branch of the Saskatchewan, which forms a junction with the north branch somewhere near Prince Albert. But to return to the hill country, we cross the Red Deer River inside of one range of the great Rocky Mountains. Here in the old days there was a beautiful plain known as Mountain Park. It would have been an ideal spot for ranching on a moderate scale. It has no doubt been long ago appropriated.

Crossing Prairie Creek and Clearwater River, we soon reach the giant north fork of the Saskatchewan River near its source. This giant river, the Saskatchewan, drains the watershed from the eastern slope of the Rockies, flows across miles of prairie thickly dotted with prosperous settlers, and finally disgorges itself into Lake Winnipeg at Grand Rapids, then by river and lake system on to Hudson Bay.

Fifty years ago, this country was but sparsely settled by the white man, and the silence of nature was seldom broken, except by the old flintlock gun of the aboriginal man. Such a thing as fixed ammunition had not made its way this far. Tried, brave, and accurate in marksmanship were those old-timers amongst the Red Men. It took no small courage to beard the grizzly in his mountain lair with no return shot, should the first prove unsuccessful, which was seldom the case. Today the big game has largely disappeared, except that protected by the government. In consequence thereof, the Red Man has to seek in another direction for a livelihood.

It was in the year 1896. May had ripened into leafy June, which in turn had given way to rosy July, and nature and beauty were evident on every hand. The afternoon hour was approaching four as I, seated I must admit rather impatiently on the hilltop, awaited the appearance of my Indian guide. Presently out of the thick bush to the southeast I beheld him approaching in the saddle and leading a pack horse. Reaching me, and with an upward glance at the sun, he said, "My brother, we shall have to move quickly; I have been unavoidably delayed." Hurriedly loading up my pack horse with foodstuffs, blankets, and other travelling paraphernalia, we turned our horses northwards and took up the all-day foothill jog-trot so familiar to the men of the hills. For the first two miles or so we rode through the Indian Reserve, ever and anon passing a home of some of the dusky sons of the hills. These, however, showed no signs of occupancy, as their owners were all out on the river flats living under canvas, a very common and healthy custom during the summer months.

Crossing the boundary line between the Reserve and white settlement, silently we jogged along, the only break being made by my guide, who now and again pointed out some spot where some of his people had been done to death by a warrior enemy during the days of tribal war. It is always a listening attitude that brings out the western man, not the firing of a lot of catapult questions.

Two miles farther on we reached the north fork of Ghost River. Descending the steep hill on the narrow bridle trail, we pushed through the bushes, forded the stream, and climbed the northern bank. Half a mile or more on, we passed the home of a hardy frontiersman who had squatted here as the influx of settlement had reached this frontier region. Following the Half Moon Valley for a mile or so, we climbed the steep hill and again entered the timber. Passing through the Wildcat Hills, we moved cautiously as this is the home of the black bear of the western foothills. All western men will certify as to the deep antipathy existing between the black bear and the western bronco. However, on this occasion we passed through unmolested, reaching the north fork of Ghost River safely. This we found considerably smaller than its sister stream, the south fork, and forded it knee-deep on our steeds. Again climbing the north bank, we jogged along a distance of perhaps two miles ere again entering the timber. The next six or seven miles proved a very rough part of our journey. There was not even a bridle trail, and we had perforce to follow the dry bed of a small creek, and a rough one at that. That we managed to accomplish this safely without denuding our pack horse of his load must surely be credited to the efficient engineering skill of our guide, for unquestionably it was one of the roughest parts of the country I ever passed through, and my experience along this line has been somewhat varied.

The sun had long set and the trailing garments of eventide were coming down upon us as we emerged upon a beautiful little grassy flat on the banks of the Little Red Deer River. Nature and long habit have conspired to make the western Indian adept in the choice of a camping ground. This was my thought that evening as I gazed out over this beauty spot of nature, encircled by a belt of green spruce with the four requisites at hand, i.e., good pasture for our steeds, beautiful clear water, dry campfire wood, and a good level place upon which to roll out our blankets to spend the night. Here we were abundantly supplied with all these.

Our first duty was to our horses, for they had carried us many miles. They were watered and picketed out. The picket pins were driven securely into the ground. Remissness on my part in performing this task in the past had sometimes caused me many miles on foot. The prowling of wild animals in the night hours will sometimes stampede the horses, and in many cases they are not easily overtaken or secured. In this instance, however, we made everything as secure as possible. Next in order was the preparation of the evening meal for ourselves. This was partaken in different attitudes consistent with comfort, that of my guide seated with crossed legs, upon which he sat with ease while he ate. All this time he preserved a stoical silence. There was one thing which impressed me. It was this: he never seemed to get far away from his rifle. Even while eating it stood against the huge bole of a spruce tree, within easy reach of the sweep of his right hand, while his eyes seemed to dart hither and thither in every direction, and his head was bent forward in a listening attitude. Supper over and dishes washed, the campfire was again replenished, not because of the cold, but on account of the myriads of mosquitoes by which we were attacked.

Steadily the darkness crept down upon us. Close to our camp we could hear the horses cropping the grass. Overhead the stars glittered and sparkled. Away in the distance the silence was broken by the cry of a mother wolf, a sure sign that others were not far off. Still we sat silently, communing with our own thoughts. My guide pulled out his pipe and charged it with tobacco and *kinnikinnick*, a willow bark much used by the Indian peoples and mixed with their tobacco. He smoked on. Presently taking the pipe from his mouth and jerking himself as if from under a strain, he began.

> Many moons ago, when I was but a young man, little more than a boy, a very dear comrade slightly my senior in years accompanied me on a moose hunt. It was the month of falling leaves. We had travelled many miles, for at that time we were almost inseparable. One dull blustery morning we struck the trail of a moose. Following it until mid-day, the trail became so warm that we had to proceed with the utmost caution.
>
> My friend was in advance, for he was always brave. We had just crossed a small prairie surrounded by timber when my friend was instantly attacked by a mother bear who had two cubs. The struggle was of short duration, for he had only a bow and arrow, which were simply useless at such close range, and his hunting knife was knocked from his hand. Ere I could get to his rescue, he lay a bleeding, mangled heap upon the ground. Retreating a few yards, I strung an arrow, and first slaying the mother bear, I later slew the two cubs, leaving their carcasses upon the ground to be destroyed by the wolves. Tomorrow I will show you the last resting place of my poor friend, for when passing this district, I always turn aside to lay a few sprigs on his grave.
>
> My brother, I have spoken.

Again replenishing the fire, we sang our evening hymn and committed ourselves into the hands of our Father. Stretching our weary bodies out with our feet to the fire, we were soon locked in the arms of repose. Sleep had come to us, and side by side in the solitude we slept on. If we woke, it was but for a moment to see that our fire was burning vigorously. The hours passed away with the scintillating, dancing Aurora Borealis overhead, until the beautiful morning light of a new day came to us. We were early astir. Breakfast and prayers over, we saddled up and were on our way again. This trip lingers in my memory as one of the hardest I ever experienced.

Climbing the hills, crossing the valleys, fording the creeks, eventually we came to a small piece of prairie surrounded by timber. Here in solitude sublime, and surrounded by a log fence, we stood bareheaded beside a solitary grave. I stood reverently for a few moments while my guide quietly broke a few sprigs from a silver birch tree and laid them on the last resting place of him who had been his friend. Then he quietly remarked to me, "My poor friend whose mangled body I laid to rest here was brave, honest, truthful, and good. I doubt not, if it is the will of the Great Spirit, I shall meet him again in the Happy Spirit Land."

CHAPTER 6
MEN OF MORLEY, 1890–1910

W̲E SHOULD LIKE TO MENTION SOME OF OUR OLD FRIENDS OF THOSE DAYS long passed into history. I am referring to friends among the Stoney Indians. We shall write of them as we found them, irrespective of other men's opinions.

CHIEF BEARSPAW

In our day, this man was a rugged old warrior, and we do not doubt that he was a good Christian man. He was one of those fearless men who adhered to what he considered just and right. We have been told by old-timer white men that in the early days before white settlement had reached this part of the country, this intrepid old man had been known to follow white travellers for three or four days at a time when they were on their way to the Pacific in order to safeguard them from the treacherous Blackfoot. In many cases the travellers were unaware of this action on the part of Bearspaw, who reveres the white man.

Perhaps there was no Indian more loyal to the good old Union Jack than he in those days. There was no uncertain sound about his loyalty, especially during the days of the Riel Rebellion of 1885. And this was known to the Canadian government and the Methodist Church.

We frequently fraternized with this man and knew him well. In this connection, one little episode remains with us today. While driving along the road

John W. Niddrie, ca. 1905, taken during his days of working at Morley.

with a salesman some eight or ten miles from the mission, we passed this old man on the road. After we reached our objective point, we unhooked and fed our horses and began to light a fire preparatory to making tea for the midday meal.

The old gentleman arrived on the spot opportunely and we were glad to share our lunch with him. Presently when all was ready, he interposed. "My brethren, this is good enough to be thankful for. Let us thank the Great Spirit." We gladly assented. There, side by side, the Indian and the young white men bowed their heads while he returned thanks for the food. This may seem trivial to the reader, but it remained in our hearts for many years.

CHIEF CHINIQUAY

This man was well advanced in years ere we became fully acquainted. Consequently I was not so well acquainted with him as with his brother, Chief Bearspaw. Chiniquay was of Cree extraction. He was not the outstanding character that Bearspaw was, yet withal he was a good old inoffensive man.

Chief Chiniquay (also spelled Chiniki), ca. 1890.

As a boy he had been brought up in the camp of Maskepetoon (means "Deformed Arm"), a great Cree chief. Except for Chief Crowfoot, who was chief of the Blackfoot Confederacy, Maskepetoon was perhaps without a peer as leader of his people. He was much admired as a peace chief in those stormy days.

As Chiniquay advanced in years, he drifted southward and eventually became chief of "C" band at Morley. He was a man of even temper, and was always approachable. We always found him kindly disposed towards the white community. Vividly today do we remember his speech upon the arrest of one of his young men upon a liquor charge. Raising his aged trembling hands, he asserted:

> Today my camp is darkened and we shall have to hold down our heads on account of the indiscretion of one of our young men. Many times have I warned all of you young men, and you have heeded me not. Now today I see one of you with chains on like a dog and he will have to suffer for his folly.

The old chief passed away at an advanced age.

COUNCILLOR JAMES DIXON
(OR, THE MAN WITH THE WOODEN LEG)

Here is a man who was respected by old and young alike. In his early days he had been a renowned trapper and figured also in tribal war. After first listening to Rev. Robert Terrill Rundle, he never was the same man again. He used all his powers for peace and goodwill amongst the different tribes.

James was a man of sterling quality and of great piety. Immediately after the inception of the Morley mission, he became the missionary's right hand. He was a splendid interpreter, a linguist, inasmuch as he spoke and understood the Cree, Blackfoot and Kootenay languages. It was at once evident that he was a man to be made use of for God and country.

In the early 1870s he met with a serious accident and in consequence thereof he had to have his leg amputated. At that time the nearest medical officer was at the Police barracks at Fort Macleod. A message was sent and the doctor summoned. On his arrival at Morley he found that the case was serious in the extreme as gangrene had set in and nothing but amputation would save his life. Preparations being made, James was told that he must get up on the table. When asked why, he was told that an anesthetic would be administered to save him suffering. He refused and sat holding his own leg while the doctor proceeded to cut it off. I was a little dubious when told this, but it was substantiated by others who saw the operation.

This good man was wont to carry with him a bell, a hand bell, which he constantly rang on the Sabbath afternoon in all his travels to his winter quarters, and he held a service for his band very faithfully.

Finally, late one fall at the end of the century, he got badly wet setting some beaver traps. On the next Sunday he was unable to get up out of bed, but faithful to the last, he had the bell rung and conducted the service in bed. In a few days poor old James went over to join the silent majority, while mourned by the whole Stoney tribe.

JONAS TWOYOUNGMEN

This man was a special friend. He acted in the capacity of councillor and later chief of the "C" band. Jonas was a man of ambition and thrift. His home and environment showed this. He mastered a smattering of the English language and was a most courteous gentleman. Perhaps Jonas' wife was the most respected woman on the Stoney Reserve.

After the Riel, or North-West, Rebellion, was over, the Rev. Dr. John McDougall took three of the loyal chiefs east in 1886 to meet and acquaint the government and eastern people of their loyalty to good government. Jonas was chosen to represent Chief Bearspaw. These chiefs toured eastern Canada, speaking in the largest buildings and churches. On one occasion when Jonas was called upon to speak, he said something like this:

We are a long way from the mountains and we shall be glad to get back home again when the time comes. We like to listen to our missionary when he told us of the Happy Spirit and tonight, since entering the church, I am assured that it is all true. I shall return to my people and tell them it is all true and that we are not alone.

PAUL RYDER, COUNCILLOR OF "C" BAND

Paul was a natural gentleman. He was well advanced in years when we became acquainted. In those old days, we often thought that Paul and his wife were a splendid example of wedded life among the Indian people. He was an earnest Christian and always on hand at the church services when at home.

He was also a good singer and assisted all he could. We were pleased to welcome him to our table at the Residential School. He was reliable, unassuming and devoted to his people, especially the rising generation. His passing was very sudden, as he had been sick only part of a day. However, we have no doubt Paul was ready for the summons when it came, and is today "Far from a world of grief and sin, with God eternally shut in."

WILLIAM TWIN, OF "C" BAND

We first met this man in the fall of 1895, in the Gap to the entrance of the Rocky Mountains on the line of the Canadian Pacific Railway. He had travelled a great deal in the mountains and was a faithful guide. He had quite a smattering of the English language. We shall never forget that Sabbath afternoon when we first met him. It was then that we learned that none of the elder Stoneys travelled on the Sabbath, much less carried a loaded gun.

In later years this man was sent to New York by the American Gun Club and Hunting Association, so he had a wide experience. At this time of writing (1938), he is nearing the century mark in age.

GEORGE MCLEAN, COUNCILLOR AND CHIEF OF "C" BAND

George was one of the younger generation, but has had quite a history. To begin with, we note his name. The significance is that when still a little boy, he was taken to Morley Residential School by the Rev. John McLean, who for some years was missionary to the Blood Indians, thus his patronymic.

We always held George in high regard and found him very willing to assist us when we held a service, and he proved himself to be an able interpreter. George was a steady man, sturdy and independent. We cannot forget the way

Joshua and William Hunter (Twin) of Morley, two of the many Stoney Indians known to John Niddrie. Date unknown, possibly 1920s.

he spoke once at a council meeting at the Morley Agency. We admired his straightforward intelligent way of dealing with the matter brought up for discussion. We have every reason to believe that George and his good wife have done their best to make their calling and salvation for the next world secure.

PETER WESLEY, CHIEF OF "B" BAND, THE NORTH RESERVE

Peter was a man of indomitable energy, ambition and thrift. It was late in life when he came to the chieftainship, but we are sure that he did all in his power to help his band. He had a large family, and did his best to have them educated, and they were certainly not without ability. Peter was what many people call "a diamond in the rough," unpolished but thoroughly trustworthy.

We always found him ready to be guided in the right direction. He had a great respect for the white man and the white man's way of life. One significant fact about this man was that, though we knew him for more than twenty years, and he lived in a country where horseback riding was the chief means of locomotion, we can never remember seeing him on horseback. Even when his band was starting off for the fall hunt, Peter would be found walking ahead of them all.

He made for himself and his family a good home. He was a great hunter and trapper in his day. He must have lived to an advanced age, as it does not seem long since he passed beyond the reach of human ken.

Well do we remember accompanying him and the councillor to the camp of a dying man. Even before we had time to sing a hymn, the poor weak man, who was on the confines of the eternal world, said, "I want Taoussa (the Chief's Stoney name) to pray for me." This was an old man with whom Peter had fraternized a great deal, and it showed the mark of respect in which he was held. The sick man passed away that night.

MOSES HOUSE, EX-COUNCILLOR

Moses was a good man in his day and generation, a faithful Christian and diligent in his duties as a councillor. He was a man interested in the rising generation and often visited our day school. The large general average of attendance was due to his faithful efforts. We often regretted his resignation as councillor, for while he was one of the old-timers, he was a man whom all respected. We are sure his life was fruitful. In both work and effort he was honest and true.

Well do we remember standing outside the old McDougall church in the gathering shadows of darkness and listening to Moses in his address to the young of his little band. In the calm evening we did not miss a word. We also remember his great anxiety to be allowed by the Department of Indian Affairs to roam up to the headwaters of the Saskatchewan River, and his gladness when such permission was granted.

COUNCILLOR GEORGE TWOYOUNGMEN

This man was a wonderful Christian gentleman of the old school. We cannot write about him as fully as we would, for he was retiring and never sought the limelight. He was, however, of undoubted Christian character and served in the dual capacity of councillor and class leader.

It was a common experience with us when passing his lodge at eventide, to stop our horses and hang our sombrero on the saddle horn while he and his good wife were at their devotions. As the Indians would remark, "George was a man of one tongue." His word was as good as his bond. He was dearly loved by his people.

JOSHUA HUNTER, OR TWIN

Joshua was the twin brother of William Twin, already described. He lived to be about a hundred. He was a class leader and ranked high in the estimation of his people. In our years on the Reserve we always found Joshua to be willing to assist us in any way he could. When we held our Sunday evening song service, we could at any time call on Joshua to address the people, which he did very effectively.

He had two fine boys who, if opportunity had offered, could have made their mark in the world. They were exceedingly clever in the schoolroom. Always kindly disposed to their teacher, they were both willing and obedient. Many times we were much interested in this old man's stories of early days amongst the Indians. We pray that he may have a great flood of light at eventide.

JOB BEAVER

This was a man essentially of the mountains. He was highly respected by all, by both white men and Indians. Job was a man to be depended on. Perhaps of all the Stoneys, he was most familiar with those of the mountains and mountain passes. Job also knew a great deal about minerals and mineral deposits, and where they could be found. He was noted for his splendid bunch of coloured ponies and a goodly number of cattle. His demise was very sudden and caused great grief in the band. He had some fine boys, two of whom were settled near Nordegg in the mountains west of Rocky Mountain House.

There were many others, too numerous to mention, all good men at heart. Councillor Big Jimmy Swampey, Big Paul Twoyoungmen, Joseph Hunter, John Twoyoungmen, Old Jimmy Jacob, Paul Jonas and the Poucette boys, together with Amos Bigstony. All or most are gone, but we have kind memories of them all.

While the Stoneys have often been judged to be a peculiar people speaking a unique language and having unique habits of life, we have always found them splendidly loyal to the government and trustworthy. Stoney Indians always proved themselves a loyal bodyguard for the protection of government officials and their families.

Now as to our object in writing these memoirs, it is this: many of the newcomers into this western country know very little of the people and times of early days, or shall we more correctly state, the conditions faced by those old-timers. Life in those old days was strenuous. Today it is luxurious. The people who today enjoy such a great measure of peace and prosperity should remember that it has very largely been purchased by the old vanguards who made it possible for them to enter upon such conditions as prevail today.

We are too apt to forget matters of this kind, and are slow to recognize the debt we owe our forerunners. Then regarding the aboriginal people of whose lives we have written, they also are to a great extent being forgotten by the rising generation who live under such improved conditions and days of peace. That we may all accord to those of whose memory we have written, "honour to whom honour" is the earnest wish of this writer.

CHAPTER 7
OXFORD HOUSE, 1910–1915

AFTER TWENTY YEARS IN THE INDIAN WORK AT MORLEY, I WAS IMPORTUNED by the late Rev. Thompson Ferrier to take up work in the Far North of Manitoba amongst the Indian people there. For some little time I weighed the matter over and sought wisdom from God in the matter. Many circumstances made it difficult for me to leave Morley. I had formed many friendships and had become very familiar with the country and its habits. In the meantime I received a number of letters urging me to accept, as the Manitoba Methodist Conference was about due to meet in the city of Winnipeg. Eventually I accepted and signified my willingness to go to the most needy place.

In due time a further letter containing a cheque for travelling expenses, amount fifty dollars, arrived, and I was advised that I had been appointed by Conference to Oxford House in the Far North. It would be necessary for me to move as soon as possible as the journey was a long one. It is a far cry from Morley, at the base of the Rocky Mountains, to Oxford House, which is situated about two hundred miles south of Hudson Bay. However, on July 26, 1910, I boarded the train and whirled off eastward to Winnipeg.

I was amazed in crossing the plains to find the difference twenty-one years had made. Many of the sidings had become little villages since I last passed this way, while many of the villages had blossomed into respectable towns. This was especially noticeable in Medicine Hat and Moose Jaw. I admired the acres and acres of waving wheat as we crossed the Saskatchewan plains. My train pulled

Mission House, Oxford Lake, ca. 1920s. Note cariole hitched to horse.

into Winnipeg station on Friday evening, July 28. Here I also found many changes, and this metropolitan city had surely become a wonderful place during my absence. When I left Winnipeg twenty-one years previously, it had a population of a scant twenty thousand souls, and now it had increased to about one hundred thousand or more, while its growth commercially and financially was something phenomenal. I was exceedingly amazed to find how it had extended and grown with churches. colleges, public buildings, and warehouses. No longer did the old horse streetcars pound along Main Street or down Kennedy Street. We had been making strides in the subsequent years and now a splendid system of electric cars was flashing about.

Here I was delayed for nearly two weeks awaiting the return of the *S.S. Wolverine* to be conveyed across Lake Winnipeg. This steamship had been chartered by Earl Grey, who was then on his way across the continent to York Factory, to ship from that point by Hudson's Bay steamer to England. Earl Grey was at that time Governor General of Canada.

Lake Winnipeg is a large sheet of fresh water. The waters of Red River disgorge themselves into it at its southern extremity. This lake is variously estimated at from two hundred and fifty to three hundred miles in length, and of irregular width, fully seventy-five miles across at the extreme north end. Its waters teem with fish: sturgeon, whitefish, pickerel, perch and many other species. It is a source of considerable wealth to the province. I understand these fish in this lake find a ready market in the United States. At its southern extremity the lake is narrow, dotted with many islands and cross currents.

S.S. Wolverine *at Berens River, 1925. This ship was used by both John and Annie Niddrie travelling on Lake Winnipeg to Berens River. It was built in 1903, laid up in 1932, and dismantled in 1936.*

Many rivers disgorge their waters into this lake. On the east side there are the Winnipeg, Hollow Water, Bad Throat, Berens, Poplar and Black Rivers, and at the extreme north end the giant Saskatchewan. This giant river drains a vast extent of the country. The Saskatchewan River, ere disgorging its waters into Lake Winnipeg, rushes over a series of rapids about six miles in length, known as Big Grand Rapids. Here in the old days of York boat freighting, many difficult and dangerous problems presented themselves to the various crews employed in these strenuous tasks.

It was Friday morning, August 11th, when we boarded the *S.S. Wolverine* at Selkirk, northward bound. The crossing of Lake Winnipeg was an eye-opener to me as I had no idea of its extent. Today it is a great tourist summer resort, or rather a summer tourist trip. The weather continued beautifully fine and we reached Warren's Landing after spending the night on the steamer.

Warren's Landing, at the extreme northern end of the lake, is the terminus of steam navigation and freight transport. Generally speaking, the freight for the remote trading posts is towed by gas boat in a barge to Norway House, which is a distributing point for the inland far-away points. From this point it is shipped by canoes as the York boat regime is now over. While the canoe may be a more expensive mode of transport, it is an admirable system, as the water courses sometimes become very shoal. In these days of improved transport facilities, aeroplane and the outboard motor engine have largely expedited

Another ship seen on Lake Winnipeg was the Grand Rapids, *shown here with fishing boats at Warren's Landing, 1921–27.*

inland freighting. Air transport may seem to the unaccustomed an expensive mode, but one takes time to consider and note there is no destruction of property in this mode, whereas by canoe there are frequently major losses.

From Warren's Landing we were conveyed by Hudson's Bay gas boat across greater Playgreen Lake and down Jack River to Norway House. It was quite late on Saturday evening when I reached Norway House Boarding School, where we met with every kindness from the resident missionary, who was also the principal of the school. Mr. Lousley, the missionary, kindly requested me to hold two services in the church the following day, both of which were well attended.

Norway House is a historical point both ecclesiastically and commercially. In the old days it was a distributing point in the Hudson's Bay Company's business. The goods were all shipped from England, landed at York Factory in bulk, and here made up by craftsmen and shipped to Norway House, where they were apportioned to the different posts north and south, and also west according to the requisitions. It was here that God gave to Rev. James Evans, who landed at that point on June 10, 1840, the Cree syllabic system by which that language is reduced to written order. His first efforts, it is true, were somewhat crude but nonetheless successful. Securing some of the lead from the interior of the tea chests at the Hudson's Bay Company's fort, he with his jackknife cut out the syllabics from this. In lieu of paper he used the inner bark of the silver birch tree, and made ink from sturgeon oil mixed with soot from the chimney. An old fur press was kindly loaned him by the Hudson's Bay

Rev. John W. Niddrie, right, with Nelson Williams of Norway House, ca. 1930s.

Company, and through this medium his first translations appeared: a number of verses of Holy Writ and a number of popular hymns were printed on birch bark. When the Indians departed for winter quarters, he rolled up the bark containing these writings in the breast of his capote coat and carried it to the Indians at their winter trapping grounds. By the light of pine logs in their camp the gospel message of salvation was read. Today this syllabic system is used far and wide by the aboriginal people of western Canada. This system of Cree writing became very popular and was easily mastered. Indeed, it has never been improved upon and other churches have adopted it.

I must not omit the fact that two of my nieces from Winnipeg decided to accompany me into the hinterland and spend the winter in my new northern home. Everything to these city-bred girls was at first a novelty and perhaps a little more than a novelty in the line and mode of travel, because this was all outside of their experiences in the city. However, ere they returned to Winnipeg the following summer, the novelty soon wore off and I must admit they conducted themselves bravely.

We found the missionary effort well to the front at Norway House upon our arrival, and the younger generation making rapid strides in education. A commodious church and boarding school for the Indian children was filled to capacity, seventy or eighty pupils in attendance. We enjoyed the kind hospitality of the resident missionaries, Rev. J.A. and Mrs. Lousely, very much for a few days. For years these good people had been labouring for the uplift of these aboriginal people in this extreme isolation.

Roscoe T. Chapin identifies this photo from the 1920s as a "loaded canoe and at least 1000 lb. of freight." Note the men with paddles in each end of the canoe, while the man in the centre is pulling on oars. John Niddrie described such travel in his writing. Too big to fit comfortably in the bow or stern of a canoe, with his large size and strength, Niddrie was well suited as an oarsman.

We remained at Norway House a few days while preparations were being made for our journey into the Far North, for we still had one hundred and eighty miles to make ere reaching our objective point. Finally we started out. Our mode of locomotion was a huge skiff, manned by four men. We started out with a fair wind and, hoisting our sail, we forged ahead until we camped the first night out at the Big Rock on Black Water Creek. I found our men splendid fellows willing, industrious, and capable. It added no little to our comfort that we had the very finest of weather.

The mist of early morning hung over the water when we again embarked at 5:00 A.M. Rowing steadily northward, we camped the second night out at about three parts of the way up to Watershed River, or in the native language, *Ee-och-e-mamis*. Following this stream another twenty or twenty-five miles, we reached the spot known as the Height of Land.

A century or more ago, all of the freight for the western inland country passed through the narrows of this small river. The goods were shipped in bulk to York Factory by Hudson's Bay Company ship and converted into separate articles and utensils, thus giving this place its name. I have been told that at one time as many as three hundred craftsmen were employed in this industry. These were shipped first to Norway House, either by birchbark canoe or York boat, the latter carrying what was termed one hundred "pieces" of one hundred

Men with burdens on a portage in the 1920s were a familiar sight when travelling by canoe in northern Manitoba. John Niddrie was admired for his efforts in carrying his share of the load.

pounds each, or five tons. Each boat was propelled by nine hardy voyageurs, eight known as "middlemen" and one steersman or guide. On approaching the rapids, one of the bow oarsmen acted as "bowsman." The whole system was both slavish and dangerous, and was responsible for a great deal of mortality. Reaching a portage, the men had to become beasts of burden, upon whose backs the whole cargo was transported, if upon the river, beyond the danger zone, or if following a chain of lakes, to the next water course. The short season, the changeable weather, the great distance to be covered, all of these kept the personnel going at top speed.

The ordinary load per each trip across these portages is two pieces or two hundred pounds. A portage strap is affixed to the load. This strap has a broad forehead band, and is pulled over the head into position. If the load be properly balanced with a good heavy top pack, away goes the man on the run, mostly, with both hands swinging at his side. It is almost incredible the weights

BAPTISMS.

Municipality of Congregation of

	No. 205	No. 206	No. 207
When born.	August 20th 1910	September 3rd 1910	September 12th 1910
Where born.	Otillia Muskago Oxford House	Oxford House	Oxford House
Name.	Otillia "	Matilda Chubb	Alice Munroe
Sex—male or female.	Female	Female	Female.
Name and surname of father.	James Muskago	Robert Chubb	Aleck Munroe
Name and maiden surname of mother.	Rebecca Beardy	Ethel Robinson	Philippa Hindley
Occupation or calling of father.	Hunter.	Councillor Oxf. Band	Trapper and Trader
Signature, description and residence of informant.	David Munroe Oxford House	Robert Chubb Oxford House	David Munroe Interpreter Oxford House
When baptized.	September 11th 1910	September 15th 1910	September 18th 1910
Signature of clergyman or minister.	J. A. Lousley Supt. Norway House	J. W. Niddrie	John W. Niddrie
REMARKS.	[illegible]		Baptized in Camp Mother too Poorly to bring Child to church

	No. 208	No. 209	No. 210
When born.	March 15th 1910	May 15th 1910	July 26th 1910
Where born.	Oxford House	Oxford House	Oxford House
Name.	Annie Nattaway	Moses Bevington	McLeod Williams
Sex—male or female.	Female	Male	Male
Name and surname of father.	Uncertain	Peter [illegible]	John Williams
Name and maiden surname of mother.	Christy Nattaway	Mary [illegible]	Elizabeth Grieve
Occupation or calling of father.		Clk H.B. Co.	Trapper and Trader
Signature, description and residence of informant.	David Munroe Interpreter Oxford House	David Munroe Interpreter Oxford	John Williams Father
When baptized.	September 20th 1910	September 23rd 1910	October 4th 1910
Signature of clergyman or minister.	J. W. Niddrie	J. W. Niddrie	J. W. Niddrie
REMARKS.	This Child was baptized in Camp cause Illegitimate	"Illegitimate" Baptized in Camp.	Illegitimate. [illegible] ashamed to say

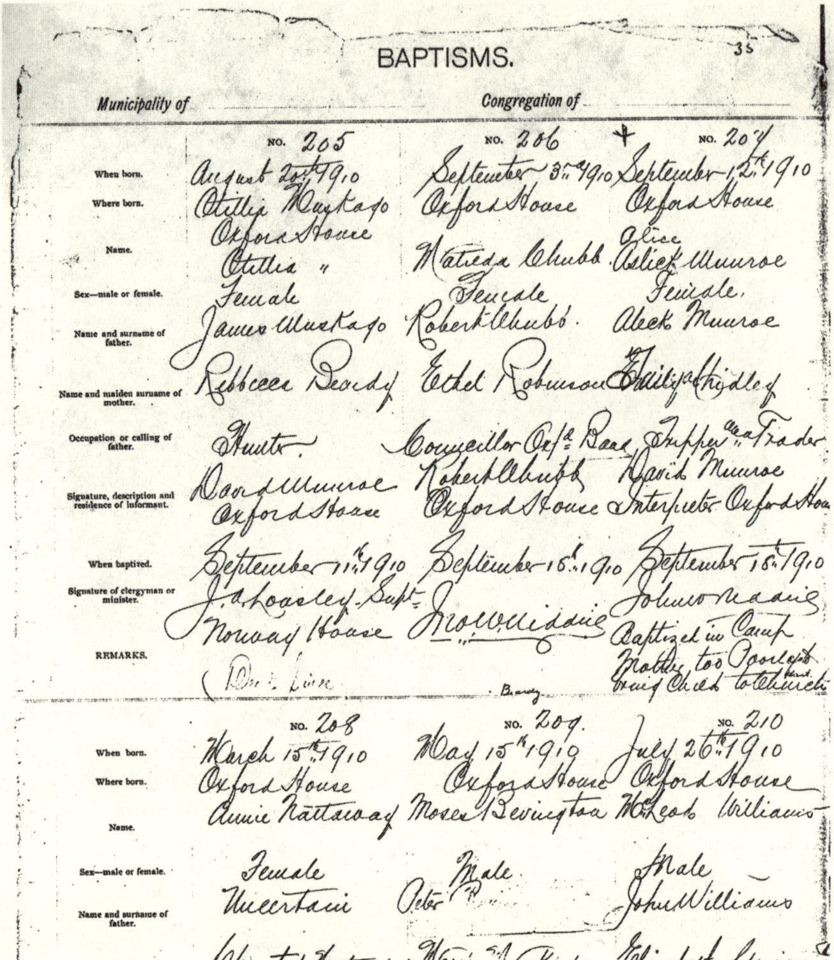

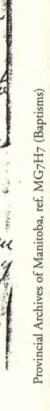

Sample records of baptisms at Oxford House, 1910, in the handwriting of John W. Niddrie.

Provincial Archives of Manitoba, ref. MG7H7 (Baptisms)

some of these regular freighters can thus carry. I have seem a slim, slight young fellow with three hundred and seventy-five pounds to a load, but the portage was not lengthy, and he was moving carefully. In hot weather the perspiration and blood from the bites of mosquitoes and other insects all very materially add to the discomfort of such mode of transport. It is a very costly mode of freighting for, after all, there is no greater asset than human power if properly handled. I have seen men comparatively young in years almost completely used up on account of attempting this work when too young.

This being Saturday evening when we reached Robinson Portage, it behooved us to look for a good camping ground at which to spend the Sabbath Day. This we found at the north end of the portage. Here we spent a very quiet, peaceful Sabbath. I held two short services, one in the morning and one in the evening. Monday morning bright and early again found us on the move at 5:30. That night we camped at Windy Lake. The weather continuing fine, we reached The Gateway at Oxford Lake for a night camp that evening. Next day at 11:00 A.M. we reached the mission house at Oxford and were for the time being at the end of our journey.

Mission work was begun at what is now known locally as "the old mission" at Jackson's Bay, about twelve miles by winter road from the present site, or twenty-five miles by summer route.

It being Wednesday evening, and formerly when a missionary was located there, they used to hold an evening service, I was asked if I would hold a service. I heartily acquiesced. The bell was rung, and as most of the people were at home at the time, the church was soon filled to the door. No doubt many of them were anxious to see what kind of a man the new "Praying Chief" was. The singing was hearty, and by securing the services of a man amongst the crowd as interpreter, the service progressed quite satisfactorily.

Immediately I began to study the Cree language and was able to make some little progress. Very few of the Oxford House people at that time spoke English. They seemed anxious to assist me in my efforts to learn the language, as I had to try to understand them and make them understand me. The band of Indians at that point numbered about three hundred, all Swampy Cree. I found them docile and easy to manage, and intelligent readers in the Cree Bibles. This encouraged me very much and brought to me great good cheer.

Oxford Lake is a beautiful sheet of fresh water, and has always been noted for its splendid quality of whitefish and trout. Some of these lake trout weigh as much as twenty-five and thirty pounds. The lake is about forty miles in length, and of irregular width. The Hudson's Bay Company post and the Mission and Church stand upon its north bank about four hundred yards apart.

I found the Oxford House Indians splendid people. Indeed, the five years spent at that Mission are a green spot in my memory. My immediate predecessor was a native and, on account of his dereliction to duty, the work

Sample records of marriages at Oxford House, 1910, in the handwriting of John W. Niddrie.

had been allowed to run down. However, I am thankful to say that matters soon assumed a different stage.

It was Saturday afternoon. The sun had passed the zenith and was casting its beams over the lake, which on this occasion reminded me of the Apostolic Sea, mingled with fire. I was seated at my desk putting the finishing touches to my sermon for the next afternoon when I was disturbed by a somewhat impatient knock at the door. Hastily gathering up the loose leaves containing my notes and putting them inside my Bible to be in readiness when required, I answered the summons. A young man of about eighteen years of age stood before me and accosted me, "O, praying chief, I have been sent to ask if you will go over to the camp on the hill and see the sick woman; she is getting so weak that we fear she will leave us tonight."

"Certainly, I shall go at once," was my reply.

Sarah W. was a woman of undoubted Christian character, one of those always to the front in the cause of Christ. Whenever there was anything to be done necessitating the assistance of the women around the church such as scrubbing, etc., she was the first to arrive with pail and scrubbing brush in hand. I had also noted her earnest attention to the sermon and expounding of the scriptures, and was aware of the fact that she was endeavouring to the extent of her ability to live the Christian life and serve God.

Putting my Cree Testament into my breast pocket along with my hymn book, I stepped across the threshold of the Mission House and took my way along the lake shore. The sun was shining brightly in the heavens, the birds were singing in the trees, and everything seemed bright and glad around me, but somehow or other I could not help, or should I say resist, a feeling of sadness as I thought of our sister on her way out, leaving a husband and a little boy to mourn her departure. Slowly climbing the hill, I entered the camp where the Angel of Death was hovering with slippered feet. The poor woman lay, gasping out the last hours of her life, on a small pile of spruce brush with the walls of the tent lifted to admit the cool air and surrounded by her friends. Room was made, and a box set down for me to be seated. Taking the poor, emaciated, fevered hand in mine, I waited for the spell of consciousness which nearly always comes ere the departure. I sang, I prayed, but the spell of unconsciousness still lasted. The weak pulse, the laboured breathing continued, sure signs that dissolution was at hand, and that the weak woman was nearing the Great Divide.

DEATHS OR FUNERAL SERVICES. 103

Municipality of | Congregation of

	No. 109	No. 110	No. 111
Name and surname of deceased	— —	Zackeus Hattaway	Mary Jane Hart
Date and place of death	Oxford House Aug. 15 1911	July 25th Oxford House	Oxford House September 2nd 1911
Sex—male or female	Female	Male	Female
Age	Only about ½ an hour	about 2 weeks	about [illegible]
Occupation or calling			
Religious denomination			Methodist
Where born	Oxford House	Oxford House	Oxford House
Cause of death and duration of illness		Convulsions	Female Trouble & Tuberculosis (3 mos).
Name of physician, if any	None	None	None
Name, description and residence of informant	Henry Robinson	James Hattaway	Her brother Willie Hart Oxford House
Date of funeral service	Aug. 15th 1911	Monday Aug. 7th 1911	Saturday Sep. 2nd 1911
Signature of clergyman or minister	Jno. W. Niddrie	Jno. W. Niddrie	Jno. W. Niddrie
Remarks	Jamie Robinson's Infant.	Charlie Hattaway's baby	This was the best girl at Oxford at this time —

	No. 112	No. 113	No. 114
Name and surname of deceased	Wm. Dan Grieve	Stanley Grieve	McLeod Williams.
Date and place of death	September 20th 1911 Oxford House	Sunday October 1st 1911 2 mile Point Oxford	October 3rd 1911 Oxford House
Sex—male or female	Male	Male	Male.
Age	about 3 years of age	about 2 Years Old	about 14 Months Old
Occupation or calling			
Religious denomination			
Where born	Oxford House	Oxford House	Oxford House
Cause of death and duration of illness	Diphtheria Semblance 5 Days.	Diphtheria Second. 1 week.	Perhaps Diphtheria 2 Weeks.
Name of physician, if any	None	None	None
Name, description and residence of informant	James Hattaway Oxford House	Benjamin Okemow Oxford House	Robert Chubb. Oxford House
Date of funeral service	Sept. 21st 1911	October 2nd 1911	October 3rd 1911.
Signature of clergyman or minister	Jno. W. Niddrie	Jno. W. Niddrie	Jno. W. Niddrie
Remarks			

Provincial Archives of Manitoba, ref. MG7H7 (Burials)

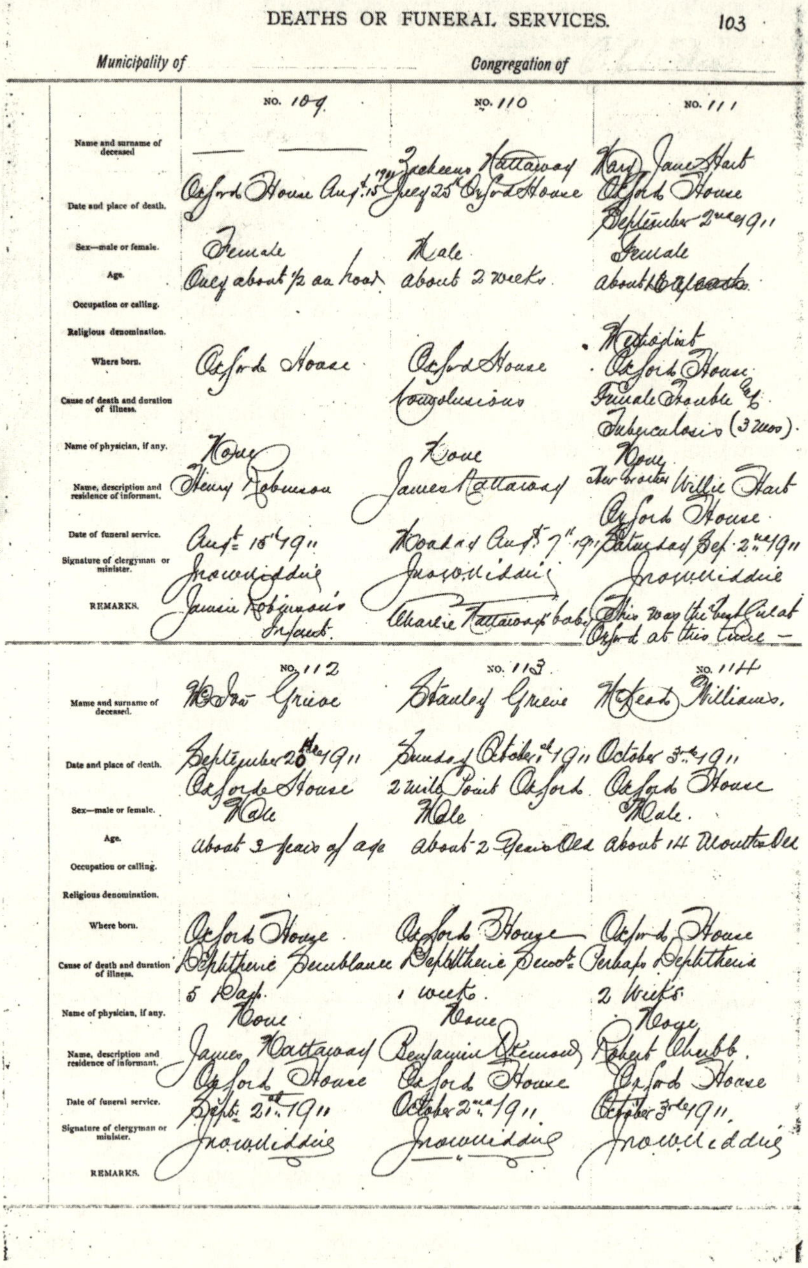

Sample records of deaths or funeral services at Oxford House, 1911, in the handwriting of John W. Niddrie. Most deaths shown here are of youngsters, as young as half an hour (No. 109). Of Mary Jane Hart (No. 111) who died at about age sixteen of "female trouble and tuberculosis" on September 2, 1911 and was buried the same day, Niddrie noted that, "This was the best girl at Oxford at this time."

After a little while she opened her eyes, and with a smile of recognition spoke the following words intermittently: "I have....just been...listening to beautiful music. It was...the song of...the angels. I am... so happy." Opening my Cree testament, I began to read John 14:1 to 6. Then again kneeling down, I prayed that this soul, nearing the confines of the eternal world, might have a great flood of light at eventide. Again seating myself, I could see that she wished to communicate something to me. Her eyes followed the circle of friends until she singled me out. Stooping with my ear close to the dying lips, for by this time she had grown very weak, I could just manage to catch the halting words:

"Tell...the people...tomorrow...that I have...no fear...in my heart, no trouble...on my...mind...for Jesus is with me...to take...me home." The last word seemed to come to me in a faint, far-away whisper, as if almost from the golden strand.

That afternoon I had gone to the camp to try to help this good woman down the River Brink, but as I left and walked homeward in the gathering twilight, I myself was made strong and comforted by the dying message. On the following afternoon I committed her body, "Ashes to ashes, dust to dust," in the little God's Acre on the hill in the rear of the Mission House.

It was a spring morning in 1913. I was ringing the school bell. Already the school children were beginning to gather in twos and threes, with a half-smiling "Good morning, Teacher," which I had for some time been trying to teach them. Looking up, I saw a young man coming at top speed along the path near the lake shore. Presently he almost breathlessly accosted me in the Cree tongue, "Come quick, the old man is dying."

Handing up the bell rope, and cautioning the pupils not to stray far away as I would return soon, I hastily followed the messenger. The distance was not great, certainly not more than a quarter of a mile. When I reached the wigwam, partly composed of birchbark, moss, and canvas, I could, ere I entered, hear the poor old woman soon to be left a widow wailing out her grief. Stooping down, I entered the wigwam. This old gentleman must have been at least eighty years of age. For many years he had been known as the spiritual leader of his people. On his knees, unable to lie down no doubt on account of some pulmonary disease, with his long white hair falling on his shoulders, he certainly presented a very patriarchal appearance. It was quite evident that whatever was to be done must be attempted at once.

Dropping upon my knees beside him, and throwing one arm around his body, I began to sing in the Cree language, "Safe in the arms of Jesus."

Willingly and bravely he attempted to join in and assist me in the singing of this grand old hymn which has been the solace and comfort of many a departing child of God. I then proceeded to offer a prayer for the departing one. Somehow or other as I prayed, a great light, a great peace seemed to flood the wigwam. It was while I was still kneeling that the message came. I could hear between the sentences of my prayer the whispering words from the withered lips at my side, the last being, "Father, I am coming." A few moments later he lurched forward out of my grasp and was gone.

I have today many happy memories of the five years spent at Oxford House, of the acquaintances which ripened into friendships strong and true amongst those dusky sons of the forest who tried to live the Christian life. With few exceptions they belong to the Swampy Confederacy. There are, it is true, one or two small bands of Saulteaux who have sprung from the great Ojibway tribe, but anyone who is a master of the Cree language can mostly understand them and make himself understood. The Swampy Cree language is dialectal, that is, a shoot off the parent Cree language. Many people assert that the Indians are a vanishing race. However, of late years there has been a very substantial increase in numbers.

One thing is without doubt: it will take them some time to fall into step with their white brethren and assume the duties of citizenship. For many years now I have been impressed with the fact that all, or nearly so, of our hope for this people lies with the young, that is, the rising generation. While we do our best to assist those of more mature years, the rising generation assimilates much more quickly and retains with much more tenacity the teachings of Christianity and the benefits of civilization. Those of more mature years have a great deal to unload ere they come into line for a newer and better mode of life, and this mode of unloading is a difficult matter, that is, it is difficult for them to eliminate the traditions, customs, and habits of centuries. In their own line they seem to excel as guides, etc. Without pencil or paper they seem to have photographed upon their brain the topography of a country, and many of them are magnificently gifted with human memory. As canoemen they are unexcelled. Travelling along through the water courses in the wilds and meeting with an accident to our craft, they will go to work and in an incredibly short space of time we have been again on our way as if nothing had happened. I question if there is any other aboriginal people as easily reached and as readily responsive to Christian teachings as these Indian peoples.

Two men carrying a canoe are shown on one of the many portages necessary when travelling by water in northern Manitoba, ca. 1920s.

They cannot by any stretch of imagination be termed a provident people, for with them it is either a feast or a famine—largely the latter, frequently. The changing times, coupled with many fatal maladies such as smallpox, Spanish flu, and the great white man's plague, T.B., have thinned the ranks and carried off thousands. Emerging from the nomadic to the semi-civilized has exacted its toll in human life.

Now a few words regarding the climate. In the Far North beyond Norway House and on to Hudson Bay the ground generally assumes its winter dress any time after the twentieth of October. I have seen snow on the ground to a depth of between three and four feet, indeed often near to the latter. Then the open-water navigation has frequently come to an end in that district from the twentieth to the end of May. For months the ground was asleep beneath this blanket of snow. The winter temperature has remained very low. Upon one occasion I noticed the temperature at Oxford House to be between 59 and 62 below zero. I read these figures on two different thermometers at the Hudson's Bay post at that point. I do know that the cold was so severe, the snow so dry that it was almost an impossibility for my dogs to drag the sleigh along, and the journey usually accomplished in two and one-half days took me upon that occasion four days and a half.

Sometimes towards spring, the morning would come upon us beautiful and bright. The wind would swing to the north and in half an hour it would be cold in the extreme. I opine this was on account of our proximity to Hudson

Bay. During the summer months the growth is extremely rapid. I believe that this is on account of the short, hot nights. Insect life obtains and reproduces very rapidly, and is a great pest to the traveller, unless precaution is taken in the way of a mosquito net. I can speak from experience and certainty, at least on this point. During the Conference year 1914 and 1915, the work at God's Lake was added to my field. That winter I made six trips to God's Lake. Each of these trips took from six to seven days. That was an exceedingly cold winter and I suffered accordingly. I also made one trip to Island Lake. The labours of life had come upon me, and I had very little time to sigh for the former fleshpots of Egypt.

Mission work amongst the Oxford House people was a grand success. Many I saw trying to live the Christian life. I also stood by the bedside of others when they departed with the smile of God upon their lips and His kiss on their cheeks, and heard them murmur, "This is the last of earth." I was sometimes very interested listening to some of the old men speaking of some of their first resident missionaries stationed at Norway House prior to the establishing of permanent work amongst them.

CHAPTER 8
ISLAND LAKE, 1915–1920

For weeks the snow had fallen until it covered the ground and frozen waters of the lake to a depth of nearly three feet on the level. It was impossible for us of the Mission House to go to the lake for a pail of water without first wriggling our feet into a pair of snowshoes. Sometimes quietly and again persistently, the snow was driven by the cruel northwest wind against the walls of the Mission House, standing on the north bank of Oxford Lake, and then swirled away to the rear, where it accumulated in ever-increasing drifts among the willows.

The short days and long nights of a northern winter seemed to drag themselves wearily along. Christmas and New Year's Day came upon us and went with nothing more of an exciting nature than a few dog-train races, which seemed to be hugely enjoyed by the few Indians and half-breeds lingering around the Hudson's Bay Company's post. Slowly, it seemed to me at first, the days began to flicker and lengthen out perceptibly as the sun swung higher in the heavens.

It was a dull gray February morning with low-hanging clouds when my Indian boy Willie, about thirteen years of age, and I packed up our sleigh containing food and blankets, hitched up our dogs, and took the trail northward, God's Lake being our objective point. I ran ahead on snowshoes, faithful Willie driving the dogs. Through the woods, across the back lake, and on to the long portage between us and Knee Lake we hurried, for ever and anon there came

Methodist Mission, Island Lake, 1921–27. Both John W. Niddrie, and Roscoe T. Chapin, whose selected photographs appear in this book, served as Methodist missionaries at Island Lake.

on the frost-laden air the one word of command, "Marse!" in Willie's clear treble voice. And "Marse!" it was to me as I dodged, now in, now out, beneath the snow-laden pine tree branches.

By and by the stars one by one flickered and died out, and the dim gray daylight came stealing over us. The clouds rose, and the keen north wind intensified and cut like a knife as we hurried along. We crossed the height-of-land and were now on the descending slope to Knee Lake, which we reached all in good time. The morning air was bitterly cold as we took up the long open stretch. I had, however, long ago learned that to travel with any degree of comfort in the rigours of the northern winter, one must clothe himself judiciously, that is, have a sufficient quantity of good warm clothing on, and yet not too much to retard active movement. The main thing is to keep the blood circulating vigorously.

The sun had by this time swung high in the heavens, although very little of its heat seemed to reach us in the frosty atmosphere of 45 or 50 below zero. The snow glittered and sparkled, but was exceedingly dry, and being so, friction made it very hard pulling for our dogs. The sleigh seemed as if it were being pulled through sand and not snow. Reaching a spot where dry wood and green spruce were in abundance, we called a halt. The dogs were pulled out of their collars and allowed to roll. The snow was kicked away a little, the ground carpeted with a few armfuls of spruce bush, the big dry logs cut down and piled on our fire. The frying pan being brought into requisition, bacon was soon sizzling and tea water from melted snow bubbling in our kettle, while our frozen bannock thawed out before the roaring fire for the mid-day meal.

Our stay at this point was short, for I was working on the principle that, "the king's business required haste." Soon again to the dogs' amazement, Willie was pushing their heads into the collars, the sleigh was tied up, and donning our snowshoes, once again we were on our way. As we travelled northward, the snow seemed to deepen, making my work of trail-breaking heavier. I had, however, long ago learned to accept all of these things as coming in the day's work, and was satisfied.

It may have been 4:00 P.M. or a little later, and the evening stars were beginning to show themselves when we pulled up on the banks of the little round lake which is said to mark the half-way point between the Oxford House post and that of God's Lake. Here we went to considerable more trouble in camp-making as we had to spend the night in the open without any other covering than the blue canopy of heaven afforded us. Shovelling away the snow with a snowshoe, we carpeted the ground to a depth of eighteen inches with green spruce brush. A few of these branches were stuck in the rear of the camp as a windbreak, the whole thing being accomplished in fifteen or twenty minutes. Then, lighting our fires and carrying our ten-foot logs, we piled them on. The making of such camps in the open involves a great deal of labour, as carrying in the night's wood on snowshoes is not always an easy task, and coming at the end of a long day's travel in trail-breaking may be termed strenuous. Then again, these open camp fires consume an immense deal of dry wood. However, this is the code of the trail, and why murmur?

The next item was the evening meal for men and dogs. These latter are fed but once a day, and that in the evening after the day's travel, two whitefish being the allowance for each dog. The fish were stood up round the big fire and thawed out. Then Willie, with whip in hand, stood over the snarling, growling pack to see that each one got justice. Then followed our supper, after which the drying of moccasins, socks, etc. was the order of the evening. The hours passed; bed-time arrived.

Hark! What was that reverberating away across the treetops and across the frozen waters of the lake? In the Cree tongue, it was the song of evening praise preparatory to prayers. Willie's beautiful tenor and my bass mingled in the moonlight and amongst the shadows of the trees. Kneeling down on the frozen spruce brush, which the roaring fire had failed to thaw, we committed ourselves into the hands of the God of Israel, who neither slumbers nor sleeps. Rolling up in our rabbit robe, lying closely as possible together to preclude the entrance of the cold air, Willie and I spent that night as we have spent many another in this land of ice and snow, with more or less comfort.

Our camp fire threw out its great lurid light, and by and by burned low; the trees cracked in the grip of King Frost; overhead the stars glittered and sparkled in the cold night air; and calm, tranquil in its chastened splendour, the moon pursued its course through the liquid heavens. Away through the woods the wolves howled, and just overhead a night owl hooted out its doleful note. Presently Willie's long, steady respiration proved that he was asleep and at rest after the hard day's travel. Yet sleep for some reason or other failed to visit my eyelids. The singing of the hymn had awakened memories that refused to be hushed, memories of other days, other friends, other scenes. Some of these friends were away across the blue waters of the Atlantic. Others had heard the voice of their Father calling them to the home of many mansions and had crossed the bourne whence no traveller returns. Others have passed away and their bodies lie out yonder in our own western foothills. The flowers play hide-and-seek over their graves, while the big fir trees stand sentinel over the rest and the Rocky Mountains, like fragments of a petrified eternity, loom up in the background.

The hours passed away. The moon set. The beautiful Aurora Borealis scintillated, sparkled and flashed around us with its rainbow tints. "Sleep that knits up the ravel'd sleave of care" had at last come to me. My last thought as I peered through the small aperture left for a breathing space was as if a great voice had proclaimed:

> Bring forth the royal diadem,
> And crown Him Lord of all.

Side by side we slept on in the frozen solitude. The stars were still sparkling when we awakened and went about the preparation for the morning meal. Soon our big campfire was again throwing out its glaring light. Again our morning meal was over. Packing up, we turned our faces northwards. The country through which we travelled that day was more rugged. Forest and lake interspersed. As we proceeded northwards, the snow seemed to deepen. Steadily pushing on, quite late that night we reached the Hudson's Bay post at God's Lake. Here we received a most hearty welcome and were hospitably entertained by the officer in charge, a young Scotchman. Very soon the news spread that the "Praying Chief" had arrived and the few Indians in the vicinity began to gather. That night I held a service in the "men's house," preaching from John 14:1 to 3.

We felt indeed glad and thankful, as we wended our way to the officers' quarters after the service, that we did not have to make camp in the open that night, for the temperature had perceptibly lowered and it was most keenly sharp and cold. We remained here all the next day awaiting the arrival of Indians to guide us to the large outlying camp whither we were bound. These men arrived late that night. Early the following morning we were astir and "Marse!" was the word as we hurriedly crossed the portage and took the course eastward along the lake. The distance was long, but we had a fairly good trail and by pushing hard made the camp late that night. Very soon again the people began to gather, and as soon as we had got comfortably domiciled in my good friend Daniel Hill's camp, we began a service. There may have been between thirty and forty people in the congregation, and as I looked over the motley group, they surely looked to me like sheep in the wilderness without a shepherd. This being Saturday evening, we announced for three services the following day.

Daniel Hill, in whose camp we were for the time domiciled, was one of nature's noblemen, a good, wholesome Christian man whose best was always to the front in the cause of Christ. Thus I found him, and thus I knew him through all the years of our friendship. Years later, when he was nearing the Great Divide, do I remember reading his last letter, in the Cree language, to his daughter, who was a pupil in the Residential School at Norway House, and his pleading with her to follow what was right and meet him in the Happy Spirit Land (an Indian term for heaven).

We had scarcely finished breakfast next morning ere the people began to arrive in twos and threes. Soon we had all who could manage to walk. Three times that day I pointed them to the Lamb of God that taketh away the sins of the world. We administered the sacrament of the Lord's Supper, and baptized those eligible for the same. Late that night I sought a much needed night's rest.

Next morning we held another service with these needy people, and again left for the Hudson's Bay Company's post, where we remained another day and held another service. Wednesday morning we eagerly turned our faces southwards and travelled almost the entire length of God's Lake. Camping once by the way, we held services with two or three outlying families. Still pushing southwards next morning, we reached the other large camp that evening. Here one service followed another in quick succession. Monday morning bright and early found us on the first stage of the home stretch. Nothing of a more serious nature happened than a shortage of food supplies, which we happily supplemented from the dogs' fish. We were very pleased to reach home late on Tuesday night, having travelled a half circle, covered somewhere about three hundred miles, and held seventeen services. Next morning, one of my class leaders called to inform me that my services were urgently needed at Red Sucker River to assist one of our boys, who was dying.

Thursday morning again found us on the trail. This time the journey was but a short one of thirty miles for the round trip. Thomas C. was a boy about seventeen years of age, one of those bright, sunny-natured fellows all learn to love. Early the previous fall the family had left for winter quarters. The boy had developed acute T.B. and had grown suddenly worse. Seeing that death was inevitable, the parents hurried homewards so that the boy might have a Christian burial, but he had weakened so much and so rapidly that a halt had to be called ere they could reach the Reserve.

Hudson's Bay Company Post, Island Lake, ca. 1920s.

I can still in fancy see the leap of joy in the eyes of the dying boy as I entered the camp. It took me some little time to steady myself and begin to try to help him "down the river's brink." The lump in my throat, the pain at my heart as I looked upon the poor, emaciated body, almost transparent hands, and woefully diminished features—all of these were better felt than expressed. I prayed, I read, I sang, I talked and tried to encourage him, all the time thankful that he was not suffering too much to heed my efforts. I remained in the camp all the rest of the day, and, when fully assured of his humble faith in God, reverently administered the sacrament of the Lord's Supper.

The trailing garments of eventide were by that time coming down upon us and warning that it was time to begin our fifteen-mile run home, but still this poor dying boy held onto my hands and begged that once more I sing and pray with him ere I left. Steadying my voice as best I could, I sang in the Cree language, "Safe in the arms of Jesus," and knelt down where the angel with slippered feet was hovering. Imprinting a last kiss on the poor white forehead, and taking a last look at the fevered cheeks where the death sweat was already showing, I sadly turned away, and he smilingly faced the Great Beyond. It was long after dark when we reached the Mission House and retired for the first really undisturbed night's rest we had had for nearly two weeks.

It was rather a disappointment to me, upon reaching Norway House at the beginning of June 1915, to find communications from the officers of our church advising me of the possibility of my removal from Oxford to Island Lake at the coming Conference. I had never entertained any such thought, but this was the

Rev. Roscoe Tranmer Chapin, right, served at the Island Lake mission following John W. Niddrie. His splendid photographs, in the collection of the Provincial Archives of Manitoba, illustrate some of the people, places, and events from the life of John Niddrie. Chapin is shown here at Kettle Rapids with his wife Etta next to him, a friend, Dorinda Sturdy, and Chapin's father at left, 1920s.

arrangement made at the Conference of 1915 in Winnipeg. I was advised at that Conference that it was not supposed that I would make any objection, and so it had been arranged. Returning to Oxford House to arrange my removal, on my way thither I met the York boats between Windy Lake and "The Big Kettle." Here I went ashore and held a farewell service on a flat rock. The boats were at that time in the charge of Abel Williams, God's good man. This was without exception one of the best men, either white or Indian, it had ever been my lot to meet. Although a young man at that time, he became Chief of the Oxford House Band and held that distinction until his death in 1918.

On July 15, 1915, I left with four canoes for Island Lake. Reaching God's Lake, I spent the day with this needy people. At that time they were located at the mouth of the Weasatchewan River. I had a very profitable Lord's Day with them, holding three services. Early on Monday morning, July 18, we left for Island Lake. The distance by canoe route from God's Lake to Island Lake is not great, but it is exceedingly dangerous, especially during "high water" season. The Island Lake river has to be navigated and in many places is fraught with danger and hard work. That night we camped near to Weasel Rapids, thankful to have passed the Kenutchwain Rapids safely. Pushing our way upstream, we reached Carrot Rapids Portage for our evening camp. Our guide was one of those men you meet so often in the north, a splendid man, and one who saw

Roscoe Chapin's memoirs, A Happy Journey Through Life, *and his collection of photographs provide an excellent look at his life and times in the 1920s. He is shown here at the oars of a loaded canoe.*

that all of the party did their share. He was also one of those guides who believe in early rising, and in some instances we had breakfast and prayer over with and were some little distance on the water by 5:00 A.M.

For five years following I had what might be termed "a roving commission," and had to minister to Oxford House, God's Lake, Island Lake, Sandy Lake and Deer Lake. This was during the years of the World War and it seemed an utter impossibility to secure men for the various fields. During those years I travelled far and wide, and estimated that I covered two thousand miles during the winter months by dog train and snowshoes, and as many more during the summer months by canoe. Sometimes the journeys in the wilds became tedious, especially when I was away on a trip as long as twenty or twenty-one days. However, I was glad to carry the message of Salvation to the hungry souls, who seemed to me like sheep in the wilderness without a shepherd.

The Island Lake Indians are a branch of the great Ojibway Confederacy, but not so pronounced as the Berens River people. Many of them have intermarried into the Cree tribes of the north, and the Cree language is wholly used in the church services at that point. I found them withal willing to learn and anxious to obey the truth, their greatest bane being their density regarding religion and ethics. My immediate predecessor had been a native man, and totally unfit to hold the position. Indeed, I had the distinguished position of being the first ordained missionary they had had. Two or three missionary teachers had preceded me but had not remained long enough at the mission to give them an opportunity to become Christianized or even to receive many of the blessings of civilization.

Even amongst these semi-pagan people I found much cause for rejoicing as I beheld them coming more and more into the light each day. There may have been some features of the work which ground harshly upon me, but the blessings outweighed the drawbacks. One has to become used to taking the bitter with the sweet, the sunshine with the shadow.

The Island Lake people were quite accomplished trappers, and it was a common thing for a man to make as much as a thousand dollars during the trapping season. However, their distance from civilization and the high cost of transport prevented them from getting much ahead materially. I have known of one man killing as many as one hundred minks alone in one winter. They were generously disposed towards their missionary, and generously supplied him with moose meat, fish, etc. Many of them were at home but a short time during the summer months, and were what might be denominated very migratory. My last Sabbath Day amongst these people was a busy one. At the morning service I baptized fifteen babies. At the afternoon service I administered the sacrament of the Lord's Supper to over two hundred, and at the evening service I married six couples.

In 1920 I was advised that the Stationing Committee of the Methodist Conference had appointed me to Berens River, and I was to be prepared to move out about the end of August to succeed Mr. Percy Jones, who was to go to Wesley College in Winnipeg. I was sorry to leave Island Lake, where I had experienced so many changing vicissitudes, mostly pleasing. However, it was for me to obey, not to criticize my superior officers.

CHAPTER 9
BERENS RIVER, 1920–1938

THE UNITED CHURCH MISSION TO THE INDIANS AT BERENS RIVER IS situated at the mouth of Berens River, about one and a half miles from the east shore of Lake Winnipeg, and about 150 miles north of the city of Winnipeg. Lake Winnipeg is about 250 miles in length. At the south end it is twenty or thirty miles in width, while at its northern extremity it is estimated at seventy-five miles.

At Berens River we have an Indian Reserve with about three hundred and twenty Indians. They are Saulteaux (pronounced Soto) and are a branch of the great Ojibway tribe. They use the Ojibway language, although somewhat dialectal. Prior to 1873, periodical visits may have been made, although few and far between, by missionaries from Norway House or other parts. In 1854, Rev. John Ryerson had strongly recommended that a mission be opened at Berens River. Almost twenty years later, in 1872, his recommendation was carried out. Timothy Bear, a native leader from Norway House, carried on the work until the Rev. E.R. Young arrived to break ground for the mission work among the needy in 1873. Consequent upon the ill health of Mrs. Young, they had to return to Ontario in 1875. Other men, devoted and faithful, followed Young, although sometimes men suitable for the work were not available. The phenomenal success attending missionary efforts in other parts of the north have not been experienced here. Unfortunately, these people have come in contact with many white men of—what shall I say?—not of the highest order.

Mothers and babies at Maria Portage, 1920s. It seems that little girls everywhere enjoy dolls—these children have papoose dolls that look like the younger children.

At Berens River I had the superintendency of the following missions: Little Grand Rapids, Pekangecum, Deer Lake and Sandy Lake. Bloodvein and Poplar River were supposed to be included. The former, however, had become wholly Romanist ere we reached our new mission, and I had Poplar River under my care for one year only.

Thursday, July 17TH dawned upon us still, quiet and beautiful. The mist of early morning hung over the river as we looked out and began putting the finishing touches to the preparations already made for our annual trip up Berens River and inland to the missions in this superintendency. For some years, annual visits have been made to these inland points.

Now a word regarding the personnel of this party. First, there was the help. Then there was our guide, John James Everett, than whom no better man could be found for such a trip. He was kind, courteous, cheerful and eminently capable on the whole trip, handling his engine (Evinrude) with a masterly hand. Then there was our bowsman, the staid and steady William Everett, whose pipe seemed to be forever in requisition. This man filled the dual capacity of bowsman and cook, and proved himself both willing and careful of all our camping outfit. These and the writer made up the party.

Breakfast and prayers over, we began to load up with food, bedding, and other necessaries for the trip, which we had packed up the night previous, to be in readiness for an early start. At precisely 7:00 A.M., John James pulled the cord that gave the magic touch to the engine and we forged ahead, the water churning up in our wake. Waving a good-bye to our teacher Mr. Street as we passed his home, we soon passed the last house in the settlement, and steadily stemmed the current.

Our first objective point was Little Grand Rapids, a distance of one hundred and six miles up the Berens River. Between Berens River and that point there are many rapids. These increase in number or decrease according to high or low water. Sometimes when there is heavy rainfall in the upper country, the river becomes swollen and in many places dangerous. At other times in dry summers, travelling is much easier and attended with less danger. Generally speaking, our freighters put the number of rapids between Berens River and Little Grand Rapids at forty-two. At all these rapids there is a foaming, churning current, and at most the canoe and all therein have to be taken out and carried across the portages beyond the danger zone. This entails a great deal of strenuous work.

Forging ahead and crossing these portages as we came to them, after crossing fourteen, we finally camped for the night between Moose Portage and the Old Fort. Here we were joined by another canoe and three Little Grand Rapids freighters. As the evening had by this time come down upon us, very soon our campfire was throwing out its lurid light. It was quite dark by the time supper was cooked and our indispensable mosquito bar was erected, for these pests were strongly in evidence. Even a plentiful supply of campfire smoke failed to drive them away. By and by the tall spruce trees were silhouetted in the glare of the campfire. As this burned down, the stars began to twinkle overhead, and we closed the day with our evening worship. Very soon the words of "My God, my life, my all" in the Cree language were floating away over the treetops. Then offering our humble prayer, we laid ourselves down in the arms of the God of Israel who neither slumbers nor sleeps.

It was still early and the smoke from the raging fires everywhere around us hung over the river when we were astir. Our kettle and frying pan were again brought into requisition and bacon was soon sizzling in the pan. Breakfast over, prayer was again offered, and at 5:15 A.M. we were stepping into the canoe, ready to proceed.

This was a day of many rapids and surely they seemed to follow in quick succession. Very fortunately for us, the river was not in flood, so this to some extent modified the danger of the trip. The labour of unloading and carrying across the portages, and loading up again, kept our time fully occupied.

Hudson's Bay Company at Berens River, 1929.

However, seventeen rapids were safely passed. Notwithstanding that I had sent thirty gallons of gasoline and a box of provisions on ahead, we still seemed to have considerable freight aboard. However, persistently pressing forward, we reached Long Lake at 8:00 P.M., where we made our second camp. These stopping places in the wilds are pretty much alike: a good landing for the canoe, with depth of water, a flat rock on which to cook and eat, good level ground on which to erect our mosquito bar and spread our blankets on the face of Mother Earth; these constitute one of these wayside hotels.

Once more rising, the sun called us to the duties of a new day. At 6:00 A.M. we were on the water and the engine continued to hum. By and by we reached the last portage on the river and were now but fourteen miles from the Mission House at Little Grand Rapids. On account of an unusually high wind, this last part of the first stage of our journey was very dangerous. We had to follow the lee shore all the way for miles and miles. By pushing along, we reached Little Grand Rapids at 6:00 P.M. Here we found our missionary and teacher, Mr. Luther L. Schuetze, and his good wife, Augusta, in labours abundant. It was surely a day of good things for Little Grand Rapids when Mr. and Mrs. Schuetze took up their work there.

Nearly thirty years ago, a summer teacher was sent to labour at this point. For various reasons, but perhaps chiefly because a suitable man could not be found, the work lapsed. It is very difficult to get the right kind of man for these isolated missions. Beyond the yearly visits of the Superintendent, for a time very little was done for the uplift of the people. This was a stronghold of paganism, and at eventide the sound of the conjurors' drums could be heard in all directions. The Hudson's Bay Company has a trading post at this point, but the people are miserably poor, especially in the matter of clothing, the cost of which is exorbitant. It is so at all these inland points.

Some three years prior to my visit, our Church appointed a yearly teacher for this place. This was a young native man from Berens River. He carried on the school work successfully but proved rather lacking in aggressiveness when the priest of the Church of Rome appeared on the scene. He was succeeded by Mr. Schuetze and his wife. Under their united efforts of teaching and living, a wonderful work of grace has been going on. In the face of many difficulties, they have been most unsparing in their efforts to teach and live the Gospel of Christ amongst the Indians of this reserve. The fruits of their labours lie all around them. They had erected a splendid log Mission House, enlarged the school building, and had about thirty children at school. Of course, many of the older people still remained pagan, but a marked improvement was evident in the deportment of the young people.

We spent the Sabbath Day with them and were delighted with all we saw and heard. As there was no church at this point, divine services were held in the schoolhouse which had been erected upon the reserve, and which was filled to capacity at every service. Rev. Mr. Barner took the morning service, and had a most appreciative audience. It fell to my lot to officiate in the afternoon. I could not help contrasting conditions with those of nine years before. Then the services were held in the old building near the Hudson's Bay Company's post, and, to put it mildly, conditions were very primitive and interest in matters spiritual quite lax. Now we were worshipping in a good school building on the reserve and the people listened with reverence and decorum. The singing, led by an organ, was hearty, and the services throughout were both pleasing and profitable. Mr. Moar, postmaster for the Hudson's Bay Company, and his good wife have given our workers at Little Grand Rapids very generous help in their work.

Early Monday morning we were on our way on the second lap of our journey. Our canoe with bow pointing eastwards was cutting the water. Our next point of call was Pekangecum, about one hundred and fifty miles from Little Grand Rapids and about one hundred and thirty-five miles across the boundary into northern Ontario. For many years Pekangecum had stood on the list of our mission stations. Owing to the migratory condition of the people, very little could be done for them. Furthermore, on account of the sublime isolation and difficulties of transport, it seemed an utter impossibility to secure the services of a suitable Christian man to carry on the work. Preferably a native man, if a suitable one could be found, was much needed to break ground. Prior to the January before my present visit, not one of the people had been baptized into the Christian faith. Our Church, however, was

Rev. Arthur Barner, left, is shown in this 1920s group picture with Rev. Roscoe Chapin, right. Barner, of the Methodist Church in Toronto, travelled during the summer with field missionaries like Chapin and Niddrie. Chapin's wife, Etta, is next to Barner. Niddrie's retirement tribute to Barner is reproduced on pp. 195–96; Barner in turn paid tribute to Niddrie (see pp. 196–97).

successful in finding the right man, and at the time of my visit a day school was operating with an average of twenty-five children in attendance. A box was sent on to the Mission Rooms at Toronto which contained medicine drums, charms, etc. These had been given up when forty-one people had been baptized into the Christian faith.

We remained here for two days and were delighted and amazed at the good work that was going on. There was only one thing that detracted a little from our happiness at this place and that was the extreme poverty of the people. Some of them, especially the boys, were almost nude. We found that the commonest pair of overalls cost five and sometimes six dollars; a pair of moccasin rubbers cost fifty cents; while a pair of men's ordinary socks cost two dollars. The Woman's Missionary Society has been sending out clothing, but it takes a great deal to make them comfortable for the winter, especially when they have not even one change of clothing. The freight from Berens River to Pekangecum at that time cost seventeen dollars per one hundred pounds.

For many years Pekangecum stood on the list of stations in the old Methodist Conference. Upon one or two occasions a summer teacher was sent in, who laboured faithfully during the summer months. Two obstacles were seriously in the way. First, the people clung steadily to the old superstition and faith of their fathers. Second, the people were very migratory in their habits, and were seldom at home on the Reserve for more than two or three months at a time.

Two years prior to our visit, Mr. James Kirkness, a native man of this north country, who as a boy had been brought up in the home of the late Rev. Enos Langford at Oxford House, offered for this work. Since then he has filled the dual capacity of school teacher and missionary. In the face of fierce opposition from the medicine men, he continued labouring and trusting in God. Such consecrated effort is never in vain. The people began to gather and listen to this new evangel which meant so much more to them than what their old faith had to offer. Under his labours, by the grace of God, Pekangecum has witnessed a wonderful work of grace. Upon his arrival to take up the work there, every last one was pagan. There was not one member of the band to whom he could look or with whom he could confer without regarding the best method of breaking ground.

But Mr. Kirkness was a man of firm faith and trust in God. Quiet, capable and unassuming, thoroughly acquainted with Indian life and habits, he began adventuring for the Kingdom of God. Steadily and quietly the power of the truth began to win its way into their hearts. The clouds of darkness and superstition began to recede. Soon there came requests for more light and instruction than the public services afforded, which were followed by baptism into the Christian faith. At the time of our visit, seventy or more souls, infant and adult, had been enrolled on the register as members of the church.

Although it was late in the evening when we arrived at Pekangecum, nevertheless we decided to hold an evening service. Soon word was carried round that two "Praying Chiefs" had arrived, and people began to gather for worship. I was again glad to listen to the message God sent through the lips of His servant, the Rev. Mr. Barner. By the time the service was over, the trailing garments of eventide had come down upon us, the wind had gone down and the canoes bearing our congregation one after another pulled out amid the deepening shadows of the gloom.

Early next morning, July 23, we were astir, and soon the people began to gather for worship. Upon this occasion the lot fell to me to conduct the service with these wandering people on God's fair earth. The morning being cloudy and threatening rain, we decided to hold the service in Mr. Kirkness' home, which comprised two Indian houses pulled together end to end. We shall long remember that service. The people were reverent and decorous, no getting up and going out

Deer Lake Indians arriving by canoe at Berens River, ca. 1932.

during the time of worship as I have seen some do in our more civilized communities. More especially were we impressed with the efforts of some of the boys and girls in their efforts to sing in Cree, and the very hearty manner in which they joined us in repeating the Lord's Prayer in the native tongue.

Service over and the rain having ceased, we left Pekangecum at 11:00 A.M. en route to Duck Lake, a distance of about twenty-five miles. We reached there in mid-afternoon. Here we planned to meet the Treaty Party and accompany them one hundred and fifty miles north and east to Deer Lake. This would now be a busy place for a day or two, Indians arriving from Pegangecum, others from Poplar Hill, traders erecting their tents to display their wares and vie with each other in securing as large a share as possible of the crisp new one dollar bills issued by the Indian Agent upon his arrival. Although most of this part of the band was still living in paganism, we held a service with them that evening at which Rev. Mr. Barner tried to turn their thoughts to higher and nobler things. It was certainly a motley group by which we were surrounded at that evening service on the hillside. However, all were reverent and quiet, although many pagans were among them.

We remained here all the next day, awaiting the arrival of the Treaty Party. Late in the afternoon, Mr. Indian Agent McPherson, his clerk, Mr. Milledge and Corporal H.A. Stewart of the Royal Canadian Mounted Police made their appearance. Treaty payments were made, followed by a Council Meeting and then we began to think of the third lap of our journey, i.e., from Duck Lake to Deer Lake, a distance of approximately 150 miles.

John W. Niddrie, with a Mr. Taylor, a forest ranger, likely at Berens River, ca. mid 1930s.

Now a word or two about the Treaty Party. In consideration of the surrender of the western lands to the government by the Indians, the government entered into contract and agreed to pay each man, woman, and child, so long as the sun shone and the grass grew and the waters ran, five dollars each year. I have always tried to time my visits to these inland points as near as possible with the arrival of this Treaty Party at the different reserves, thus making sure of seeing all of the people. The Treaty Party consists of the Indian Agent, his clerk, and a Mounted Police. However, there are always one or two free traders along in order to try to pick up one of the new crisp one dollar bills in which treaty is paid, and it is surprising how little the poor Indian has to show for his money when it is all gone.

We had now left the river course and were following the chain of lakes, hence the portages were much longer and harder to navigate. Resting all day Sunday, we held a service with our little company. For two reasons this was the hardest stretch of our whole trip: first, because of extremely low water caused by lack of rain; and second, there are really no proper roads across the portages until one gets near to

John W. Niddrie, centre, with cane, among Indians at Berens River, ca. 1932.

Deer Lake. The roads here and there on the route are merely what are termed hunting trails. Then, the continued forest fires have caused many deadfalls, over which one has to lug canoe as well as the rest of the travelling paraphernalia.

However, by persistent effort we reached Night Owl Lake for our first night camp. Next morning bright and early we were skimming across this beautiful sheet of water. Crossing eight portages, we camped on the banks of a beautiful lake above a series of rapids. Here we had a splendid camp and a good night's rest. Continuing next morning, we hoped to reach Deer Lake that day but were held up within seven or eight miles of our objective point by an exceedingly high wind. Next morning early we made another attempt, this time a successful one. Upon that occasion we had to circle the lake for miles and miles and travel on the lee side. Then one more portage and we sighted the Hudson's Bay Company post. Between us and the post we had one rather difficult channel to navigate. This gave us considerable trouble on account of the heavy gale blowing at the time. However, by lightening our load and making two trips, we accomplished this and were soon amongst the Deer Lake

Indians. Here we received a most hearty welcome, my right arm being almost converted into a pump handle.

For some years these people had been agitating with a view of moving to Sandy Lake. The plaints had been "no fish at Deer Lake," "no ground for gardening," etc. This summer a deputation from Ottawa was sent out by plane to locate them on the land they wished for a reserve. The men and only a few of the women had come in from Sandy Lake to receive their treaty money. For a number of years, one of the Band, Adam Fiddler, has been recognized as the spiritual leader of the people. He has very faithfully performed his duties, holding two services every Sunday and one on Wednesday evening when at home. He has also initiated a number of young men into the work, and even these have been a great help.

We held a service in the church Sunday night, Mr. Barner preaching. At this service, fifteen babies were baptized and three couples married. We had a full house. The singing was hearty and everything passed off satisfactorily. After the service was over, they handed me ninety-six dollars in one- and two-dollar bills collected from their treaty money for the Mission and Maintenance Society. Considering how poor they are and that they see money only once a year, I might be pardoned for saying this was consecrated money.

Early next morning we were astir and packing up. Here came to us the parting of the ways as the Treaty Party was to turn southwards and homeward, and we to proceed another one hundred and fifty miles farther into the wilds of the north. The wind was very high, making it quite difficult to get away from the shore. But John James again proved himself the right man in the right place, for we soon found ourselves listening to the hum of the engine and accustoming ourselves to the rocking and swinging of the canoe in the big swell. One of the Sandy Lake men who had come in for treaty asked permission to accompany us in his haste to reach home on account of a sick child. We were very glad to include him in our party as he was familiar with the rapids and dangerous places in the various channels. He proved himself a first-class man: capable, quiet, and agreeable.

We camped that evening at 9:30 P.M. about eight or nine miles upstream from Mink Rapids, having made a big day's travel. Next day was beautiful, quiet, and still as we found ourselves afloat on this big inland river, the Severn. We had but one short portage to make, that being Mink Rapids, and covered even a greater distance than on the previous day. We camped that night on a point not far from where the people were located. Next morning early we were amongst the people. Here we found faithful Adam and many of the women and children. Indeed, very few of the men had yet returned from Deer Lake. As the day was somewhat cloudy and rain threatened, we waited for a time, and then managed to hold a service at which practically every soul in camp was present. Again we held a number of baptisms.

As it cleared off somewhat in the afternoon, we paddled down to the site of the new church, where the beginning of a building 40' x 43' had been made. Logs had been hewed, foundations laid, and other preparations were going on. It was very uphill work, building at this place. The people were very poor, transportation of material was very high, and food scarce. However, Adam signified his intention of persevering with the work.

Next morning early we began the first lap of the home stretch. Camping two nights, we reached Deer Lake. Here we held another service, baptized more children who had come in our absence, and administered the sacrament of the Lord's Supper to those in attendance. That night we camped near the Hudson's Bay Company's post and were the guests of the manager, Mr. Hutcheon, who showed us every kindness. The following morning again found us on the move with our faces southwards, and with nothing of a more serious nature than high winds and low waters. We pressed onwards, reaching Berens River six days later. We had travelled by canoe approximately one thousand miles, made one hundred and forty-seven portages extending from a few yards to three miles in length, and been away from home twenty-four days.

Now a word or two about the rising generation of the Indian people. We have now for many years been concentrating upon the rising generation. We have felt that all our hope—or nearly so—rests with these young people. We have done our best to assist the older ones to a clearer view of the teaching of the Word of Life, but in many cases we have found that the crusting of centuries of belief and habit handed down to them from their ancestry very difficult to overcome or remove. The young people are much easier reached, and are much more assimilative, as they have not to unload the customs and beliefs and traditions of their ancestors.

We are quite ready to admit we have great respect and admiration for the consecrated men and women who today are found in our residential institutes, spending the best energies of body and mind in their work. All honour we say to those devoted and faithful workers. It is quite true—and we must be honest about it—that we do not all see eye-to-eye in this great work. We might modestly say that we have had a slight experimental knowledge of this work, having been in charge at the Morley Institute for seven years. Many times since those days we have wondered if an improved day-school system would be successful amongst the pupils and parents on the different reserves. If education were made compulsory by the Department of Indian Affairs, and

Berens River United Church, 1960, destroyed by fire in 1966.

with improved instruction in the way of midday meals, transport to and from school, and some other grants made; these reinforced by good consecrated effort on the part of the teachers, all of whom should be of undoubted Christian character and willing to work with the children in their homes or visit them when sick, it seems to us as if this might be made a success. The pupils of such an improved day-school system might be brought more into contact with the problems of the Reserve and could not help but carry much that is good in their teaching to their homes and parents.

This would, to a great extent, be a solution to the education of the rising generation on the reserves. The education of the Indian is all right, but sometimes we wonder if the system is equally so. An improved system such as we have here described would be a great uplift to the parents in their homes. Under these conditions, when the graduating time comes for the pupils to leave the school, there would not be the danger of a rebound such as often succeeds the discharge from a residential school.

I laboured here at Berens River for eighteen years and on June 30, 1938 was retired from the active Indian work.

CHAPTER 10
ANNIE NIDDRIE: THE CAREGIVER, 1927–1938

THE STORY OF THE REV. JOHN NIDDRIE WOULD BE QUITE INCOMPLETE without recognition of the part played in it by his niece, Annie Niddrie, who was his helper and homemaker for twelve years. Born in Morley in 1892, three years later she moved with her family to a pioneer homestead in Eagle Valley, near what is now Sundre, Alberta. There she grew up, attended the little school her brother had helped to build, and aided her mother on the farm. She became engaged to a neighbour, Henry Ferris (brother-in-law of Annie's brother William), and no doubt expected to follow the well-trodden way of a pioneer farmer's wife. Instead, Henry marched off to the Great War, where a German bullet or a stray bit of shrapnel ended his life.

Annie's destiny as a caregiver, however, was not destroyed; it was merely altered in ways she could scarcely have dreamed. Until she was twenty, she remained at home, helping her folks on the farm. Then she and her younger sister, Fanny, were off to Edmonton for some further schooling. Incidentally, all three of her brothers also continued their education after leaving the little Eagle Valley school.

Fanny soon returned to Eagle Valley to marry Walter Muir, a local farmer, but Annie remained in Edmonton until 1927. During much if not all of that time, she lived with her brother John's family, helping her sister-in-law Verda with the six Niddrie children born to John and Verda from 1912 to 1924.

In 1927, a call came from her uncle, John W. Niddrie, requesting her to come to Berens River to keep house for him. En route to Berens River, she received another marriage proposal. That she gave it serious consideration is evidenced by the fact that she wrote to John and Verda for advice, which they did not feel they could offer. In the end, she continued on to Berens River, where she looked after her uncle for twelve years until he died. Even then, her career as the caregiver was not over; in fact, it was just in mid-stride. As her following recollections indicate, the federal government found work for her immediately, a role that lasted from 1940 to 1957. She managed a home for native women too old to look after themselves, and she was very proud of her success in doing so. At the closing of the home, the United Church paid tribute to Annie's "years of devoted service to all the Indian People of Berens River, Manitoba."

That same year, Annie turned sixty-five, usually considered the age of retirement. One might have expected her to return to Alberta, which was teeming with relatives: her sister, two brothers, their spouses, nieces and nephews, and their mates and children. But of the next four years of Annie's life we know little, except that she did not leave Berens River, which had become her beloved home.

However, in 1961, the caregiver's services were once more needed. Fanny was very sick, actually terminally ill, so Annie returned to Eagle Valley and from April 1961 to August 1963, she cared for her younger sister. Then at last, Annie

Annie Niddrie and her wood pile at Berens River, ca. 1950s.

was able to lay down the burden of caring for others. Until her death in 1982, she lived in Edmonton, a city that included three generations of her close relatives as well as many old and newly acquired friends. All of these and her church activities filled her life, which ended on February 19, 1982, the day after her ninetieth birthday.

She is buried in the Eagle Valley Cemetery, close to her parents and her only sister, Fanny Muir. The cemetery is only a short distance down the road from the Niddrie homestead. Her grave there is one of many that carry the Niddrie name.

Like her Uncle John and other Niddries, Annie put a great deal of family history on paper. His work was typed, hers was handwritten, but other differences are more important. Both made errors in spelling, punctuation, and grammar which have been corrected. But her uncle wrote about John W. Niddrie, the missionary. Not once does he even mention her name despite her twelve-plus years of devoted service to him and his cause. Annie wrote about life in a mission field, her life and his, and that of all the people around her, as seen in the recollections which follow.

Every coin has two sides. If the Rev. John Niddrie's memoirs form the obverse of one coin, Annie Niddrie's recollections, written about 1970, are its reverse.

A second piece about Annie Niddrie concludes these memoirs. It was written by Harry N. Everett, born in Berens River on April 2, 1914. He was regarded as a son by John W. Niddrie, and Everett himself considered that he was adopted by the missionary. Born Harry German Everett, his name was changed to Harry Niddrie Everett. His mother was Cree, from York Factory, and his father was "more French than native." Harry Everett's first language was Saulteaux, and he often used his knowledge of the native tongue and English to interpret for John Niddrie.

ANNIE'S RECOLLECTIONS
By Annie Niddrie

FROM WINNIPEG TO MORLEY

My father was Scotch and my mother English. They were married on April 30, 1883 and sailed for Canada the following day. It took a month to make the voyage. Upon arrival in Canada, they immediately bought and operated a dairy in Winnipeg. My father's brother, John W. Niddrie, a sister Maria, and my grandmother came to Canada about two years later and also made their home in Winnipeg.

During the next seven years, three sons were born to my parents: Willie on November 3, 1885; John on October 2, 1887; and Fred on March 27, 1890. My parents left Winnipeg in the spring of 1890 and went to Morley, Alberta, forty miles west of Calgary, with the purpose of starting a stock ranch. I was born on February 18, 1892 at Morley. My sister Fanny was born at Morley two years later in February 1894. Four years after my family moved to Morley, there was a drought. The Ghost River was several miles away. All the water they used had to be pumped out of a well which almost went dry at times. The cattle were bellowing for water. Hay was scarce and good pasture couldn't be found. The cattle were suffering so my dad sold the ranch and moved out to the Big Red Deer district, seventy miles north of Morley. In the fall of 1894 the Niddries packed their belongings up in three wagons driven by three neighbours, left Morley and went to their new home on the Big Red Deer River. The creeks just teemed with fish, mostly trout.

Annie Niddrie's home where she was born in 1892 at Morley.

LIFE IN EAGLE VALLEY

There were many things to contend with: lakes, rivers, sloughs and huge stretches of small timber. Reaching the desired spot, about half a mile south of the river, they made camp and staked out a place for a house. There were spring creeks bubbling up out of the rocks everywhere. The grass was up to the horses' sides and the scenery was beautiful to behold. This is where we were to be raised and live for many years.

The Red Deer River was a treacherous one; anyone going out in a boat risked drowning. Homesteaders were coming in from every direction. The only way to cross the river was with a team of horses and a wagon or democrat. The latter often overturned with the strong current and screams could be heard from those in trouble. My father and brothers would rush to the scene on horseback. They had long ropes and rescued the drowning and those in trouble. When the snow melted on the mountains in the summer, there were often terrible floods. I have seen the river a mile wide many times. It cut new channels, tore fences, barns, gates and posts out and made a wreck of our place. Later on, there were ferries across the river in many places.

My dad started to hay in the first summer and when it rained, which was frequently, he worked on the house he was building. Mother Earth was the floor and it had a sod roof. When it rained, it just poured through the roof. My three brothers slept under the kitchen table in times like this, and my dad pitched a tent over their bed and my sister's and mine. The flour and groceries had to be kept dry also.

Annie Niddrie, left, with sister Fanny, riding sidesaddle at family homestead near Sundre, Alberta, prior to Annie's move to Berens River, ca. 1920s.

Next summer, my dad started to build another house. It was T-shaped and each part 20 x 30 feet. It was four years before it was finished. There wasn't a board to be had closer than Calgary, and that was only a dot on the map. Two houses stood in Olds. It hadn't started to grow yet.

At the end of June, three Morleyites—Coleman, Niddrie, and Fletcher—moved their cattle out jointly to the Big Red Deer River. Mr. Coleman was in the southwest end of the valley, Niddrie in the northeast, and Fletcher was three miles east.

None of the land had ever been surveyed and the settlers were called squatters. Other than Mr. Coleman and Arthur Fletcher, our nearest neighbours were eight miles away. The McDougall ranch was west on the north side of the river. Mr. Muntz, who moved in that fall, was eight miles down the river. Alberta was a territory and didn't become a province until 1905, after it was surveyed in the early 1890s. Such a thing as a township line had never been heard of. The cattle roamed the range anywhere they wished to go. There wasn't a fence to be seen. Bears and wolves were everywhere. A huge grizzly bear killed three of Mr. Coleman's best cows one night. Later on the Indians shot it, and it now stands in the Banff museum.

There were no modern conveniences in pioneer days, and no electricity. We used coal oil lamps and the coal oil had to be brought from Morley in a wagon, as well as all the implements we used on the ranch. We had no refrigerators, no washing machines. We washed all our clothes on the washboard by hand. We carried all the water we used in pails from the creek and heated it in pots on top of the stove. We burned wood in the cook stove and the heater. There were no furnaces to be had, no wash boiler and no bathroom, and no sewing machines. My mother made all of our clothes by hand: shirts, overalls and underwear, her own dresses and aprons. My sister's and my dresses were made out of denim. It was heavy material and lasted longer. We had a better dress which was kept in case of anything special turning up.

The old sod-roofed house stood for several years, as did the newer one. They left their share of hallowed memories. They had provided a shelter, a church, a stopping-place, a hospital, a school and a place by the side of the road to any who came to its doors. Our doors were never locked. These homes provided the only church accommodation until Eagle Valley School was opened in 1905.

My mother played a noble part in pioneering. She fed the hungry, bedded them down when necessary, fed and stalled their horses. She had a heart of gold and loved everybody that crossed her hearth. In return they loved her, especially her own family, who adored her. She had a serious heart condition and died June 21, 1909 at the age of forty-eight; she was buried in the Eagle Valley Cemetery.

My father had two teams of small horses and a small hand plough. He broke ground and tried to grow potatoes, but the ground was hard and cold. He didn't gather more in the fall than he planted in the spring. The ground eventually became tillable and we raised wonderful crops. We got a binder and had to stook the grain and have it threshed with a crude machine which was pulled by horses. The ranchers always had a "round-up day" in June. They gathered all the calves in a corral and branded them with a hot iron. My dad's brand was N_ on the left shoulder. They cut a V-shaped nick in one ear. By doing this, the ranchers always knew their own cattle.

The land was thrown open for settlement in the early 1890s. My father filed on a quarter-section of land which was S.E. quarter, Section 1, Township 34, Range 5, West of the 5TH Meridian. The quarter-section adjoining it to the south was government land which he bought for $1.50 an acre. When filing on a homestead, a person had to pay ten dollars, live on the place for six months a year for three years, build a house and break ten acres a year for three years. He then received the title to the land.

Our nearest post office was twenty miles away. We often went without mail for three months, until my brothers were old enough to go alone and get it.

Our nearest school was twenty miles away also. My parents were very concerned over this situation. They taught us almost every night. Children were growing up everywhere without an education. Eventually there were enough children in Eagle Valley to keep a school open so the Department of Education gave permission to build a school in the centre of the district. A carpenter,

William Niddrie, brother to John W. Niddrie, and wife Hannah, after their move from Morley to their homestead farm near Sundre, Alberta, ca. 1902. Their children, left to right, are Annie, Fred, William, John and Fanny. Fred farmed in the area and served as an MLA in the Social Credit government under Ernest Manning. William died at age thirty-three in the Spanish flu epidemic of 1918. John retired in 1953 as the first principal of Westglen High School in Edmonton.

Mr. William Reed, a carpenter from Michigan, was put in full charge of building the school. Other help was mostly volunteered by single men. Miss Ethel Middlemiss was very efficient and the first teacher to teach in Eagle Valley School when it opened in 1905.

The educational system was vastly different from what it is now. We had standards instead of grades. Standard Five was the last one in the public school. The teachers were anxious to teach Six and Seven, and any getting their Standard Eight and going to Normal School for six months received their teacher's certificate and could teach anywhere in Alberta. Most of the pioneer teachers came from the East and great credit is due to them. My oldest brother, Will, never went to a public school, but he, John, Fred and Fanny all attended Alberta College and received a splendid education.

My father started a Sunday School on the west side of the river in a new school, Rockwood. It proved a real blessing to the newcomers.

Dr. J.H. Riddell, a Methodist minister, was very concerned over the educational situation. He went out among the settlers and down east soliciting money to build a college to help the pioneers get an education. The money was raised and the college built. It was right beside the little Methodist church that the Rev. George McDougall, first missionary among the Indians in Alberta, built in 1873 on 101 Street in Edmonton. The church was the first one in Edmonton and was used as the first school. The nails and spikes used in the building of this church were all square and had been welded that shape by a blacksmith. The church still stands today.

We never bought a toy in our childhood days. My mother made rag dolls for us, painted their eyes, nose and mouth with ink, and made the ink with ink powder. We just loved these little rag dolls. We played by the hour with them.

Buttons were a great attraction also. Fred, Fanny and I pretended we were ranchers. My brother Fred was "Niddrie." I pretended I was "Mr. Coleman" and my sister Fanny was "Fletcher," a neighbour. We divided the buttons equally. Each button was supposed to be a cow and each one had a name. We made fences with slivers of sticks and really had some ranch on our kitchen floor!

When we played outside, we each had a smooth stick. This was our horse; it soon became as shiny as glass. We tied a string to the thick end and kept it tied to the fence. After we played a while we would go into the house and ask my mother for some bread and butter, which she readily gave us. We entertained ourselves and enjoyed doing it.

When my brother John was old enough to have a pocket knife, he had one of his own. He cut willows along the side of the creek in a certain length and we built houses, stables, fences, etc. and had a real ranch laid out. Many a time he cut his hands and bore the scars until the day he died. When he grew older he loved to do carpenter work and at death left many things which reminded us of his handiwork.

We never wore shoes in the summer. We went barefoot, played in the ice-cold water, sand and stones. Our feet and legs became chapped and bleeding. We would bathe them in warm water at night, put Vaseline on them, and were all set to go again the next morning. These are precious memories we still hold.

In those early days, my mother wouldn't see another woman for several months at a time. The Muntz family lived eight miles to the east of us. Mrs. Muntz and my mother were wonderful friends. When either one of them needed help, the other one always came to the rescue. Mr. Muntz contracted tuberculosis. Thinking fresh air would cure it, he spent the last winter of his life in the woods making lumber, but in January he passed away, a true and noble man gone to his long rest, his pioneering days over. I must mention Mr. Thos. Byron here. He was Mr. Muntz's partner on the ranch and later on left the Big Red Deer and settled down in Vancouver, where he spent the remaining years of his life.

There weren't any churches in those days. My three brothers, Will, John, and Fred, went into the bush, cut poles down and carried them out and built a small church, probably eight feet square, just the walls, no roof and no seats. Will was the minister. He stood in the centre and announced the hymns and led the singing; his favourite was "Stand Up For Jesus." John's favourite was "Dare To Be A Daniel." At John's funeral the minister referred to this hymn and mentioned how he had been a Daniel in his life's work.

Fred's favourite hymn was "Ring The Bells Of Heaven." Although he couldn't carry a tune, Fred's voice was often heard chanting this hymn and made us realize there is joy in heaven. Our little service over, we returned home until the next Sunday, when we returned and had a similar service. Our faithfulness will probably be recorded in the great hereafter.

In the area where we lived, wolves were seldom known to molest horses or human beings, but one day one of our neighbours, Will Gastle, was going along the road in a wagon. A wolf came right up to him. Will picked up a large stick that was in the wagon box and struck the wolf on the head, but didn't kill it. The wolf became furious and went on its way, roaring. My brother Fred came along the same road. He had been roaming the hills looking to see if the cattle were all right. All of a sudden he realized the wolf was following him. He turned into a neighbour's place, Frank Ross'. He stopped and had his supper. Frank took his rifle and went part way home with Fred. Not seeing anything of the wolf, Frank turned back. In a few minutes Fred saw the wolf following him again. The horse was terrified and simply ran wild. He jumped a bridge that measured twelve feet across and didn't leave a mark on it. They came to a gate and the wolf sprang at them, but got caught in the barbed wire fence. This saved both horse and rider. Animals are afraid of fire, and the wolf could see the lights in our house and smell the smoke from the stove, so he turned and retraced his steps. The horse was a terrible-looking sight the next day. Instead of being white he was just streaked with black sweat marks.

Several years after my dad settled on the Big Red Deer, the government put a steel bridge over the river. But when the high water came down off the mountains in the spring, it took the bridge out, just leaving an odd post. A few years later a ferry was put on the river. An elderly man lived in a small house on the one side of the river and ran the ferry. The heat in the spring brought the snow down off the mountains and the river rose to a terrible height in the night. The house floated away down the river with the man fast asleep inside. It caught among the trees about a mile down the river and came to a stop.

The elderly man somehow got out of the door and clung to branches until he came within hailing distance of my brother-in-law Walter Muir's place. Walter saddled two horses and swam them to where the victim was standing,

Fanny (Niddrie) Muir, left, farmed with her husband Walter Muir, not far from where she was raised near Sundre, and Annie Niddrie, 1961, after Annie had returned to Alberta to care for her sister.

holding on to a tree. Though cold and chilled, he climbed on horseback and again they swam the horses to shore. As Walter stepped down from the horse, a crowd of people who had gathered on the bank cheered him. The patient was taken into the house, put in dry clothes, and sent to bed. He had been in cold water for hours, but didn't suffer any ill effects from this experience.

We had never owned a lamb. One time, my brother John went to stay with Mr. Coleman's two maiden sisters while Mr. Coleman made a trip to Morley. Upon returning, Mr. Coleman brought home a small lamb and gave it to John. We all loved it and were kind to it. We had a cow that was blind and the lamb stayed right beside her all the time. If the cow went to pasture, the lamb went; if she went in the shade, the lamb did. One day a coyote caught the lamb by the throat and left it in bad shape. We tried to feed it milk by using an old teapot to pour milk down its throat from the spout, but the lamb's throat was badly damaged and we couldn't save it. It had grown into a sheep by this time and my dad used to shear its wool, which my mother used for many things.

THE MOVE TO BERENS RIVER

My father, William Niddrie, passed away on January 21, 1921 and a year later my sister Fanny and I left the farm and went to Edmonton. On June 21, 1922 she and Walter Muir were married and returned to our old farm. I remained in Edmonton for some time, then went to Berens River, Manitoba.

Annie Niddrie, ca. 1920, before moving to Berens River.

My uncle, the Rev. John Niddrie, desired that I come and help him with the church work and keep house for him.

It was October 9, 1927 when I left Edmonton en route to Winnipeg, from there on to Selkirk, Manitoba. Reaching Selkirk, I scanned with interest the scenery up the Red River. Three boats were tied to the dock. The *Wolverine* and *Keenora* both carried passengers as well as freight to the north end of Lake Winnipeg. The *Bradbury* was a smaller boat which had a steel rudder. This boat was used for many purposes, especially to break thick ice and let other boats pass through.

We headed twelve miles on the Red River and into Lake Winnipeg. There, a huge space of open water lay ahead of us. It took almost twenty-four hours for us to reach our destination. A strong wind had blown up and most of the passengers were sick all day.

Three ships which are part of the rich history of shipping on Lake Winnipeg are left to right, the S.S. Wolverine, *the* S.S. Bradbury *(Government Fishery Boat), and the* S.S. Keenora. *Both the* Bradbury *and the* Keenora *are restored and on display at the Marine Museum of Manitoba in Selkirk.*

Annie Niddrie, left, with Mrs. Eric LeDrew, wife of a teacher, and her son aboard the S.S. Keenora *at Berens River, ca. 1950.*

NIDDRIE OF THE NORTH-WEST

The Keenora, *left, and the* Bradbury, *right, are restored and on display at the Marine Museum of Manitoba in Selkirk, their days over of shipping on Lake Winnipeg. The* Bradbury, *built in 1915, served variously as a fishery patrol vessel, lighthouse tender and icebreaker until 1973.*

My uncle stood on the dock waiting for me. I hadn't seen him for years, but he hadn't changed a bit, only he looked older. Berens River rises two hundred miles inland and empties into Lake Winnipeg close to where we had just landed. When I put my trunk in the boat, two Indian boys began to row. I was terrified lest the boat would sink, but nothing like that happened. The Indians understood the weather, when and when not it was safe to travel.

The scenery up the river was beautiful. The green and gold leaves on the trees were a sight to behold. Little did I realize that this would be my home for the next thirty-three and a half years. I never had a lonesome day in all those years.

Alberta, where everyone rode horseback, was vastly different from Lake Winnipeg and Berens River, where everybody rode a boat or canoe. There was only one motor at Berens River at that time. In the fall, many families went inland before freeze-up to trap during the winter months. They did not return until after break-up in the spring. Fishing and trapping were the only ways to make a living. In summer, men would row a boat out several miles at dawn, and lift their nets. The fish was sold to buyers for four and five cents a pound. The older people made fish oil, smoked fish and moose meat, made pemmican and dried berries for the winter. Cranberries and mossberries were plentiful. At freeze-up, they fished for winter use. Hanging ten fish by the tail on a willow stick, they placed this between two trees. These fish were used for their own use and also to feed the sleigh dogs. A stick of fish sold for one dollar.

Annie Niddrie, likely before her move to Berens River, ca. 1920s.

There were only a few horses at Berens River and those were used to haul wood to homes in the winter. A cord of wood could be bought for a dollar.

The mail had always been brought across the lake with a dog train until shortly before I went out there, when Jacob Green began to haul it with a team of horses. Mr. Jesmer succeeded him and brought mail and freight for the Hudson's Bay store from Riverton, a distance of one hundred and ten miles.

REV. JOHN NIDDRIE AND NEIGHBOURS

Rev. John Niddrie was the missionary. He had helped to raise seventeen Indian boys, even though he had never married. He and two of the Indian boys would take a cariole and dog train in the winter and would travel hundreds of miles visiting the different reserves inland. They would spend two or three days at each place. They slept under the starlit sky on spruce boughs close to a camp fire. In the summer they went by canoe. This was a hard trip for an older man.

Winter scene with dog team and cariole, Berens River United Church in background, ca. 1930.

He preached to the Indians for forty-eight years and did wonderful work among them. I was the organist for many years, helped with Sunday School, sat up with the dying when there wasn't anyone else to do it. This was just a missionary life among the Indians in northern Manitoba in pioneer days.

There had been many managers at the Hudson's Bay store, but a Mr. and Mrs. Paterson arrived the same week as I did and stayed several years. Mr. Kemp came the same fall and started to erect the buildings at the Log Cabin Inn. Corporal Stewart and his family arrived a year later. He was the first policeman to be stationed at Berens River.

In the pioneer days there wasn't a doctor, nurse or hospital there. The Indian Department sent medicine out to be dispensed by both of the churches. Brother Leach taught the Catholic School and dispensed medicine faithfully for several years, visited the sick, and will long be remembered for his understanding and love among the Indian people. Father De Gramphre spent many years as missionary for the Catholic Church on Lake Winnipeg.

Mr. Street taught the United Church day school for seventeen years. He took a keen interest in the church work. Later, he transferred to Little Grand Rapids and Fisher River, and later on passed away at the Soldiers' Nursing Home in British Columbia. His wife survived him by several years.

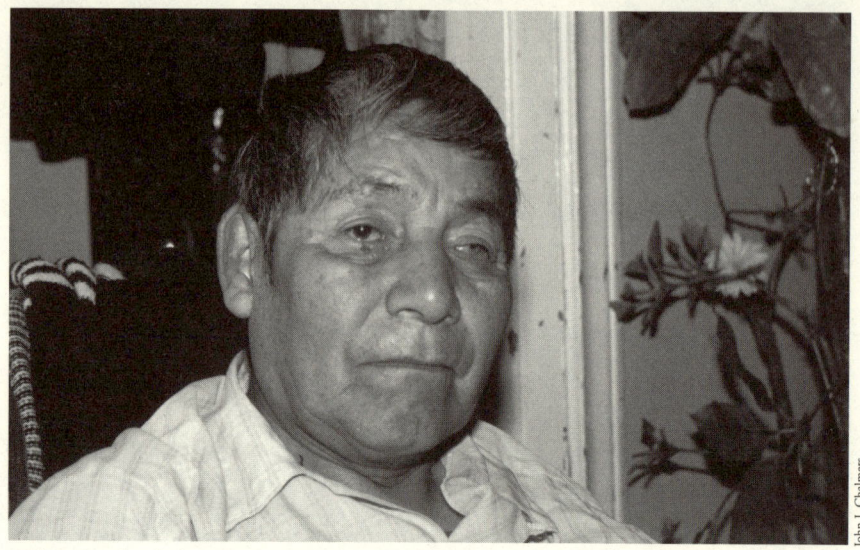

Wilson Goosehead of Winnipeg in 1999. He recalls knowing Annie Niddrie when he was young.

SOME CHIEFS AND OTHER NATIVES

There were three chiefs by the name of Berens. The oldest one was Jacob Berens. In 1875 Jacob Berens signed the first treaty, Number 5. As he could not read or write, his name was always signed, "Jacob Berens, Chief" and he placed his mark, "X" after Chief. His son William became chief after his father's death, carrying on his duties until he was about ninety years of age. In his time he had seen terrific changes. Trapping and fishing were much poorer. He lived to see tractor trains coming across the Lake with huge loads being taken up to the Berens River mines. This made work for many of our Indian men. William Berens' loving wife, Nancy, was ever at his side, serving their people on the Reserve. She celebrated her one hundredth birthday in Manitoba's Centennial year, 1970.

William Everett Sr. came to Berens River from Norway House. He was born at Trout Lake. When he was eighteen years of age, he made a trip down to Norway House and for the first time in his life heard the story of Christ. Later on, he came to Berens River and was an interpreter in the United Church for over thirty years. His wife Maggie was a wonderful midwife and helped the women in sickness and trouble. Alex Everett was a Councillor and will ever be remembered for his splendid work on the Reserve.

Dick Green, Jacob Green's father, was a real pioneer and was among the faithful ones in the early days. Much more could be said about many of the older people who were respected, loved and admired, but space will not permit. The pioneer people who lived forty years ago did not have any comforts. Today

John W. Niddrie standing in garden between mission house and river, Berens River, ca. mid 1930s.

there are high schools, higher education, highways and cars. Times have changed and today the Indian people are living in a modern world. The older Indians were so honest and truthful and the very soul of honour. There was no drinking and no working on Sundays. It was a hallowed day.

The first fall I was there was lovely. The whole earth seemed to be hushed in stillness. The winter was long, cold and deep in snow. We had to walk every place we went, and it was difficult. We would walk five miles and back to the other end of the Reserve to visit the sick. Everybody was waiting for spring. Finally, Easter came and it was twelve below. What a day! I said, "The ladies in Edmonton will be wearing their spring bonnets today!"

Summer came. Beautiful blue sky, sun, rain. The manse stood on the bank of the river and made a pleasant sight. There were men and women rowing boats and canoes everywhere I looked. I learned to row a boat, do bead work and make moccasins. Excitement was flowers. We made a huge garden. Mosquitoes and black flies were terrible. Grasshoppers were a plague.

HARD TIMES, SICKNESS, AND ACCIDENT

This was the Depression. Times were very hard. Men would row a boat four or five miles out on the Lake at dawn to lift their nets before the wind got up. They would sell the fish for four or five cents a pound. To feed a family, a cord of wood was sold for a dollar. People were short of food and clothing. Many times the babies were raised on water which the whitefish had been boiled in, and they thrived on it. Some babies were raised on water in which bush roots had been boiled. Nature took care of the Indians or they would have all died. The women's groups from outside sent huge bundles of second-hand clothing and quilts. I don't know what they would have done without this help. This was a real blessing to the Indians.

We had so much work to do, and the days were not long enough. There was sickness everywhere. T.B. spread like wildfire. I saw five people in one family die between August and March. There were no doctors, nurses, hospitals or sanitariums in those days. The Indian Department supplied us with medicine and we dispensed it and visited the sick day and night, and learned how to care for them. I had never had training, but the nurses helped us and we soon learned how to handle it and saved many dying people. It was a worthy cause.

Sanitariums were built and T.B. patients were compelled to enter them. A few weeks later T.B. was completely under control. T.B. hadn't been heard of before the white man came.

Mrs. Kemp ran the Log Cabin Inn at Berens River, had cottages and served meals to the tenants when necessary. The *S.S. Keenora* brought freight out every week, and Walter Green took it from the dock to Mrs. Kemp's. Once he was carrying a case with thirty dozen eggs up the steps. The case slipped and fell on his hand, bruising it terribly. Each day it got worse and worse. It was expensive to hire a plane to take him to town so the policeman came up to my place and asked me to go to Walter's house with him and see what was the best thing to do. We gave him a morphine tablet to still the pain. I got a pail of hot water and set it on a foot stool. He sat in an arm chair and we put his hand and arm in the water. Blood poisoning had set in and red streaks went up his arm. We started treatment at 9:00 P.M. and it took until 2:00 A.M. to get the infection out. When the water cooled off, I took a dipperful out of the pail and put another dipperful of hot water in its place. The next morning it had broken open and a terrific amount of pus and discharge was draining. It took about a month to get this terrible sore healed.

It was winter and a six-year-old boy was playing outside. His uncle drove into the yard and tied his dogs to a tree; the little boy got too close to the dogs and they grabbed him. Almost any sleigh dog will bite when it has a harness on. After the harness is off, most of them are quite tame. The people in the house saw the dogs were mauling something and rushed outside and found it was the boy, Johnny. The boy's scalp had been torn right off his head; only a strip about an inch and a half at the bottom of his head held it on. What a sight! The Catholic teacher, Brother Leach, came to aid them, then my uncle took over the case. We handled carbolic salve in the dispensary. It is a strong disinfectant and he saturated the head with it to guard off infection. Johnny's dad had gone to look at traps in the morning. He returned in the evening and immediately started to make a sleigh with a bed attached inside so he could lay

The M.S. Keenora, *originally the* S.S. Keenora, *last of the great cruise and freight ships on Lake Winnipeg, reposes in restored grandeur at the Marine Museum of Manitoba. The* Keenora *was built at Rat Portage, Ontario in 1897 and retired in 1965. Rescued and restored in 1972, it was placed in the museum in 1974 and underwent a major restoration in 1982–83.*

Johnny down. They started across the lake, a distance of 100 miles. There was a hospital at Half Way where they stopped for doctor's aid. The doctor said the child's life had been saved by someone who used the carbolic salve. They took the boy to Winnipeg, where he remained for several months, then returned to Berens River.

In the fall, the parents went to their trap lines before the rivers and lakes were frozen over and remained there until open water next spring. When crossing the portage, Johnny's rubber boot rubbed his toe. His dad brought him over for us to look at it. I immediately knew that T.B. had set in. He was taken to Winnipeg again and his toe amputated. He came home once more and was taken back to the trap line. A severe cold set in his chest, and a few days later he passed away. Johnny's dad hewed a coffin out of a tree and placed him in it. They brought him home for the last time, and he was laid to rest in the Berens River graveyard.

SUBSTITUTE TEACHER

Mr. Street, a teacher and a dedicated man to the Indian work, spent seventeen years teaching school. His work will never die down. For some reason, his wife had to go to Winnipeg but refused to go out unless her

Cultivating the garden at Berens River, subject and date unknown, possibly 1930s. John Niddrie's church is shown in the background.

husband went with her. Boats were going up and down the Lake and there were passengers of every description on board.

The church recommended that I take over the school until it was closed for the holidays. We had a good bunch of children. Some of them were very clever while some of them were slow. One young boy was slow and the teachers regarded him as retarded, but he was not. They never tried to teach him anything. He didn't know how to add one and one or two and two. I felt something should be done so I got the older children to teach the young ones and I concentrated on him. It was astonishing how fast he learned. By the time school was out, he could read all through the primer reader.

Years later, a monthly paper published out there stated that he had taken the service in the absence of a missionary. Patience and virtue go a long way.

A MISSIONARY GOES TO HIS REWARD

My uncle, Rev. John Niddrie, had many sick spells after I went to Berens River to stay with him. He once had quinsy, which is a gathering in the throat; unless it is lanced or cold compresses are applied to it, nothing can be done until it bursts of its own accord. It took from one Saturday until the next Saturday before it broke, then my uncle was free from pain and choking distress. He couldn't even lie down or swallow during that time. He was a very large man and heavy to move. I sat up with him for seven days and nights.

Annie Niddrie, left, with younger sister Fanny, at Berens River, 1942.

He had many spells with gallstones. Some of the spells would last two and three days. I could not leave him alone when he took these spells. He never recovered from the last one. His mind wandered and he talked at random. I sat up from Monday to Friday waiting for him to draw his last breath and at 5:00 A.M. Saturday he was taken. I was all alone. The Indians had gone to their spring hunt of muskrats. I sat by a table with a small coal oil lamp all those nights. I was completely exhausted. The news of his death spread and I got all the help I needed. He had been a wonderful missionary, probably the best in northern Manitoba, and is remembered by many.

TRANSITION

I had worked with the Rev. John Niddrie for twelve years when he passed away at the age of seventy-six in 1940 and was buried in the Indian graveyard at Berens River. "The prayer of a righteous man availeth much." His work on this earth was finished and he went to his long rest. Does mission work pay? I say yes.

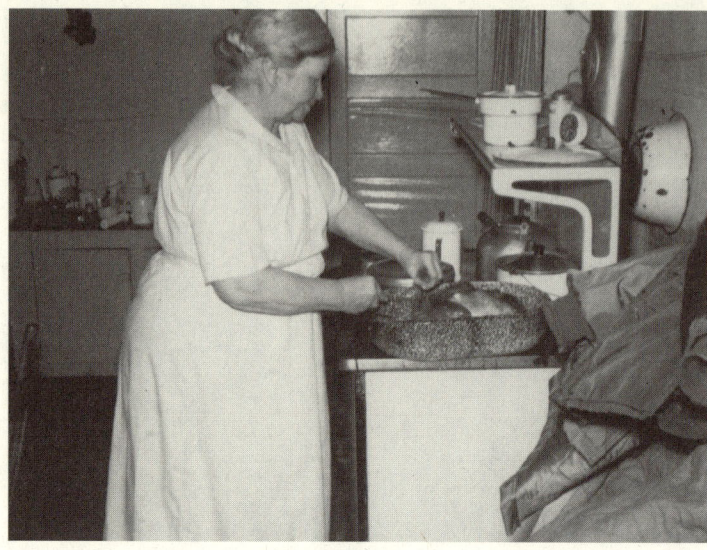

Annie Niddrie in the kitchen with a Thansgiving turkey at Berens River, likely 1959.

At this point I bought a boat and motor and did very little walking from then on. I learned to handle it, paint and chink it, and it was my pride and joy.

The older people were in such drastic shape for food that the Indian Department opened a home for them and I was put in full charge of it. I worked under the policeman and could take in any patients he would allow me to have. I ran it for seventeen years. The oldest one was ninety-three years of age and the others were in their eighties. They were a happy bunch of old people. In the fall of 1959, three of them died inside of a few weeks. The pension plan had come into effect and they received the same pension as the white people. After they had financial help, their relations wanted to look after them, so our home was closed down.

My sister, Fanny, who lived in Eagle Valley, became very ill and I desired to go and stay with her so I dug up my roots once more and left the home I loved in April 1961 and came back to stay with her. She passed away on August 21, 1963 and is laid to rest beside her husband Walter in the Eagle Valley Cemetery. One after another has slipped away and a new generation is rising to take their place.

REMEMBERING NAN NAN
By Harry N. Everett

In the late fall of 1927, Nan Nan arrived on the last trip of the *S.S. Wolverine*. There were a lot of people to meet the boat, as they had heard for weeks that Rev. Niddrie was getting his niece from Edmonton, who was coming out to help him at Berens River as housekeeper for one year. It was late in the fall evening before the *Wolverine* arrived, but we had been there early in the afternoon, as we never knew what time the boat would arrive. Shortly after the boat was tied up, the purser, Tom Peers, came down the gang plank with a lady right behind him. I was thirteen years old then and that was the first sight that I had of Miss Annie Niddrie. Her blue eyes were the first things that I noticed, as they reminded me of my grandmother's eyes.

When all her luggage had been unloaded, she wanted to know how we were going to take her big trunk up to the mission. Her uncle had told her how far it was up the river where the mission house was located, and had also told her we had to go either by canoe or skiff. She did not want to get in the canoe, so Mr. Street, the teacher, took her on his skiff. She wanted to know if her trunk would be safe in the skiff. She was afraid the trunk with its weight would tip the skiff and she must have held her breath when the trunk was loaded.

We had a lot of visitors at the mission the next few days as everyone wanted to take a look at the minister's niece. She said the first thing that she noticed with the Indians was that they were all so clean with their clothes and sat on chairs when they came in the mission house. She said she was used to Indians wearing blankets and sitting on the floor when they came in the house, and they had their hair cut instead of wearing long hair in braids. She was taken up with my grandfather from the first time she met him. He used to interpret in church and Rev. Niddrie used to take him home for dinner every Sunday, so they got to know each other very well.

Harry N. (for Niddrie) Everett, of Winnipeg, Manitoba. Born in Berens River in 1914, Mr. Everett is shown here at age 85 in 1999. One of his many jobs was to serve as Purser from 1959–65 aboard the S.S. Keenora, illustrated on page 127.

I remember the first Sunday she was there. I always sat at the last pew by the door. There was a middle aisle in the church with pews on both sides. I guess everyone was waiting, especially those that had not seen her yet. When she came in, she had a dark-crimson velvet hat with a few ornaments on it and her coat was dark coloured with a fur collar. She went right up to the front and chose the second pew from the front on the left side facing the pulpit. That was where she always sat all the time she was at Berens River, or at least till that old church was pulled down.

That first winter she was there she must have written miles of lines on paper. She would make carbon copies and put the heading on the letters after. When she put the letters in the envelope and sealed them she would sit on the sealed envelopes and we used to find that very funny. She was a faithful letter writer. All the years I was away at school in Winnipeg, she would write every week or every chance she had to send mail out. In the summer we got mail once a week but in the winter it was every two weeks or twice a month. If anyone was going south or if a plane stopped to refuel at Berens, mail was sent out by them.

I don't know if she ever got lonesome. If she did, she did not show it. That first fall she used to go over with Mr. Street to visit Mrs. Street, and after school Andrew and I would go over with a skiff, rowing to bring her back. She would sit at the back, hanging on each side of the skiff, and we would kind of rock it and she would yell at us to stop it. When we got close to shore, we would row

Keenora *landing at Berens River, June 1933.*

harder, and she would yell for us to stop but of course we would row harder till the skiff hit shore, which had a soft ground. Rev. Niddrie would hear her screaming in the house and he would laugh at her, as would John James Everett, who lived across the mission. He had a hearty laugh and you could hear him laughing. I guess we were real stinkers to scare her like that when she was not used to water and boats.

I never saw a lady work so hard as Nan Nan did all the years she was at the mission while I was there. On the hottest days in the summer she would be canning raspberries with the kitchen wood stove going full blast; she also canned saskatoons and at times blueberries. There were very few wild strawberries at Berens. In the fall she would can crabapples and apples, and if we got moose meat she would can that too. I never saw anyone fry moose meat like she could. When the people from Grand Rapids came down for freight on the canoes, they sometimes killed a moose and they would always drop off a hind quarter.

Rev. Niddrie used to tease her a lot and tell her stories which he would stretch at times. He used to like moose nose and Tom Boulanger always brought some down for him from his trapping ground, along with beaver tail which Nan Nan would never touch. She did not believe that people made soup out of ducks, and Mr. Niddrie would tell her that the people ate the beak and feet also.

But the first batch of bread that she made was something we never ate before. All the years she was at Berens she must have baked tons of bread.

Annie Niddrie and her house at Berens River, ca. 1950s.

Many a sick person had a loaf of her bread. When we made toast out of her bread we would cut it about an inch thick and toast it over the red hot coals in the cook stove. It was very, very good. The meals she used to cook! Sometimes there used to be six extra boys for supper and she never knew who was coming. What a mother she would have made if she had children of her own. She was like a mother to me. After my wife died and the girls were small and staying with their grandparents at Berens, they used to go over and stay with Nan.

When Sylvia, my daughter, was born and we brought her home from the hospital, Nan took over in helping Sylvia's mother. I think she did more, like bathing. She would open the oven in the cook stove and bathe the baby beside the oven. If anyone came in while she was doing that, she would holler at the person to close the door and say, "Don't you see that I am bathing the baby!"

It was not long after that she got a baby girl from Mrs. Cochrane and she kept the baby for the winter. So she had two babies to look after. Sometimes I used to wonder how she kept going the way she worked from morning till night. In the summer she used to get a break on Tuesday afternoon as I used to take her down to meet the boat. By this time she was used to canoes and boats. She later got her own boat and outboard motor and was really proud of them. This was after she left the mission and was on her own looking after the elderly people. I did not see much of her after 1941, as I was away working in different places, but she still used to take time to write to me and give me all the Berens River news and tell me how the girls were getting along. Before she kept the baby, she had a young girl about twelve years old that she looked after for the

Annie Niddrie at Berens River, date unknown, possibly 1950s. After overcoming her initial fear of water and small boats, her own boat became a source of pride with Annie and gave her a sense of independence.

winter at the Mission. This was so the girl could go to school as she lived quite a way from school. That was the same reason that Andrew McDonald used to stay at the Mission. He would go home Friday after school and come back to the Mission house after school on Monday.

When Rev. Niddrie was unable to get around to visit the sick and handle the medicine that the Indian Department used to send out, Nan looked after that too, that is, dishing out the drugs and visiting the sick. Most of this she did walking and she never had a decent pair of shoes that fit her. Sometimes Mrs. Street would go with her on these visits. The church ladies from the East used to send bales of used clothing and that was where Nan used to get her shoes. This she also handled in dishing out to the needy. She would be in the middle of doing some of her own work and had to drop it when her uncle asked her to dish out some clothes. She would go upstairs to the room she used to call "the junk room." That was where all the clothes that came were kept.

The only thing that she did not do at the Mission was the laundry. There was a Mrs. Ross who came once a week and did the washing, but Nan did the ironing. We never had a water tank to store water in and we only had two water pails. I used to see that they were full before I left for school, but at times they would run out of water and Nan had to go down to the river and fetch the water. It was not bad in the summer, but in the winter when it was cold she had to chop the water hole open and struggle up the hill with the pails of water, and the snow did not help. What she did not mind was feeding the horse and watering it when I was not there.

For the first few years she was at Berens River in the spring, before the ice was gone and the first boat came in with supplies for the stores. There used to be a lot of groceries that would run out at the stores and we had to live on potatoes and onion gravy when we did not have fish. Whenever my Dad got fish he used to see that the Mission got some. The Hudson's Bay store used to save flour for the Mission, but nothing else. We would be out of butter and other staples and had to use lard on our toast and bacon grease that Nan used to save during the winter.

I thought after the first spring, when she saw how we lived and ate during break-up, that she would have gone back to Edmonton, but not our Nan Nan. They don't make ladies like that anymore, who help out the way she did and not get anything out of it for herself. And all the church work she did, too; when Tashie and Gordon were away on Sunday, Nan would play the organ. She did that for years. She also used to sweep the floor of the church and ring the church bell on Sundays when no-one else was around. But I will never forget her bread and her fried moose meat and the gravy she used to make after frying the moose meat. She used to say that the gravy from moose meat was the best.

I never saw her mad, but she used to say that she was spitting mad enough to talk Saulteaux. There were a lot of babies at Berens River that were named after her.

It must have been in the fall of 1932 that her teeth were bothering her so much that she caught the last plane going south after the last boat had gone south. She had to stay in Winnipeg till the first trip that the mailman made across Lake Winnipeg. I was glad that she was there as I used to see a lot of her. After she left to go to Berens again, I really missed her and was lonesome. She travelled with the mailman who had a team of horses with a canvas caboose on the sleigh. I think it took them five days to go from Riverton to Berens River. The last night before reaching Berens they had to sleep in an out camp; before, they always stayed with some people. I made the same trip with the mailman in 1934 so I know all the places she stayed. At Rabbit Point they stayed with two trappers at their camp. After that, whenever she had a chance, she would send some of her homemade bread to the two trappers. She had a heart of gold.

At times, late in the summer evening, she would go out for a walk around the graveyard as it was close to the Mission house. When she would get back her uncle used to ask her if she had taken a cheerful walk around the cemetery. After the Streets moved quite close to the Mission on the same side of the river, she was able to go and visit Mrs. Street. She did not have many people that she could visit. The winter was the worst for her, as she was pretty well shut in outside of her sick visits.

Annie Niddrie with Schuetze family goats at Berens River, with church in background, ca. 1940. Rev. Luther Schuetze succeeded John Niddrie as the United Church minister at Berens River in 1938 and served there 1938–42.

It was while I was in school in Winnipeg that I got a letter from her telling me that she had a letter from Lance Snelgrove. He was the forest ranger in the summer and ran an outpost for the Hudson's Bay Company in the winter. He had asked her to marry him. Nan said she did not know how many sheets of paper she tore up in trying to refuse the offer. She always figured that the minister and his wife from Poplar River had a lot to do with the offer, as they used to come down to Berens and always talk about Mr. Snelgrove—how good he was and what a kind man to be with. They too were isolated at Poplar River.

I think it was about 1938 that we moved out from the Mission house to our own place. The Schuetzes from Little Grand Rapids were coming to the Berens River church and Nan was going to stay with them. They had a place right by the house for Rev. Niddrie so Nan could look after him from there. We still saw her quite often, as we used to take up cooked stuff for Rev. Niddrie that he liked—like wild duck, fresh whitefish, and sturgeon. After it had been cooked, Sylvia and I would rush up there while the things were still hot so Rev. Niddrie could eat whatever we had for him.

We used to see Nan then and at times she would walk over to our place for a visit. She was alone with her uncle when he died. That was the first, but not the last, time that she had to lay out someone after they had died. After we moved and I was in Winnipeg, we would stay with Nan at her old folks place whenever we had a chance to go to Berens. One night we were there and one of her old ladies died, so my wife Jean and I had to help her in fixing up the old lady's body.

I used to tell her that I could never thank her enough for the things that she did for me and my girls. One thing that she told me I will always remember when I am getting dressed: no matter how good your clothes are, if your shoes are not polished, you are not dressed. Yes, I owe her so much. After Nan died my mother passed away too, and it was just like I had lost two mothers in the same year.

Nan was never late for anything, she was always ahead of time. When she used to come to Winnipeg and stayed with us on her way to Thompson or Edmonton, either going by train or plane, she was always in a hurry to get to the station or to the airport. She used to enjoy going to see Sylvia and the family as she said it reminded her of the north all the time. She always referred to Berens River as the north. After she left Berens there was many a person that missed her. We will always remember Nan Nan and all the things that she did for us. I guess a person could write page after page of her good qualities.

CHAPTER 11
THE LETTERS OF JOHN W. NIDDRIE

WHILE JOHN W. NIDDRIE'S MEMOIRS PROVIDE PERSONAL HISTORY, accounts of his travels and a look at his work as a missionary, it is his correspondence which sheds light on some of his day to day operations and concerns. Whether writing to government officials, colleagues, family or newspapers, his letters provide an additional perspective into the life and thoughts of the man. Although somewhat reserved and formal in his writing of memoirs, it was in his correspondence that Niddrie revealed more of his thoughts and character.

THE ALBERTA YEARS

The following letters provide some general insight into the concerns about the operation of the McDougall Orphanage and School under John Niddrie's principalship. From financial operations to crops at the Morley settlement, many things had a bearing on the Institution. Although often the subject of a letter by itself, the availability of an adequate water supply is frequently mentioned in other correspondence. Two people to whom John Niddrie wrote frequently were Rev. Dr. Alexander Sutherland in Toronto, General Secretary of the Methodist Church in Canada, and the Hon. David Laird, the Indian Commissioner in Winnipeg.

McDougall Orphanage
Morley N.W.T.
26/7/98

Rev'd. A. Sutherland, D.D.:

Your letter dated July 20TH to hand with cheque of I.A. Dean enclosed for which I am extremely obliged. With this letter I enclose receipt for same. I am sorry that I am still unable to furnish you with a financial statement as Mr. Dean's books have not yet come to hand. Hence my delay in making my monthly financial statement which you instructed me to make on the 20TH of each month in your letter under date of June 16TH.

I am pleased to say that matters are progressing favourably. We have got two new pupils which makes a total of 31. I expect two or three more this week which will leave us room for *a few more*. I am thankful to say that all of our new ones are doing remarkably well, especially at the English language. I am sorry the boys are mostly young, for while they are very useful they are not strong enough for ranch work or hauling water. However, what we lose in one way, we hope to gain in another, for I find that the results of camp life are much easier effaced when we get them young.

I am afraid that our crops, etc. are not going to amount to much, owing to the careless way in which the land was prepared for seeding in the spring. Our crop of green feed (for hay) will be very light and our roots, with the exception of about 1/4 of an acre of turnips, will be an utter failure. I find also that amongst the stock there has been shameful neglect, which will be felt next spring.

I have been informed by some members of the staff that sometime during Mr. Dean's stay here he rec'd a grant of $300 from the W.M.S. for the furnishing of the McDougall Orphanage, that a portion of this had been spent, and that the balance returned to you. Could you please inform me at your convenience if this is the case, and if there is any money funded for this. We require some furnishings for the house and as I have no idea whatever re the state of affairs in this line, and having examined the few papers left here by Mr. Dean, cannot find any statement of any kind relating to this. I am sorry to trouble you about it but thought it best not to expend any of our regular funds for this purpose without your sanction. While we are practising all economy possible, we find a few articles required as the removal of Mr. Dean's furniture renders this indispensable.

I was told by the Agent representing the Gov't here that a tender has been submitted to the Indian Commissioner re water supply for the Orphanage.

I must now close to catch the next mail
With Kind Regards
I am yours Faithfully
John W. Niddrie

December 28th, 1898

The Indian Commissioner
Winnipeg

Sir:

I beg to call your attention to the fact that the windstorm which prevailed all day yesterday has stripped the shingles off one half of south side of the roof of the school house in connection with the Institution, and also upset or overturned the Boys Closets carrying them a distance of some 30 or 40 yards into a coulee.

Could you kindly issue instructions to have these repaired at your earliest convenience. We have a carpenter, Mr. A.K. Sibbald, in our settlement who has been employed by the Department here on previous occasions.

I have the honour to subscribe myself,

Your Obedient Servant
John W. Niddrie

No doubt the following exchange was cause for frustration. The simple matter of obtaining adequate school desks was met with a blunt refusal to provide them.

McDougall Orphanage Morley
May 10th, 1899

The Indian Commissioner
Winnipeg, Manitoba

Sir:

The desks in our school room here are very old and are not at all comfortable for the pupils in the school. Will you be kind enough to inform me if you think the Department would be willing to supply us with regular folding school desks and if so, should I apply to the Department at Ottawa for desks the same as those used in Red Deer and Calgary schools.

I have Sir the honour to Subscribe Myself
Your Obedient Servant,
John W. Niddrie
Principal

Office of the Indian Commissioner
for Manitoba and the North-West Territories,
Winnipeg, 15 May 1899

Principal,
McDougall Orphanage,
Morley.

Rev. Sir,

I beg to acknowledge receipt of your letter of the 10th instant re school furniture, and to say that the Department has repeatedly refused of late to provide school desks to Boarding Schools, and it is consequently useless to submit your request for its consideration. Even such schools as Duck Lake and Emmanuel College, which are practically industrial, have been refused this privilege.

Yours truly,
D. Laird
Indian Commissioner

> Office of the Indian Commissioner
> for Manitoba and the North-West Territories,
> Winnipeg, 23 Aug. 1899
>
> Principal
> McDougall Orphanage,
> Morley
>
> *Confidential.*
>
> Sir,
>
> I beg to inform you that the following persons are to be placed on the patronage list for supplies at Calgary:
>
> > *Hardware*, A. McBride & Co., Calgary Hardware Co.; *Dry Goods*, A. Allen & Co. and Glanville & Robertson; *Clothing and Gents Furnishings*, Calgary Clothing Co., J. Diamond, W. Diamond, and Glanville & Robertson; *Boots & Shoes*, J.B. Kelly and F. McDonald; *Groceries*, J.G. Vanwart, A.W. Ward, Worden Bros.; *Meats*, T.G. McLelland; *Farm Implements*, J. Lee Johnson, Vanwart & Co.; *Drugs*, W. McLean, C.A. Wallace, J.G. Templeton, O.H. Bott; *Lumber & Wood*, Vanwart & Co.; *Livery*, R.A.G. Bell; Blacksmiths, McTavish Bros., Jarret Bros.; *Carpenters & Bridge Builders*, H. Church, D.J. Gunn, J. Creighton; *Furniture*, Neilson Furniture Co., F.F. Higgs; *Printing*, J.V. Binning; *Harness*, Saunders Macartney and Corcoran.
>
> The patronage for hardware should be divided between the two firms.
>
> > Yours truly,
> > J.B. Nash
> > Secretary to the Indian Commissioner

The expansion of the facilities at Morley and the increase in pupil enrollment appeared to be proceeding well. However, not all aspects of the school were uneventful, and concern was expressed by the principal about two boys who had run afoul of the law.

Morley
November 9TH, 1899

Rev'd. A. Sutherland D.D.
Toronto, Ontario

Rev'd. Dear Sir:

Your letter dated October 24TH to hand a few days ago, also one of later date from Mr. Shannon with cheque to cover amount applied for, for which please accept our sincere thanks.

I am sure you will be pleased to hear that the new building is now well under way. Two or three more weeks will complete it. I am pleased to say that the contractor, Mr. McNeill of Calgary, is doing first class work. I will now proceed to touch on some points of your letter.

In reference to the transfer of pupils from this Institution to Red Deer School—In May of 1897 three boys were sent there from this school, and I am sorry to say it has not proved satisfactory at all. To my certain knowledge these boys have run away 3 times since sent up there, and about 2 weeks or a month ago two of them were arrested here by the police, and taken to the Barracks at Calgary, and sent from there under the escort of one of the N.W.M.P. to Red Deer. All of this has conspired to make Red Deer School very unpopular amongst our Indians. Then again there are reasons for which I could not feel justified in encouraging pupils to be transferred to Red Deer. Please do not think me uncharitable or prejudiced in this matter. I would very much rather recommend Brandon as a suitable place. There they would be far way from the influence of camp life. Furthermore, too much care cannot be taken in attending to the morals of these children, and the growth of any habits that will prove detrimental to them. I often feel that unless our pupils here get a good grasp of the truth, and become established in the "Good Way," a very large proportion of our work will be effaced after their leaving here. Our main effort is and has been here to get these children to think and act for themselves on the matters pertaining to a better life, and I am thankful to say that in some measure our weak efforts have been blessed.

In regard to the Government setting apart Lot 7 for this school, I have written asking if they would confirm the report and have not yet received a reply. Miss Clement, our teacher, will be leaving us at the end of this month. I am sorry to be compelled to make a change, but must suit personal feelings for the benefit of the Institution. During the last 17 months matters in regard to the schoolroom have not been satisfactory, and the progress has not been what I could wish for. My experience amongst the Indians is that to make a success of the work you must "*Push, Push, Push.*"

The health of the children is good, and their ability to learn and use the English language is wonderful. Then again, some of the boys are becoming very useful on the Farm, and also the girls in housework. I will now close in order to catch mail, and will write you again in a week or two in regard to New Building, pupils, etc.

Hoping You are Well
I Am Yours Sincerely
John W. Niddrie

Expansion of the school and increasing enrollment placed additional demands for adequate facilities and necessities for the boys and girls. As seen in the refusal to provide desks for pupils, the government, either through the office of the Indian Commissioner in Winnipeg or the central government in Ottawa, was not meeting all needs. As he had done on other occasions, John Niddrie requested help from the W.M.S., the Woman's Missionary Society. Its creation had been authorized in 1878 by the General Conference of the Methodist Church.

McDougall Orphanage and School
Morley December 6th, 1899

Mrs. D. Briggs
Toronto, Ontario

Dear Madam:

My object in writing this letter must be my apology. I am informed that you are president of the Supply Committee of the W.M.S. of the Methodist Church, and as we have enlarged our building here, and wish to provide capacity for 30 more pupils, I am writing to ask if you could possibly come to our aid in the matter of bedding and clothes for this number. More especially are we in urgent need of sheets and quilts. I have written the Indian Department in Ottawa requesting their assistance in the furnishing of our new building and have had a reply to the effect that they had no funds available for this purpose. I want to say in conclusion that we have at present 40 pupils, and our new wing will provide capacity for 30 more. Boys' clothing ranging from the age of 6 to 13 is required. If you could in any way help us I should feel extremely obliged, and can assure you would appreciate it very much, as we hope to open our new wing at New Year's.

Apologizing for taking this liberty,

I am yours Respectfully
John W. Niddrie
Principal

For a principal on the frontier charged with the care and education of the children enrolled at the McDougall Orphanage, it must have been a source of some annoyance to be subjected to the direction of a distant Indian Commissioner and government who provided instructions on simple matters within the responsibility of the principal.

Morley
December 19TH, 1899

The Indian Commissioner
Winnipeg, Manitoba

Dear Sir:

Could you please allow the pupils of this Institution to visit their friends and attend the Yearly Feast, held on New Year's Day. This is no "Sun Dance"—only a friendly gathering, well and quietly conducted. If you could grant this favour I should feel extremely obliged. It has always been customary for them to attend in the past, and they are now anxiously waiting your decision in the matter.

I have the honour to subscribe myself,
Your Obedient Servant
John W. Niddrie
Principal

Office of the Indian Commissioner
for Manitoba and the North-West Territories,
Winnipeg, Dec. 22ND 1899

Principal,
McDougall Orphanage,
Morley.

Rev. Sir,

I beg to acknowledge receipt of your letter of the 19TH instant and to authorize you to allow the pupils of the McDougall Orphanage to attend the Stony Year Feast to take place on New Year's Day. I may point out that the same favour having been granted last year, the parents, instead of taking the children back to the school direct, went by the Agency, and were a source of considerable annoyance to the Agent, it being ration day. You will see that they are all brought back to the school without involving the Agent into any trouble in the matter.

Yours truly,
D. Laird
Indian Commissioner

The request for support from the W.M.S. was answered with a donation of clothing, for which the following letter of appreciation was sent.

Morley
January 4TH, 1900

The Auxiliary of the W.M.S.
Shetland, Ont.

Dear Friends:

Some time ago I rec'd a post card from Miss Edith L. Dobbin of Shetland, Ont. advising me of the fact that a bale of clothing, etc. had been shipped to our address from North Bothwell by your Auxiliary. The same has arrived here all right, and in first-class order. The goods, which were of first-class quality and most suitable for our children, are indeed a very great help to us, and I cannot sufficiently express our gratitude to you for your great kindness in making such an excellent donation to our institution, but pray the Father (who has promised that a cup of cold water given in his name shall not lose the reward) may abundantly bless and reward you for remembrance of us.

We have 41 pupils in our Institution at present and expect to get 25 more into our new wing, which is almost completed. Our work has its discouragements, but our Father has abundantly blessed us in the past year. Pray for us please, and with much Christian Love,

Yours in the Faith,
John W. Niddrie
Principal

However, direction from the office in Winnipeg was not confined only to the deportment and privileges of the pupils. Advice was provided also on custodial matters and plant management on what were no doubt regarded as commonplace or commonsense issues. Whether the following comments were regarded as gratuitous or not, it is easy to imagine that they were unnecessary, particularly by those who were closest to the operation and used to coping with the rugged life in the foothills.

Office of the Indian Commissioner
for Manitoba and the North-West Territories,
Winnipeg, 30 Jan. 1900

Principal,
McDougall Orphanage,
Morley, Alta.

Sir,

I beg to acknowledge receipt of your letter of the 24TH instant in regard to the ventilation of the new dormitory, and to note the contents of same. Good ventilation, I believe, is best arrived at by having registers near both floor and ceiling, and one point should not be overlooked, that, in order to obtain a proper evacuation of foul atmosphere, a supply of pure air must be at hand. Nothing can take the place of aeration by means of open windows. Artificial ventilation, though required for changing the air when the windows are necessarily closed, is insufficient, even under the best of circumstances, unless the room is from time to time thoroughly refreshed and purified by the sweep of the free winds through all its windows widely opened. Such an atmospheric washing should be secured three or four times daily in all weathers; at recess, particularly, it should be insisted on, banishing

John Simeon family in front of their house on the Stoney Indian Reserve at Morley, 1908.

teachers and pupils from the room meanwhile, if necessary. They will more than make up in the brightness of the remaining hours for the time they may thus lose. Immediately after school, morning and afternoon, the process should be repeated for a longer time, and just before school, also, if the room can be warmed again quickly enough.

Yours truly,
D. Laird
Indian Commissioner

As principal, John Niddrie had many responsibilities beyond staffing of all teaching and support positions, providing an education for the children, and looking out for their well-being. The Institution had undergone expansion and increased enrollment during his principalship. Ordering supplies, painting and maintenance, acquisition of fenceposts and erection of fencing, management of crops and provision of water were among his responsibilities. So also was obtaining adequate provisions for staff and students. Just as Winnipeg had advice for air and ventilation of the facility, so too did the office of the Indian Commissioner have suggestions about providing an adequate supply of beef.

Office of the Indian Commissioner
for Manitoba and the North-West Territories,
Winnipeg, 8 Aug. 1902

Principal,
McDougall Orphanage,
Morley.

Rev. Sir,

I beg to acknowledge receipt of your letter of the 5TH instant in regard to your beef supply, and to say that nobody here is aware that issues were made to the McDougall Orphanage in former days—at any rate the grant of $72.00 is supposed to cover all the cost of maintenance of pupils at the boarding schools of which the McDougall Orphanage is one, notwithstanding the Regulations of the Department which rank it as an industrial school by a mere clerical error.

I could suggest, however, one or the other method which follow of obtaining your beef supply at a fair rate and in such quantities as will not allow it to spoil. Either to arrange with the Agent and Contractor to have the quantities needed handed over to you on ration days at contract prices, or otherwise to allow your beef account to run on until it can be wiped off by handing over a live animal, which will spare you the trouble of killing and having an excessive quantity on hand during hot weather. I think this could be arranged so that everybody concerned will be agreeable to the transaction.

Yours truly,
D. Laird
Indian Commissioner

DISAGREEMENT WITH THE INDIAN AGENT

It appears that late in 1898, the Acting Indian Agent, Mr. Bangs, had been critical of some of the conditions at the McDougall Orphanage, and had reported as such to David Laird, the Indian Commissioner. Laird, in turn, passed on the information to John Niddrie, which is where the following trail of correspondence begins.

Office of the
Indian Commissioner
for Manitoba and the North-West Territories
Winnipeg, 7 Dec. 1898

Principal
McDougall Orphanage
Morley, Alta.

Sir,

I beg to inform you that Mr. Acting Agent Bangs of the Stony Reserve complains that the boys of the McDougall Orphanage are not as clean as they should be, and to call your attention to the necessity of their being well looked after in this as well as in all other respects.

Yours truly,
D. Laird
Indian Commissioner

Niddrie's first response was to write in his own hand at the bottom of the letter, "This is utterly false. All the pupils are washed and dressed 3 times a day, and change their clothes every Saturday. John W. Niddrie."

A few months later, the disagreement between the Indian Agent and Niddrie still continued, as Niddrie's following letter indicates.

McDougall Orphanage Morley
May 18TH, 1899

The Indian Commissioner
Winnipeg, Manitoba

Sir:

In reply to your letter No. 122/68 of May 10TH, I beg to inform you that Mr. Acting Agent Bangs' report to the effect that, "the pupils are allowed to keep very dirty," is not correct. On December 7TH you wrote me re a similar Report made by him which was also incorrect.

All of the pupils here wash three times daily, are bathed all over every Saturday and have their clothes changed. No pupil is allowed to come to the table at meal times unwashed. If between meal times some of the small pupils (for we have a number of these) get their hands dirty it would be difficult to remedy this. I beg to assure you that it would take a better man than the Government Representative here to keep these pupils any cleaner than they are kept usually. Matters on his Reserve here go to prove this. In an Institution like our it is much easier for outsiders to criticize than to remedy.

In pursuance of your instructions I will to the very utmost of my ability keep them clean, but am very much hurt to think that you should have a wrong impression on this matter.

Your Obedient Servant,
John W. Niddrie
Principal

A few months later, Niddrie's level of frustration had increased to the point where he was no longer prepared to tolerate what he considered false statements by the Indian Agent.

Morley
September 12TH, 1899

The Indian Commissioner
Winnipeg, Manitoba

Sir:

I beg to acknowledge receipt of your letter No.77/68 of September 9TH, in which you quote a paragraph of the Acting Agent's Report reflecting on the management and cleanliness of this Institution and calling for explanations for the same. Before giving these I will just say that this man is as unreasonable as he possibly can be. Since I assumed the principalship here, it would appear it has been his aim to make matters as unpleasant as possible for myself and some members of my staff. Now I beg to inform you that this must cease, as I do not intend putting up with any more nonsense from him.

I. Now in regard to the boys' clothing, I enclose a sample of material used for these. They are lined with Factory Cotton. Each boy has two suits, and they are washed and changed every week. I attend to this matter myself and can vouch for the correctness of this statement. Furthermore, your Acting Agent makes use of the words, "The clothes of the boys are not as carefully looked after as I would like."

Now in my humble opinion, this is a piece of sublime impertinence. I have never yet considered what he likes. I have been actively engaged in the Indian work for more than five years and have always tried in every way to meet the wishes of the Indian Department, the Missionary Society, and work for the benefit of the people, and with one exception, that being the Govt. representative here. I am sure both Indians and whites can testify to that.

II. As to the general untidy appearance of the outside premises, I have to conclude that your Representative does not understand what he is talking about.

I have lived within 4 miles of this Institution for the last ten years, and never have I seen the outside premises more tidy than they are now.

It is true that the recent rains made the yards very muddy and disagreeable, but otherwise everything is all right. However, were I to take a pattern of the outside premises and yards of the Stony Agency at Morley, part of the report alluded to in your letter would indeed be true. I am sorry to have to write in this strain but necessity compels me and trust that you will understand matters sufficiently to at least give me justice, which is all I ask for.

> I have the honour to subscribe myself,
> Your Obedient Servant
> John W. Niddrie
> Principal

John Niddrie was just a few days short of his thirty-sixth birthday, old enough to have full confidence in the work he was doing and mature enough not to be easily intimidated. He had been in the west long enough that he was no longer a greenhorn, and bore the responsibility of serving as principal of the Institution. He had also enlisted the support of Rev. John McDougall to vouch for him, and on the same day that he wrote the preceding letter to the Indian Commissioner, Niddrie wrote the following to Rev. Sutherland. It was clearly time for Niddrie to assert his own authority.

Morley
September 12th, 1899

Rev'd. A. Sutherland D.D.
Toronto, Ontario

Rev'd. Dear Sir:

Quoting paragraph 3, page 2 of your letter of June 6TH, 1898.

"So long as you are in charge you will be the responsible head of the Institution and while it will be right and proper to keep in close touch with Mr. McDougall and the Indian Agent," etc.

Now I am sorry to complain of the conduct of the Indian Agent. Following along the line of your advice, I have tried to work in all harmony with him, and for the sake of the work. I have conceded a great deal, but am sorry to say that Mr. Bangs has harassed and worried us very much, and has sent in reports to the Commission that have been very wide of the truth. I have today written the Commission a plain statement of facts relative to this and I beg to inform you that some steps must be taken to avoid this unpleasantness and untruthfulness, as it seriously interferes with our work here.

If there was any truth in his reports, I would not care, but as this is the third time he has made a similar report, all of which have been false, I am sorry I cannot allow it to pass without calling your attention to the matter and asking your advice. Mr. McDougall can vouch for the correctness of my statement.

Will you please have forwarded to my address Financial Blank Forms and Monthly Report forms. Have not heard anything yet re the funds this quarter.

In a hurry to catch mail,
With Kind Regards,
Yours Faithfully
John W. Niddrie

Over a year later, the matter appears to be still unresolved, as indicated by this letter, once again from Indian Commissioner Laird to John Niddrie.

> Office of the
> Indian Commissioner
> for Manitoba and the North-West Territories
> Winnipeg, 13 Nov. 1899
>
> Principal
> McDougall Orphanage
> Morley, Alta.
>
> Rev. Sir,
>
> I beg to acknowledge receipt of your letter of the 9TH instant re the duties of our Agent at Morley when visiting the Orphanage, and to enclose you a blank form which he has to fill after each visit. There are other things to which he should not close his eyes not shown on the form—this depends a great deal on circumstances. I should be obliged if you would state your grounds of complaint so that I may see my way to have same removed if any undue interference has been shown.
>
> Yours truly,
> D. Laird
> Indian Commissioner

After more than ten years at Morley, the frustration with the Indian Agent caused Niddrie to consider resigning from his job. Again he felt compelled to defend his work in this letter to Sutherland. Another concern was Niddrie's salary as principal and he compares the work he does with the situation at Red Deer. However, it would seem that the imminent departure of Mr. Bangs has caused John Niddrie to reconsider leaving his job; in fact, he would spend another ten years at Morley.

> Morley
> March 7TH, 1900
>
> Rev'd. A. Sutherland, D.D.
> Toronto, Ont.
>
> Rev'd. Dear Sir:
>
> Your letter dated March 1ST to hand yesterday afternoon, and in reading it over find that a few points referred to require some explanation from me.

I. Rev'd. Mr. Woodsworth's Report in regard to Gov't Representation. Since assuming Principalship of this Institution, the Indian Agent has in some cases harassed us very much, and made all sorts of unreasonable and unkind Reports about our work. So much so that I had fully decided to tender my resignation at the end of March Quarter to take effect June 30TH. In your first letter to me after I came here you advised me to work in all harmony with the Indian Agent. This I tried very hard to do, but with indifferent success. What his reasons are for the unpleasantness which he has exhibited, I cannot say, but this I can assure you: he has never in any way assisted me in my work. When I came here end of June '98, Mr. Dean had 18 pupils on the Register, 17 of which were here at that time. Today we have 50 pupils and sufficient (10 more) in sight to fill the New Wing. In all my efforts to secure these, I have "struggled along unaided." Chief Jonas Bigstony and other of my Indian friends being very loyal to our work. I have been informed by the Chief referred to that Mr. Bangs had advised him not to advocate the sending of pupils to the Institution. I must, however, say that he has taken no notice of this, and whenever I have visited him in his Camp on the Reserve (which has been quite frequently) I have found him willing to listen and anxious to help so far as he could, and furthermore he has always, as also all of the Indians, expressed this appreciation of the Good Work being done here. In turning up returns of former years you will find nothing like the number of pupils as these, nor anything like the regular number in attendance. *We have no card of truancy or run away*, something unparalleled previously. I am not writing you this in an egotistical spirit, but simply to show you the measure of success we have had, and for which we are thankful. Notwithstanding the opposition of man, God has prospered the work of our hands.

I am informed that Mr. Bangs is leaving the Stoney Agency soon, and I hope and pray a good man may be sent to relieve him.

II. In regard to the Bell: This was brought from Rev'd. John McLean's old Blood Mission at Fort Macleod and the Gov't has nothing whatever to do with it. Mr. Steinhauer and Mr. McDougall are willing to let us have it. If the Indians agree will this be sufficient?

III. In regard to purchasing a wood range. I am positive it would suit and be a great saving to the fuels. In the meantime, I will

Three Alberta Indian chiefs in Toronto, August–October 1886 with Methodist missionary Rev. John McDougall, left. Chiefs left to right are Samson (Cree), Pakan or James Seenum (Cree), and Jonas Goodstoney (Stoney). Standing at right rear is Rev. Robert Bird Steinhauer, another Methodist missionary and colleague of John W. Niddrie, whom Niddrie knew from his days at Morley. McDougall hired Niddrie to work at Morley, and Niddrie also maintained contact with Steinhauer throughout his life. Steinhauer, born in 1861, died in 1941.

look around for an opportunity to dispose of it to advantage, and when the new Gov't representative comes will ask him to recommend the change to the Indian Commissioner.

IV. Salary: If the Exec. Com. sees fit to advance my Salary $100 per annum, that would make it $500. Would this compare with Mr. Somerset's at Red Deer? I am informed they have at that Institution 62 pupils. In a week or two, we will have *sixty*, no assistant Principal, nor as much help in any way, and much more work, as all of our pupils are very young. Excuse me placing these matters so plainly before you. My sole object in doing so is to make you understand matters as they are. I feel that I cannot let this opportunity pass without informing you of the efficient, industrious and loyal way in which our matron Miss Buehler has stood by me in every instance since I came here. In fact, we have what may be termed a very Good Staff.

There is one more matter which I must allude to before concluding. I was told yesterday at Morley P.O. that the Inspector had been up and had expressed a wish to have the Millward Post Office here. I have said nothing about it as Mr. McDougall strongly objects. I have been further informed that having said office here would mean an income of over $100 per year, which would help out considerably with the Institution. The Mail is carried twice a week and would not mean any extra expense to us as the bags go up for our mail nearly every day. I have nothing whatever to say in the matter. Would you be kind enough to express your opinion in the matter.

> With much Christian love,
> I Am Yours Sincerely,
> John W. Niddrie
> Principal

FINDING A COOK

John Niddrie's many responsibilities included staffing the school with both teachers and support personnel. On June 20, 1898, he wrote the following to the *Calgary Herald* newspaper.

> Please insert the following advertisement in your daily paper 3 insertions—
>
> Wanted Good Strong woman as Cook, must be willing to teach Indian children in this Department, and of undoubted Christian Character
>
> Apply
> Principal
> McDougall Orphanage
> Morley

When the newspaper advertisement produced no results, the following was written a few days later to Rev. Dr. Alexander Sutherland in Toronto. Not only was hiring a cook of concern, but other staffing problems and difficulties also existed at the time. As well, the major problem of having an adequate water supply was reported.

McDougall Orphanage Morley
July 4, 1898

Dr. Sutherland

Dear Sir:

On June 24TH I wrote informing you of my arrival at the Orphanage and also informed you of our cook's indication of leaving this Institution, and that we had advertised in the *Calgary Herald* for one to fill this position. We feel it impossible to obtain one here. Mr. Dean has been paying our present cook $20.00 per month, which I consider a very high figure, but for which she would now, having reconsidered the matter, be willing to stay on. I had hoped to be able to secure some one at $15.00 per month who would suit us, thus saving the amount of $5.00 per month, but am unable to do so. Our matron, Miss Buehler, knows of a Miss Walker who has been at Red Deer for a year, and thinks she would be a suitable person for us. Mr. Somerset has been paying her $15.00 per mo. Do you know anything about this person? Miss Buehler is writing her. Will you please instruct me what to do re this matter at your earliest convenience. In the event of not securing the services of Miss Walker, should I keep our present cook at $20.00? Mr. Dean's books have not yet come into our possession and I cannot furnish you with our state financially.

I am sorry to say that we have found matters rather unsatisfactory, and outside on the Ranche is a state of such neglect. A farm instructor had been employed here (and was paid $25 per month) who has had no energy whatever and who has allowed matters almost to go to ruin. We have not a respectable fence on the place, and previous to my coming here neither sheep nor pigs had been kept off the crops. I also find on the farmer's list 16 cows milking. Now while they may have milked this many at one time before the transfer of the two big boys to Red Deer Industrial School, (who were registered here 25 and 39) I found on my arrival here 4 cows milking, the farmer Mr. Grier's excuse being that he did not come here to work.

With the increase of pupils now in the school I must get some more cows in out of the land and milk them. I have secured the services of a good strong youth at $6.00 per month to assist on the Ranche and haul water. This latter is a very big job. I have been hauling as much as 200 gallons per day, and with an increase of pupils in the near future will be quite an improvement to our work. Formerly a much smaller quantity was required but with Mr. Dean's improvements (if I may call them such) we cannot get along with a small quantity. I put the water question very plainly and forcibly before the Indian Department representative here, and he has promised to do his best in placing it before the Commissioner.

New pupils have settled down very well and are fast becoming useful and acquainted. Our matron, Miss Buehler, is a very superior and energetic person in the house, both economical and practical. Our clothing and boots and shoes supply are just about run out. Could you please recommend a firm in the East when you write me? I am thankful to say that spiritually we are in good condition here now. Please pray for us, and with much Christian Love and apologies for thus trespassing on your time,

I am yours Faithfully,
John W. Niddrie

About a month after first advertising for a cook, the position was still not filled, but some progress seems to have been made in securing an adequate supply of water, as reported to Dr. Sutherland.

McDougall Orphanage Morley
July 16th, 1898

Dr. Sutherland
Toronto

Rev'd. and Dear Sir:

I write to acknowledge receipt of your letter dated 20th June with draft for $500 for which I thank you very much, also letter dated July 9th with instructions re Cook. I am sorry that I have been unable to answer the former and acknowledge the draft sooner owing to the press of work on the Ranche. Whichever way I turn there seems to be so much work to do, and so little time at my disposal in which to do it. Then hauling water has taken us so much time. However, I am sure you will be pleased to know that we are making some progress with the Government in the way of bringing water into this building. The Indian Agent has been here with another party and measured the distance to a spring in Mr. Ricks' field (to the west of us) and upon the whole I believe and hope some steps will be taken in this direction in the near future. I have not involved myself or advanced any theory further than pressing for immediate action to this matter every visit the agent makes here.

Re the Cook, I have spoken to her since receiving yours of the 7TH and have had to engage her for 3 months more, that is 3 mos. from Aug. 1ST. She had the offer of another situation and would not engage here for a shorter time, thus *I hope I have done right*. Matters in the house are very agreeable and I am very thankful for the influence we are gaining over the children. Ours indeed is a grand busy work. May God ever help and prosper us.

There are a great many difficulties to contend with on the Ranche amongst stock, agriculture, etc. I am sorry that I cannot say much about these as you might not understand me, and I might appear uncharitable towards Mr. Dean. I will therefore do my best to conquer the work and hope by and by to give you a better account. I may just say in conclusion that I have not yet heard from Mr. Dean, further than a telegram which I had from him asking me to ship his household goods at once to Wetaskiwin which I will do as soon as possible. Our children have all got over their coughs and are now doing very well. I have opened an account with the Molsons Bank, Calgary, and will follow your instructions re paying accounts by cheque.

I will write you by and by and inform you how we are getting along on the water question.

With Much Regard
I Am Yours Faithfully
John W. Niddrie

About a month later, John Niddrie seems to have been given a lead to follow in locating a cook, and began correspondence with a potential employee.

August 30th, 1898

Miss E. Weber
Didsbury

Dear Madam:

The position occupied by our Cook here will be vacant after Oct. 31st. Hence I am writing you to explain matters, and also to ask if you would be willing to occupy this position.

In the first place, the person employed as Cook in this Institution must be of undoubted Christian Character. Knowing you to be that, we should feel very thankful if you could decide to accept the situation and prove capable in the same.

We have in the neighbourhood of 40 pupils and a staff of 7 including the Cook. Two strong girls are detailed to assist in the Cooking and Kitchen every day. These would be under the personal supervision of the Cook, and as they are good intelligent girls would to a very great extent lighten the labours of the same. The management of the Dairy would also devolve upon the Cook, but at this time of the year is light and no heavy work in connection with it, as the boys do all the churning, etc. etc.

The wages paid is $15.00 per month. We could secure the services of a cook from the East, but would prefer having you if agreeable, our Matron, Miss Buehler, having an acquaintance with you and your family. I may just say in conclusion that the duties are not nearly as formidable as they appear, but thought it best to explain matters plainly, and save any misunderstanding. Please answer at your earliest convenience.

Yours Respectfully,
John W. Niddrie
Principal

Miss Weber appears to have been interested in the position of cook, a situation that no doubt provided some encouragement for Niddrie's search, and the following was written.

September 10th, 1898

Miss Weber

Dear Madam:

I am sorry that press of work has prevented me from answering your letter sooner. We shall be pleased to engage you as Cook for one year at $15.00 per month and fare paid to and from Didsbury. Will that suit you?

    I informed you in my letter that the situation would be vacant after Oct. 31st. Should anything occur to the contrary, could you manage to come before that?

Yours with Respect,
John W. Niddrie

But for some reason, Miss Weber was not available for the term offered and the following letters indicate a willingness for compromise to secure her services for whatever time she could make herself available.

September 17th, 1898

Miss Weber

Dear Madam:

Yours of the 12th to hand, and while I am sorry that you cannot see your way through to take an engagement with us for one year as Cook, I beg to state that we will accept your proposal for six or seven mos. term and hope if matters prove satisfactory to both parties you may find it convenient to prolong your stay.

    Kindly hold yourself in readiness to come on Nov. 1st.

Yours Respectfully,
John W. Niddrie

October 17th, 1898

Miss E. Weber
Didsbury

Dear Madam:

Our cook wishes to leave us next Thursday to go and visit her friends before the end of the month, and I am enclosing cheque, value $5.00, for your travelling expenses. Could you come to us with as little delay as possible?

Please write and inform us when you can come and I will meet you at Station.

Greatly Obliged,
Yours With much Respect,
John W. Niddrie

It appears that Miss Weber worked in the position for only a few months, as by the summer of 1899, the search was on again.

Morley
July 21st, 1899

Miss Shaw .
Trout Lake
West Kootenay, B.C.

Dear Madam:

Having heard through Miss Wellwood that you were open to take a situation, I beg to inform you that we are in need of a cook for this Institution, duties to commence about August 15th. The wages paid are $15.00 per month and should the applicant suit and remain in said position for the period of two years, Railroad Fare to Morley will be paid. Should you think anything of this situation, please write me at once and I will furnish you with further particulars.

Respectfully Yours
John W. Niddrie
Principal
McDougall Orphanage
Morley

Apparently Miss Shaw was not sufficiently attracted by the prospect of working as a cook in Morley, but another possibility arose, this time locally.

Morley
August 1st, 1899

Miss Mumford
Morley Station

Dear Madam:

Having heard that you propose leaving your present situation, I beg to inform you that we are in need of a Cook for this Institution, duties to commence August 14TH. Wages $15.00 per month. Should you think anything of this position, will you be kind enough to drop me a line at your earliest possible convenience.

Respectfully Yours,
John W. Niddrie
Principal

Miss Mumford, it seems, was not interested in the position after all, but it appears that Miss Shaw had not lost interest totally, as indicated by the next letter to her.

Morley
August 11th, 1899

Miss Shaw
Trout Lake B.C.

Dear Madam:

Your letter dated July 25TH came to hand some time ago and I beg to make the following proposition. As I have enquired of Mr. Steinhauer who has just returned from visiting his friends in the North about a week ago and cannot find out anything about the Bears Hills Boarding School, if you could in the meantime come to our School we would be very thankful and would be willing to let you go as soon as the School at Bears Hills is opened. I have no doubt but we could arrange to pay half Railroad Fare if you remain one year, and I honestly do not think that the other School will go on before next year. However, if it should do so you would be at liberty to go and we would endeavor to arrange the matter of fare allowance as satisfactory as possible to both parties.

Please write at once and state your decision.

Yours Respectfully,
John W. Niddrie

It is easy to imagine that by now the principal believed good help is hard to find!

HIRING MISS WALSH

In the summer of 1899, it became apparent that a replacement teacher would be needed at the McDougall Orphanage. At the suggestion of John McDougall, Niddrie began correspondence to secure the services of Miss Mary A. Walsh, a popular teacher at Morley previously, but who had left for Ontario, where John Niddrie was able to reach her.

Morley
June 26TH 1899

Dear Miss Walsh:

Will you please let me know at your earliest convenience if you would be willing to come back again to teach school at McDougall Orphanage, and if so, when you could make it convenient to come. Mr. McDougall visited us a few days ago and suggested that I write you to this effect. Should you be willing to come, I will write you again stating a few particulars. In the meantime, it might be well for me to say nothing here until I get your reply.

Hoping this will meet with your approval,

I Am Yours Respectfully,
John W. Niddrie

Obviously Miss Walsh was interested in returning to Morley, as indicated by Niddrie's next letter, some six weeks later.

Morley
August 10TH 1899

Miss M.A. Walsh
Orono, Ontario

Dear Madam:

Your letter dated August 7TH to hand today. I was very pleased to hear from you. I wrote you on June 26TH asking if you would be willing to come back to the Orphanage as "*School Teacher.*" As I never received any reply I am afraid I was rather uncharitable in thinking that a certain member of our staff who left us here might have said something unfavourable which might have prejudiced you against coming to us. However, I am thankful this is not the case, and that you are willing to come back. I delayed writing Dr. Sutherland re the matter in hope of hearing from you.

We have made no other arrangements, but having now heard that you are willing to return, will make a move as soon as possible.

I presume you are aware that the Salary is $25.00 per Month and should the teacher remain 2 years the fare out is refunded. The duties of the teacher you are also quite cognizant of.

The teacher is not asked to do anything outside of schoolroom work, her own room and taking charge of the girls in turn with the other lady members of the Staff after supper and every second Sunday.

We have 40 pupils. Some of these you are acquainted with, and others have come since Mr. Dean left. A great many of the pupils are in the primary class and I think a little Kindergarten work would be a great help to them. The oldest boy we have is about 13 years of age and Beckie Beaver is our oldest girl.

Matters in the schoolroom in the way of progress are not very satisfactory, hence I must recommend a change at once. We will all be very thankful if you can see your way to come back, and I promise you we will do our utmost to make matters agreeable and to make you comfortable.

With Kind Regards,
Yours Respectfully
John W. Niddrie

Although Niddrie had the responsibility of staffing the school, he kept Dr. Sutherland informed of the circumstances. Miss Walsh was obviously held in high regard, and while Niddrie may or may not have passed his compliments on to her, he had no hesitation in advising his colleague of the opinion he held.

Morley
August 14th, 1899

Rev'd. A. Sutherland D.D.
Toronto, Ontario

Rev'd Dear Sir:

I feel it my duty to write and acquaint you with the fact that it is highly necessary that a change be made in the matter of a School Teacher for this Institution. Our present teacher, Miss Clement, completed her term of two years here last June. For some time I have thought of recommending a change here, but am now fully decided that the sooner the change is made the better.

In view of this, I have written Miss M.A. Walsh, formerly Teacher here, and she has written me signifying her willingness to return and again take charge of the school-room. For different reasons I would like to have her come.

I. I have examined a great many schools both "White" and Indian in the N.W.T. and have been employed in this capacity, namely teaching myself for years, and never have I met anyone so capable as a Teacher as Miss W.

II. Whatever she may have been or may not have in any other capacity in this Institution: as a teacher she was a great success. Of this I am confident.

III. Since coming here, the Indians have very often asked me to write you asking for her return as School Teacher here. She was very popular, both with parents and pupils, and was the means of leading some to a better life who have passed away.

As I know you do not favour the re-engaging of staff, I have endeavored to make matters as plain and pointed as possible, and hope you will write authorizing us to engage her on the terms that our present Teacher has been working on. In the matter of Book Learning, our Indians are becoming quite interested, and I am sorry to say that some of the pupils I brought here from the No. 1 Day School last summer are very little, if any further advanced than they were here.

There are other reasons for which a change must be made.

Hoping to hear from you at your earliest possible convenience re this matter and with

Kind Regards—Hoping You are Well
I Am Yours Very Faithfully
John W. Niddrie
Principal

The school was expanding, and while construction and furnishing of the enlarged facility was to proceed, it became apparent that the school might not receive all it needed for the pupils. As correspondence continued with Miss Walsh, John Niddrie began to inquire about the possibility of her assisting him by calling upon the W.M.S., the Woman's Missionary Society, to furnish some of the things needed by the children.

Morley
September 5TH, 1899

Miss M.A. Walsh
Orono, Ontario

Dear Madam:

Your letter Aug. 26TH to hand a few days ago, and should have written you sooner but for the fact that I have been suffering from a severe attack of quinsy.

From your letter I fear you have got a wrong impression of the School. You will have no trouble whatever in controlling the pupils, but their education in the school-room is very indifferent and lately has not been made interesting to them in any particular. I should very much like to have you come now, but all things considered, perhaps it would be well to have you come Nov. 1ST and should you be able to do anything for us with the W.M.S. I can assure you we will appreciate it very much and will not soon forget it. Sealed tenders for the New Building will be closed tonight and a considerable sum will be required for furnishings, etc.

The extension will accommodate 20 additional pupils. We have a different class of pupils here altogether from those that were here in Mr. Butler's time and I am confident you would like them very much. We have some most promising boys and girls.

Since writing you last I have had a letter from Dr. Sutherland in which he informs me that I must be responsible for the engaging and discharging of all of the Staff of this Institution. Now in conclusion I will just say that so long as I am here in the capacity of Principal I will do my utmost to make matters both agreeable and comfortable for you and all of the other members of the Staff. This has been my aim since I assumed the principalship, although I am sorry to say that some members of the staff have not appreciated it. "*Unity is Strength.*"

Stoney Indian boys at Morley photographed by Mary Walsh, ca. 1901.

We shall expect you by Nov. 1ST and please write and inform me the day you expect to be at Morley and I will meet the train with the buggy.

Hoping You are Well
Yours Respectfully
John W. Niddrie

At last the services of Miss Walsh were again secured. Not only did the principal look forward to her arrival, so did the children.

Morley, Alta.
October 12th 1899

Miss M.A. Walsh
Orono, Ont.

Dear Madam:

Your letter dated Oct. 3RD to hand, and I note your decision to commence your duties here Dec. 1ST instead of Nov. 1ST. Following along the line of your suggestion it will in all probability be the better way. I have no wish whatever to part with any ill feeling existing between our present teacher and myself. This is something that all through life I have endeavored to avoid.

We are "toiling on here" as usual. By Dec. 1st our enlargement will be in good running order. If you know of anyone likely to have any "Cast off Children's Clothing" (mostly boys) we would be very pleased to get them, providing that they were fairly good, that is, worth paying freight on. We are in need of overcoats for the larger boys about 12 and 13 years old. In regard to reduced fare will you please write Dr. Sutherland asking him to recommend this to the Railway Co. and should you wish me to pay same in advance let me know, and I can have funds on hand and forward you a cheque for the amount.

The children are looking forward with pleasure to your arrival. Almost every night in the Dormitory, Abraham and David ask, "How many more weeks till Miss Walsh be coming?" I would be very sorry to leave these children now. I think I may say without being egotistic that we have got a very good grip on them.

Must close in order to catch mail. No. 1 going west is now due at 10:00 A.M.—No. 2 going E. at 5:35 P.M. much better than formerly.

> Hoping you are well
> Yours Faithfully
> John W. Niddrie

Miss Walsh did arrive to teach again, and with her camera she recorded images of Morley which grew in importance as the decades passed.

WATER SUPPLY—A SERIOUS PROBLEM

In other correspondence, John Niddrie refers to the serious problem of obtaining an adequate water supply for the Orphanage. It was an issue which seemed to be difficult to resolve, even though Niddrie had proposed a solution by obtaining spring water from another property. Meanwhile, water had to be hauled daily, and as the Orphanage increased in size and enrollment, the demand for water increased.

McDougall Orphanage Morley N.W.T.
August 3RD, 1898

The Indian Commissioner
Winnipeg

Dear Sir:

I write to call your attention to the water supply in connection with this Institution. These are our circumstances. We have no water whatever, excepting what we haul. For different reasons this is most serious as well as exceedingly detrimental to this school.

In the first place, the health of the children is certainly not improved in any way by the use of this "hauled water." Then again in the event of a fire breaking out I would very seriously fear the consequences to this frame building. Coupled with this there is the expense of hauling water every day.

There is a spring in Mr. Ricks' field a short distance to the west of this building where I think a good supply could be had. If you could do anything for us in the way of bringing this water into the house we should feel extremely obliged.

Hoping to hear from you re this matter soon,

I am Sir, Your Obedient Servant,
John W. Niddrie

Morley
February 22ND, 1889

The Secretary
Department of Indian Affairs
Ottawa

Sir:

I beg to call your attention to the water question in connection with this Institution. We have no supply of water whatever, except that which we haul daily, and as we have had a very narrow escape of a serious fire, I feel very anxious to know if the Department could do anything to help us in this matter.

Last fall the Department Surveyor, Mr. Ponton, was instructed to come here and take the level of a spring which is situated in Mr. Ricks' field about 600 yards to the west of this Institution. It was found that the head of this spring is some 75 feet above the level of the School. We have hauled water from it all winter, and find there is almost an unlimited supply of water which cannot be excelled in quality.

Mr. Frank Ricks, who was settled on this land, has moved over south of Bow River. If he were agreeable, would the Government be willing to exchange him land elsewhere, and thus secure this land for our Institution and be enabled to bring water into it in abundance at a very reasonable figure?

We have at present 43 pupils, and you can scarcely conceive the disadvantages we are put to through lack of a proper water system. The continual fear, and wear upon men and horses, is very hard.

If you can do anything for us in this matter I should feel extremely obliged. I see Mr. Ricks quite frequently, if instructed by the Govt. I could approach him re the matter.

> I have, Sir, the honour to Subscribe Myself,
> Your Obedient Servant
> John W. Niddrie
> Principal

> Morley
> April 22ND, 1899

Secretary, Department of Indian Affairs
Ottawa

Sir:

I beg to call your attention to the water question in connection with this Institution. We have absolutely no supply excepting that which we haul daily, and in a school like ours with 41 pupils you can scarcely conceive the inconvenience and extra labour we are put to through the lack of a proper water system.

I wrote you the matter of February 22ND, but rec'd no reply. In letter of that date reference was made to Mr. Ponton the Surveyor's visit here last Fall, spring in Mr. Ricks' field, etc., etc.

Will you please inform me if you think the Government would be willing to do anything in this matter? It will be impossible to do the work here as it ought to be done without water being brought on to the premises, and in case of a fire breaking out, the loss would be very heavy, as this is a frame building and high winds prevail.

Hoping to hear from you soon re this matter,

> I have the honour to Subscribe Myself,
> Your Obedient Servant
> John W. Niddrie

Although Niddrie was in conflict with Acting Indian Agent Bangs on other matters, it was still necessary to set aside those differences and communicate with him about a water supply.

> Morley
> June 3rd, 1899

E.I. Bangs, Esq.
Stony Agency

Allow me to call your attention to the water question in connection with this Institution.

We have absolutely no supply on hand excepting that which we haul daily; and in an Institution like ours with 41 pupils, you can hardly conceive the inconvenience we are put to through the lack of a proper water system. It is an utter impossibility to do the work here as it ought to be done under existing circumstances. Moreover, in a District like this where high winds prevail, should a fire break out I would very seriously fear the consequences to a frame building like ours. If you could do anything in the way of recommending the Govt. to bring water into the building I should feel extremely obliged.

> Yours Faithfully,
> John W. Niddrie
> Principal

Some three months later, progress seemed to be made in getting a positive response from the Department of Indian Affairs in Ottawa. The following letter, all in one sentence, was received from the Secretary of the Department.

Ottawa, September 9th, 1899

John W. Niddrie, Esq.,
Principal
McDougall Orphanage,
Morley
Alta.

Sir:

I have to acknowledge the receipt of your letter of the 23rd ultimo again calling the attention of the Department to the water supply of your school and in reply I beg to say that the Department is pleased to be able to inform you that the right of obtaining water for Lot No. 7 on the Morley Settlement has at last been obtained for the Department of the Interior and instructions will now be given to the Commission to have the work necessary to conduct the water from the spring to the Orphanage building proceeded with at once.

Your obedient servant,
[illegible]
Secretary

Another two months passed, and there still seemed to be no progress.

Morley
November 19th, 1899

The Indian Commissioner
Winnipeg, Manitoba

Sir:

Some time ago I was notified by the Dept. of Indian Affairs at Ottawa that it was their intention to have the water conveyed from a spring on Lot 7 (to the west of us) to this building, and that the work would be proceeded with at once. Since then I have heard nothing more in regard to this. Could you inform me when the work is likely to commence? The enlargement of our building is fast approaching completion, and we will in a few weeks be in a position to take in 23 more pupils and I am anxious to have a proper water system in working order by that time.

Your Obedient Servant,
John W. Niddrie
Principal

Now, at least two years after Niddrie first began expressing his concerns in writing, the lack of a decent water supply persisted.

Morley
Sept. 21st., 1900

The Indian Commissioner
Winnipeg, Manitoba

Hon. Sir:

Allow me again to call your attention to the water question in connection with the Institution. I wrote you on July 23RD stating the terms upon which Mr. Ricks would allow us a water privilege on Lot 7, Morley Settlement, but have not received any reply.

Would you please inform me what the Government's disposition is in the matter, as we are sadly hindered in our work here through lack of a proper water system.

Hoping to hear from you by return,

I have, Sir, the honour to Subscribe Myself,
Your Obed't. Servant
John W. Niddrie
Principal

Morley
April 15TH, 1901

Rev. A. Sutherland, D.D.
Methodist Mission Rooms
Toronto

Rev. and Dear Sir:

The question of water supply is still a very great drawback to us in our work here. I have written the Indian Department so many times in regard to this matter that I am weary of doing so. At one time there was a probability of their complying with my request and of bringing it into the house. Later on there was every likelihood of our obtaining the north half of Lot 7 on which the spring is situated, but through the inopportune interference of someone, Mr. Ricks asks an enormous figure for this land and further charges us $50 per year for the privilege of hauling water from this spring.

Methodist Church at Morley, prior to construction of steeple, photographed by Mary Walsh, ca. 1901.

Now what is to be done in regard to this matter? There is no other water near enough for us to keep up a supply. Even under present circumstances it entails an almost inconceivable amount of work upon us hauling water and keeping up a supply. I might point out that in the past not nearly as much water was required as now.

Faithfully Yours,
John W. Niddrie
Principal

Another year has passed, and despite any promises to remedy the situation, water still has to be hauled as no improvement has been made. In this letter, which deals with other matters and concerns, Niddrie makes almost only passing mention of the water problem. However, it appears that the problem has been raised at a higher level in government.

July 24th, 1901

Rev.'d. A Sutherland, D.D.
Toronto

Rev'd. Dear Sir:

Enclosed herewith please find financial statement of McDougall Orphanage to June 30th, 1901. I am sorry that I did not mail this to you more punctual, but owing to the Department allowing the children a short holiday, a great deal of the work which the boys performed has devolved on me during their absence.

During the Fiscal Year 1900–1901 we have had a great deal of sickness and death. We have at times been very much discouraged in our work and the Department of Indian Affairs has done so little for us. We have so many small children who require constant attention and during the months of February and March mostly all of the pupils were laid up.

In regard to improvement re progress of the pupils, I am thankful to say that this has never been better. Too much cannot be said in favour of the general conduct and morals of the pupils. We have felt all along that to make our work a success we must be earnest and faithful on the Spiritual Side of the work, and I am pleased to say that "Our Father's" blessing has been given to us. More than one half of the girls and the same number of boys are "Standing up for Jesus" and are living consistently according to the light they have. We never have any cases of runaway, in fact, during the years I have had charge of the School, we have had very little if any cause to complain in this respect.

Our two eldest boys are 14 and 15 respectively (all the rest are young) and they have volunteered after harvest to assist me with the ranch work, and thus dispense with the necessity of keeping a ranchman. It will be a grand training for the boys.

I am writing the Hon. Clifford Sifton again today in regard to the water supply, also making a very plain statement of our work and financial expenditure, and earnestly requesting an advance in the per capita grant. So soon as I receive a reply I will write informing you of his action.

During the year we have had the main building and school house painted (3 coats). I gave a note personally for the material and have succeeded in getting the Government to grant $300.00 which will cover this and repair sewage and drainage and complete the log buildings we erected last winter. When the drainage is attended to and if the Department would put water into the building, the school would be in perfect running order. The former will be immediately attended to with part of said grant. This requires attention in the very worst way and during the recent heavy rains the basement and yards have been in a very muddy state.

In regard to funds—could you conveniently send by return of mail $800.00 on last year's expenditure and $400.00 for month of July the fiscal year? I am sorry to trouble you so urgently, but am anxious to straighten accounts up at once.

With Kind Regards
Faithfully Yours
John W. Niddrie

The problem of an adequate water supply has endured now for years. The following letter raises unanswered questions, but it appears than Niddrie has now had his knuckles rapped for raising the issue where someone has considered it inappropriate.

Morley
November 5th, 1901

Rev'd. and Dear Sir:

Referring to your letter of October 28th re two letters from Indian Department in regard to sewage, drainage, and water supply, I cannot understand clearly how "I have missed the point." I have written so many times about these matters that I had become almost desperate and while I knew that these remarks were supposed to be made in a separate communication, I made them in the annual report thinking that perhaps by thus doing, the Department would take steps to remedy the evil.

We were in a fair way to secure Lot 7 (to the west of us), upon which the spring is situated, and this might have led to the getting in of the water, but for the inopportune interference of someone.

Yours Faithfully
John W. Niddrie

MISS WELLWOOD—A JOB AND A HUSBAND

The following letter was written to Miss Mary Jane Wellwood, who was at the time teaching at the Red Deer Industrial School in Red Deer, Alberta. Somehow, John Niddrie had learned that she might be interested in a change of position.

Morley
June 1st, 1899

Miss Wellwood
Red Deer

Dear Madam:

Having heard from our Matron, Miss Buehler, that you are somewhat unsettled in your present situation I write to inform you that we are in need of a Sewing Teacher in this Institution. Duties to commence on July 1st. Should you be wishful to make a change I shall be very pleased to hear from you as to salary, etc. and will answer any communication by return of mail.

Yours Respectfully,
John W. Niddrie
Principal

Niddrie wrote the following a few days later. In it, he tries to come up with a way to offer acceptable pay, and suggests that until the position is accepted she be discreet about it with her present employer.

Morley
June 8th, 1899

Miss M.J. Wellwood
Red Deer

Dear Madam:

Your letter dated June 5th to hand, and in reply beg to state that we should be pleased to have you come as soon as you can.

In regard to salary, I am sorry that we are at present not allowed to pay more than $15.00 per month, but as we have some talk of an extension to our school, I would do my utmost to get a rise for you. All things considered, I think you would in all probability like the change after you get settled here. At all events we should try to make you comfortable here. As to your coming I beg to make the following suggestions. If you could manage to come to us on or about July 12th, your time here could commence July 1st and, as our pupils go to camp in August, you could then have one week's holidays. If you prefer holding to your original plan of coming July 20TH, please let me know and we shall try to make some temporary arrangements until that date. However, perhaps it would be as well in the meantime to say as little as possible to the Principal of your Institution in regard to what I have suggested in this letter.

Hoping to hear from you as to your decision soon,

I am Yours Respectfully
John W. Niddrie
Principal

Mary Jane Wellwood did accept the position and John Niddrie reported his success at hiring her in the following letter.

Morley
June 19TH, 1899

Rev'd. A. Sutherland D.D.

Rev'd. and Dear Sir:

I beg to inform you that I have secured the services of a Sewing Teacher to fill the vacancy of our Miss Jackson, who having completed her two years engagement at the end of this month leaves for the East. The person who succeeds her is a Miss Wellwood who has been at Red Deer Industrial School for two years, but who is leaving there on July 1st and who I hope will suit us. In trying to be as charitable as possible with our present seamstress, I must say that it has been rather difficult to get along pleasantly with her sometimes, but am thankful that matters now can change. Wages of the one who succeeds her are $15.00 per month.

I am anxiously awaiting a reply to my letter written you at Conference. All are well here and matters progressing favourably.

Yours Faithfully,
John W. Niddrie
Principal

Within two years of the young teacher's arrival, romance followed. Two young brothers, Arthur and Frederick Kent from Ontario, had found employ-

William Kent, born 1907 and shown here in 1999 at the Morley church, is the son of Mary Jane Wellwood, hired as a sewing instructor at Morley. Kent's parents were married by Rev. Robert B. Steinhauer, and their wedding certificate was written by John W. Niddrie.

ment at the settlement. On April 8, 1901, Mary Jane Wellwood and Arthur Edgar Kent were married at Morley by Rev. Robert B. Steinhauer.

THE MANITOBA YEARS

John W. Niddrie decided at age eighteen to serve the Lord, while still living in England, having moved there from his native Scotland. His first work in Canada in the service of the church was at Morley, Alberta, where he functioned as a lay minister, and continued in that capacity when he moved to Manitoba. In 1915, he travelled to Winnipeg to attend the annual conference of the Methodist Church. It was at that conference where at the age of 51 he was ordained as a minister of the church on June 20, 1915 and could now officially use the title Reverend.

Three days earlier, a Winnipeg newspaper carried an account of Niddrie's trip to the city to attend the conference. Upon his arrival in Winnipeg, he

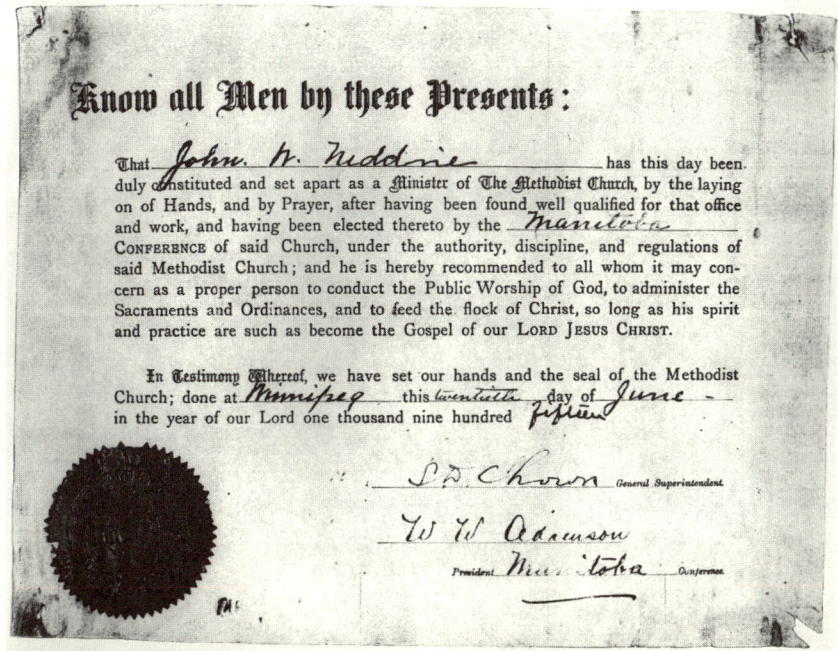

John W. Niddrie's ordination certificate, dated 1915.

stayed with his sister, Maria, whom he had seen rarely since leaving her in Winnipeg when he moved to Morley in 1889. Now married to a man named Cornelius deWinter, Maria was erroneously named as Mrs. Winters in the following account.

OVER THREE WEEKS MAKING TRIP FROM NORTHERN POST TO ATTEND THE CONFERENCE

Tanned and weather beaten, with the quiet blue eye of a man used to the great distances and the solitudes, Rev. J.W. Niddrie, missionary at Oxford House, a lone post in the northland, has arrived in the city after an arduous trip through the wilds. He started on May 25 and in company with Willie Hart, an Indian native of the Oxford House region, he made the trip successfully, arriving as was his desire for the opening of the Methodist conference. Mr. Niddrie is the guest of his sister, Mrs. Winters, 439 Martin Avenue, Elmwood, and the visit is of special interest as

John W. Niddrie, centre, ca. 1930s, likely at Berens River, with Esaias Boulanger, left, and Willie Hart, right, both mentioned in Niddrie's writing. Willie travelled with Niddrie to Winnipeg in 1915 when he was ordained as a minister in the Methodist Church.

this is only the second time for the brother and sister to meet during the last 30 years. Mr. Niddrie is of Scottish birth but imbibed his Methodism in England. He looks forward to the time when these two great denominations will form one vast Christian society in this dominion.

Rev. Mr. Niddrie has been in touch with the Indians of this country for a period of 23 years, and 10 of these years have been spent in active missionary work. He has been with the Oxford House Indians for five years and before this he was with the Stoney Indians in Alberta. The Oxford House Indians are Wood Indians and he finds them less proud and arrogant in spirit than the Stoneys of the prairies.

Modern in Dress

The young Indian who came down with Mr. Niddrie, Willie Hart, is a bright, alert lad and has a remarkable talent for drawing. He has been with Mr. Niddrie for the last five years and plays the organ in the church at Oxford House. The Indians up there are quite modern in their manner of dress and Mr. Niddrie notices little difference in this respect between Oxford House and Winnipeg.

The Methodist mission at Oxford House has been in existence for 65 years and no other denomination is engaged in missionary work in that vicinity. The Methodist mission has absorbed all the Indians and the mission has been extended to God's Lake. Mr. Niddrie makes periodical trips to this post, which is 60 miles distant using canoe or dog sleds, according to the season.

Expects Mineral Development
Mr. Niddrie is not of the opinion that the Oxford House region will ever be of great value from an agricultural standpoint, but he has faith that some day the mineral wealth of the region will be uncovered and will be of immense value. He says that the Indians before the war were making good money, from $500 to $1,000 per year. This money was made in fur trapping and in freighting for the Hudson's Bay company and other traders. Now the war has seriously disturbed the fur business and prices have suffered as a result. Last year there would have been destitution among the Indians, Mr. Niddrie says, if the government had not come to their assistance.

Oxford House is 600 miles north of Winnipeg and 225 miles south of York Factory.

There are 340 Indians in the region. They are fish-eating Indians and the old-time members of the tribe live practically on a fish diet. The younger ones are beginning to want a little variation in the way of bread.

The Methodist Yearbook of 1915 lists John W. Niddrie as the only minister ordained at the annual conference, when he was "Ordained for Special Purposes." It appears that he was regarded as a probationary minister prior to 1915. The statistics for his responsibility at Oxford House showed 68 Methodist families with 123 persons having full membership in the church, 3 infant baptisms, 4 marriages solemnized and 21 burials attended.

In the following letter to his friend and colleague, Rev. Robert Bird Steinhauer, whom he had known from his days at Morley, Niddrie begins as westerners often do, by commenting on the weather and the crops. In addition to describing some of his activities, Niddrie comments upon some of the problems and successes of the missionary work. He questions some of the things the church has done, and while recognizing the accomplishments of some comrades, he is critical of others, and scornful of certain fellow white men.

Berens River and Inland United Church Missions
Via Selkirk, Manitoba
Rev. J.W. Niddrie
MISSIONARY

September 10TH, 1928

Rev. R.B. Steinhauer B.A.
Saddle Lake, Alberta

Dear Brother Steinhauer:

It seems a long time since you and I exchanged letters. Indeed I really think you owe me one; in reply to my last to you. However, if I make a break in the ice (even if it is fall), perhaps you may find time and inclination to answer me. I hope Mrs. Steinhauer, yourself and family are all well and happy and enjoying the many blessings of Our Heavenly Father.

We have had a very dry summer here; and while there is nothing like agricultural pursuits carried on, our gardens have suffered very much and indeed are almost worthless. This through lack of timely rain. It is generally reported that weather conditions were quite favourable for crops outside in Manitoba, so it would appear that the dry weather we have experienced here is purely local. However, the feeling of fall weather is already upon us and indications point towards an early winter, so far as we can judge at present.

Our work here at Berens River is somewhat varied. At the beginning of July I started off on the yearly official visit to the Missions inland in this Superintendency. We made the trip by canoe and were away almost a month. The distance covered was between 6 and 7 hundred miles. The Missions at Little Grand Rapids, Deer Lake, Pekangecum and another outlying point were all visited and a few days spent at each point. Our Church has been ministering or rather, shall I say, sending her men to make periodical visits to Pekangecum for 25 or 30 or perhaps even more years, and still every last mother's son of the people are pagan. Not one at this place has yet been baptized into the Christian Faith.

However, we are sending in a good Christian man as Missionary Teacher this summer and the people seem to be taking a great interest in him; and we are therefore hoping for great things. It is simply absurd to think of sending a white man in on the ground floor to break ground at a place like Pekangecum. In the first place, the people do not understand one word of English and again a white man has no idea of the mode of the Indian life at such a place. These people are all purely Saulteaux. It must, however, in justice to them, be confessed that heretofore they have evidenced no desire for the white man's religion: they have always treated us with great kindness and courtesy. Some of "Our Powers that be" have been highly incensed with me for making the statement that, "The reason the Pekangecum Indians are such good moral people is because they are so far away from the deteriorated degenerated white men." Whether we like it or not, there is a great deal of truth in this statement.

At Deer Lake conditions are quite different—in this way. One of their men, Adam Fiddler by name, carries on the Mission work, holding two services every Sunday and one each Wednesday evening. For this work our Church pays him 150 dollars per year. Even with the utmost stretch of imagination you could not call this man cultured, or even possessed of excessive intelligence, and yet he has done a wonderful work for The Lord. It is simply amazing. The people came to services while we were there (indeed it is a continuation of services all day) and they sing, sing, sing. Oh how they do sing. This is a very good sign.

At one of our Sunday services we were led in the singing by three organs and six male voices (a choir). It is simply wonderful. They erected their own Church at their own expense. They have carried the work on now for thirteen or fourteen years. They have purchased their own organs. The only grant that I have ever known made them was 150 dollars to enlarge the original Church. It just happened to be Treaty Time when we were there this summer and after the Treaty Party had gone and all of our work was done and we were preparing to leave the next morning. This man, Adam, came in and threw down a roll of bills as the Missionary Subscriptions all unsolicited. He said, "Count that." It amounted to ninety-six dollars—ninety-six in one-dollar bills given out of their penury—and remember at that place flour costs forty dollars a sack. Tea three dollars a pound. Blue overalls seven dollars and fifty cents a pair, moccasin rubbers five dollars a pair. This giving speaks for itself and also Adam's work.

We sent in a new man to Little Grand Rapids last year and he has done a most excellent work. This is a hard place to work. So many conjurers and Witch Doctors, etc. etc. However there is a great turnover. The building was filled to capacity at all of our services and at the close when they started off home we counted 18 canoes all loaded with people. They handed me through their Missionary thirty dollars missionary givings all unsolicited.

We are indeed thankful for the signs of the times. Now regarding our Home Mission and work here, there are many discouraging features connected with the work. One of the worst being the destroying influences of the Scum of White Fishermen. We do earnestly pray and believe for a great change here. We have a splendid Day School of nearly 40 children. Two years ago one girl passed Entrance to High School. This year one girl and two boys passed entrance examination and received certificates of entrance to High School. Then we have a prospective class of 4 for next June. We have also some very clever and intelligent pupils in grade 6, although they are only 10 and 11 years old. We are aiming at efficiency now.

Have you heard anything about a new Cree Hymn Book? I had a letter from this man, Rev. Stevens, informing me that he and Rev. Gaudin were appointed a committee to prepare a new book.

I sent him a few copies at his request which will need a great deal of revising before they go in print as I am no Cree scholar. I can read it freely enough, but you would laugh at my construction of sentences. Of course, this is "Bush Cree." I am told that Rev. Gaudin, who claims to be an expert in the Cree language, is now preaching in English at Norway House through an interpreter. I never heard any particular flow of Cree from him. Of course, I suppose Stevens is better, but Joseph Everett tells me he cannot talk proper Cree. I am wondering what the new book will be like?

How is your work going on at Saddle Lake? Things should be in good shape there as you must have some good men. Anyway, I have found work amongst the Crees better and easier in every way than amongst either the Stoneys or the Saulteaux. Well, My Dear Old Friend, I must now close with very kind regards to Mrs. Steinhauer, yourself and all the family. May God give you multiplied peace and joy.

Yours faithfully,
J.W. Niddrie

John Niddrie never forgot his beloved homeland and cherished his early memories of Scotland. He kept in touch with Oban by reading copies of *The*

Oban Times, which were received by another Scot and then passed on to him. Occasionally Niddrie wrote to the editor of the newspaper, and some of his work appeared in print in his home town.

As usual, he referred to himself in the plural form when making a statement. "We have now spent forty-four years in this, the country of our adoption," he wrote in one published letter dated March 1, 1929. "We have in Canada many daily, weekly and periodical papers. Many of these are excellent, and we love to read them because of their sterling worth, splendid diction, and reliable authority; that is, provided they reach us, in this isolate territory."

He went on to say, "Somehow or other, *The Oban Times*—our own hometown paper—always brings a ray of sunshine into our lives upon its arrival."

A few years later, he was obviously moved by an obituary in the newspaper which brought back memories of a friend fifty-eight years earlier when Niddrie was a lad of thirteen. His letter in its entirety appears as follows.

    The United Church Mission, Berens River, Manitoba, Canada
                                                          March 10TH, 1934

To The Editor, "Oban Times," Oban, Scotland

Dear Sir:

> Living as we do, in this country of magnificent distances with its commensurate solitude, our facilities for receiving and transmitting mail are not at all as frequent as are those of our friends living near the great centres of civilization. We, however, receive mail and sometimes newspapers of a more or less ancient date.
>
> Through the kindness of a good friend and brother Scot, "The Oban Times" are passed on to us after their arrival here. With the greatest interest we peruse the columns of your splendid paper, trying to trace the names and some of the happenings in the Dear Old Highlands of Scotland. To those who may not have passed through a like experience, it might be inconceivable how many scenes of the past rise up before us as we thus meditate.
>
> In your issue of February 3RD, 1934, we read in the column of Deaths the following:

> "At Glengorm Isle of Mull, on January twenty-fifth 1934, Colin Fletcher, late Manager of Ulva, and third son of the late Alexander and Catherine Fletcher, Glenaros, Aged 67 years, husband of the late Margaret Cameron...Sadly missed."
>
> The reading of this obituary has awakened within us mingled memories of joy and sadness. Gazing back through the mist of the years—or perhaps to be more correct—on a beautiful sunshiny day in the month of May 1876, we for the last time walked by Colin's side along the high way from the School at Salen to the cross roads near the old Aros Bridge. Side by side we sat in the schoolroom; side by side we stood in the same class. All these memories rising up before us today stand out like a broad band of light. Many years intervene, many changes have come, and to quote from the far-famed Burns, "Seas between us brade hae roared / Since the days o auld lang syne."
>
> Yet as we today gaze back from near the sunset of life, we think with fond memories of our boyhood friend Colin, who never failed us. Our hearts today go out in sympathy to the loved ones left behind, and while we may be an utter stranger to some of these, still we feel that we owe this simple tribute to the memory of one we always loved.
>
> I Have Sir, etc.,
Rev. J.W. Niddrie

Niddrie's life in Alberta and Manitoba left memorable impressions which comprised the bulk of his memoirs as he wrote them in 1938–40 following his retirement. But as with us all, the memories of childhood remain vivid throughout one's life. Almost a year to the day of the foregoing letter to the editor of *The Oban Times*, John Niddrie wrote the following to that hometown newspaper on March 15, 1935.

> Today from near the sunset of life, with your excellent paper before us as we write this, with the article on the Island of Mull and the beautiful eulogium to your contributor by Mariead Oig, we pause and reflect—or should we say, pause and retrospect—back through the intervening three score years we pass with a bound. An unseen hand seems to sweep away the mist of the years and we stand a bare-footed boy on the shores of Loch-na-keal again.

> In fancy we hear the waves dash on the rocks, and a vision carries us to the little isle of Eorsa and the Gribun Rocks. A slight turn of the head and there is brought within our encompassing vision the naked peak of Ben More, towering heavenward; while away behind us, tier upon tier, rise the beautiful pink heathery hillsides.
>
> Distance intervenes and years have passed, but forget these pictures we never shall: no, not while reason stands enthroned and memory holds her seat. All Highlanders should surely be very appreciative of your contributor's pen in depicting so minutely and correctly the rocks, hills and glens of the grand old Isle of Mull.

Looking at old photographs of John Niddrie in his later years, still tall and imposing with his big handlebar moustache, now white, but much heavier than the strapping young man seen in early pictures; and while reading his single-spaced typewritten pages, many scorched by fire on the edges, it is easy to conjure up an image of the man. He sits there at his table with a simple typewriter, writing out the memoirs of his life as a missionary. Never married, but never alone, and never one to complain of his rugged life, he recalls with photographic clarity the scenes of his youth and the more recent events of his life in service to native people.

But not all his writing was of memories. On Saturday, December 10, 1932, the *Winnipeg Evening Tribune* published a full-page feature on the front page of its Magazine Section entitled "The Puzzle of the Indian Tribe." It was written by Matthew Halton, a name to become well known in Canadian journalism. John Niddrie took exception to both the text of the article and to what he felt were inappropriate illustrations, which bore more resemblance to the reader's imagination of what life in ancient Egypt would look like, rather than contemporary life among Canada's native people in the North.

Here is an excerpt from Halton's article:

> At our very door, in that vast hinterland of waters and wooded wilderness which is Northern Ontario, there are settlements of pagan Indians, carrying on the traditions, primitive arts, religion,

and habits of living which their ancestors practised before Christianity was born.

It is a little settlement of a few hundred people who are like the white man only in that they wear his clothes; who worship in temples built of birch bark; whose religion is a strange and complex mixture of an ancient animism which originated in Egypt before the dawn of Christianity; who are extraordinarily healthy and virile; live lives of practical communism, based on an elaborate ritual; and have developed a beautiful art and craftsmanship out of the crude materials of their savage surroundings.

They are a section of the Saulteaux Indians, an Ojibway people speaking a dialect of the Algonquin tongue with related tribes in Manitoba. They call their settlement Pikangikum, which is several hundred miles from civilization, and accessible only by canoe. It lies in that part of the Patricia district of northwestern Ontario which is about 400 miles north of the American boundary and about 80 miles east of the Manitoba line, a section which has as much water as land, and where the lake and river islands and mainland are so densely wooded that an aerial picture of the region looks like a carpet.

Untouched by Missionaries
The story of this strange tribe was told to me in Philadelphia by Dr. A. Irving Hallowell, professor of anthropology at the University of Pennsylvania, who spent the summer with these Indians, studying their manners and customs, and whose announcement of what he saw and learned there has caused a sensation.

Niddrie responded with this letter to the editor of the Winnipeg newspaper, correcting what he felt was inaccurate reporting and even spelling. The letter was published in the January 21, 1933 issue of the newspaper.

The United Church Mission, Berens River
January 4TH, 1933

To the Editor
The Evening Tribune, Winnipeg, Manitoba

Dear Sir:

Living here as we do on "The Ragged Edge," our facilities for receiving and transmitting mail are not as expeditious as some of our more favoured friends living outside; hence our delay in writing you this letter for insertion.

In your issue of December 10TH, first page, Magazine Section, there appears an article from the pen of Mr. Matthew Halton entitled, "The Puzzle of the Indian Tribe," together with some caricatures which may be attractive, but are not much to the point in dealing with the above named article.

We have not the pleasure of an acquaintance with Mr. Matthew Halton, but were pleased to meet and become acquainted with the learned Doctor A. Irving Hallowell, of Philadelphia University, last summer, and he did us the honour to call and visit us in our home here.

We also loaned him a book on The Indian Work and its workers. He was then on his way inland to Pekangecum. Mr. Matthew Halton, quoting from information received from Doctor Hallowell and his last summer's visit to Pekangecum makes some rather incorrect statements. The title of his fourth paragraph on the above subject reads, "Untouched by Missionaries."

Mr. Editor, will you please allow me to say that such a statement is, to say the least, incorrect, and quite misleading. We have been in the Indian work over forty years, and spent the last twenty-two in the North Country, and prior to that, we years before saw "PEKANGECUM" on the list of Conference stations. It is quite true that the different missionaries made only periodical visits to that point, presumably annually, prior to our coming to Berens River twelve years ago.

The veteran Indian missionary, Rev. Mr. Stevens of Fisher River, had made a number of visits to that point and spent days at a time with the people. Then in the last twelve years we (ourselves) have made ten annual visits to Pekangecum, sometimes accompanied by our General Superintendent, Rev. Mr. Barner of Toronto and sometimes alone. At all of these visits religious services were faithfully held.

Then in paragraph five we read, "Here a hundred miles away from our cities and railroads is a people who have never heard the name of Christ; and most of which has never seen a white man or heard a word of English."

May I once again, Mr. Editor, state that the above is most incorrect and misleading. As already stated, we ourselves have made eleven visits to this people, and at all of these visits Christ as The Saviour of the world was faithfully held up before the people. Then in Nineteen hundred and twenty-eight, a Missionary Teacher (who filled the dual capacity of Missionary and Teacher) was appointed by Conference to Pekangecum.

Two services are held every Sunday and one on Wednesday Evening when the people are at home. A successful Day School is operated, with an average of from twenty-five to thirty pupils graded all the way from one to four. In the last three years over one hundred children and adults have been baptized into the Christian faith. Further be it noted, all of these belong to the Pekangecum Band of Indians.

Quoting again, regarding the people, "hardly ever seeing a white man or hearing the English language," this is certainly incorrect. Years ago the late Indian Agent, Mr. H.O. Latulllipe, accompanied by Mr. Milledge, visited this band and paid the annuities to Pekangecum Band. All of the aforementioned gentlemen addressed the people in the English language, using an interpreter.

Mr. Editor, I have never yet heard of any of the Indians at that point being deaf and dumb, consequently they must of necessity have heard the language of the white man many times.

Mr. Editor, as to our object in writing of these facts, it is legitimate and right that your readers and the public generally should receive correct, first hand knowledge, and the Missionary Board of our Church has made an annual grant for travelling expenses to many of these places.

I Have Sir, etc.,
Rev. J.W. Niddrie

As John Niddrie reached what he called the sunset of his life and began to assemble his thoughts and recollections in written memoirs, he remained a faithful servant to his church, loyal to his God, and true to the Indian people among whom he worked for over half a century. His memoirs were a personal statement, but when the daily press printed what he considered inaccurate and misleading statements concerning life among the Indians, Niddrie then used the press itself for public rebuttal.

The Rev. Mr. Barner mentioned in Niddrie's foregoing letter to the *Winnipeg Evening Tribune* was the Superintendent of Indian Work of the United Church. In May 1936, The *United Church Record* published the following tribute to Mr. Barner, written by John Niddrie and dated June 18, 1935. Niddrie didn't hesitate to criticize what he felt were misleading statements in the newspaper, he didn't balk at giving praise and compliments where they were due. Rev. Barner was someone Niddrie had known for many years, going back to his early days at Morley. Although written as a tribute to Barner, the following piece also provided Niddrie with an opportunity to work in a little bit of sermonizing!

SUPERINTENDENT OF INDIAN WORK RESIGNS: A TRIBUTE TO DR. ARTHUR BARNER
By Rev. J.W. Niddrie, Berens River, Man.

May we, who are comparatively unknown to the outside public of our Church and seldom mentioned in the columns of its periodicals, crave a small space in your splendid paper to give expression to our deep regret because of the resignation of the Rev. Arthur Barner, D.D., from the Superintendency of the Indian Work.

It is now many years since we first met at Morley, Alberta. He was then Principal of the Indian Industrial Institute at Red Deer, Alberta. Later, or to be more accurate, in June, 1918, we were instructed by the Rev. T. Ferrier, Chairman of what was at that date known as the Lake Winnipeg District, to meet Dr. Barner at Norway House and take him by canoe round the north end of the district. Since that date, and all through the subsequent years, we have at intervals travelled hundreds of miles in these northern wilds with Dr. Barner in the Master's service.

We are to-day perfectly sure that we are expressing ourselves correctly, and also our contemporaries in the Indian work, and have our hand on the pulse of each of these, when we state that in all his travels and visits to Indian Missions, Dr. Barner has been as a tower of strength to cheer and encourage the men upon the various fields. His entire devotion to God and the work; his very perfect gentlemanly Christian spirit; his wide and genuine sympathy with those on the fields under his supervision, always brought comfort and cheer to all in their strenuous tasks for the Master. The memory of this man of God, with his kindly smile and cheerful optimism, will remain wherever he has gone as "ointment poured forth."

Dr. Barner is eminently possessed with the spirit of love to mankind. To-day the human heart thirsts for love and hungers for human sympathy. Heart-broken and weary, men gather around some great-hearted man, just as pilgrims crowd around a winter's fire. True religion, says Christ, is love. Love is gentle towards those with hollow eyes and famine-stricken faces. Love is kind towards those who have tragedy written in the sharpened countenance. Love is patient towards those who have lost fidelity, as a man loses a golden coin. "*Love is the Fulfilling of the Law.*"

That Rev. Dr. Barner and his good wife and family may long live to enjoy the rich blessings of Our Father, is the prayer of his many friends.

[Dr. and Mrs. Barner left Toronto on Monday, April 27TH, for the West, and will make their home in Vancouver. They carry with them the best wishes of their many friends. —ED.]

It was obvious that just as John Niddrie held Arthur Barner in high regard, Barner likewise had a good deal of respect for Niddrie and wrote the following tribute to him. No date was given on Barner's handwritten account, but it was likely written sometime in the 1930s, possibly in 1940 as a tribute to Niddrie after his death.

REV. J.W. NIDDRIE
By Arthur Barner

The first time I came in close contact with Rev. J.W. Niddrie was in the year 1904. At that time he was Principal of the McDougall Indian Orphanage as it was called. It was really an Indian Residential School situated on the Stoney Reserve about 40 miles west of Calgary, Alberta. Mr. Niddrie went west as a teacher and worked with the McDougalls for many years. Father and son had great confidence in him and he served the cause of the Native people with zeal and efficiency. He learned the native language so that he could preach fluently and explain the scriptures to the people in their own tongue.

About 1910 the Government and Church decided that the Residential School should be closed as the building had served its day and conditions were not favourable at that time for erecting a new building. Mr. Niddrie had received an invitation and hence asked to go to Northern Manitoba. He was stationed in the Lake Winnipeg District of the Methodist Church. He served the people at Oxford House for several years, but his activities were not confined to that place, for in those years the conference found it difficult to secure supplies for the outlying Missions such as God's Lake and Island Lake. J.W. Niddrie was renowned as a travelling missionary. He spent weeks every summer along with his canoe men, travelling the lakes and rivers and preaching the Gospel wherever there was a Reserve or a group of native freighters as they camped on their long canoe journeys. Those were the days of the "armstrong" method of travel before the outboard motor was in use.

He was a heavy man, weighing considerably over 200 lbs. and the only convenient place for him was the centre of the canoe, but that was the position for the man with the oars. In this way J.W. Niddrie became renowned as an oarsman. Then many portages must be crossed on such journeys. The canoe and all the baggage must be "packed" across these on the backs of the canoe men. Some missionaries would gladly leave such work to the Indians, but not so Mr. Niddrie. He carried the heaviest load, thus fulfilling in a real way the injunction of the scriptures, "Bear ye one another's burden and so fulfil the law of Christ." In these ways he became known all over that part of the Great North Land.

About the year 1920, the Manitoba Conference stationed J.W. Niddrie at Berens River and there he completed his ministry.

Many journeys were made during the summer months to the inland Reserves such as Little Grand Rapids, Pekangecum, Deer Lake and Sandy Lake. Thus the people in very isolated places were reached with the Gospel message.

J.W. Niddrie was a fearless preacher and a careful bible student, so he became guide, philosopher and friend to the native people through all that territory. As the people travelled down the Berens River to visit the outside world it was a common thing to see their canoes tied up just below the Mission House, which was erected close to the high bank of the river, while they visited the Minister and they all knew from experience that it could be truly said of him as it was said of his Master and Lord, "He came not to be ministered unto, but to minister, and to give his life."

In the later years of his life, a niece, Miss Annie Niddrie, joined him and took charge of the Mission House, bringing comfort and true companionship to him. Together they secured a building close by the Church and opened a home for old people of the native tribes. Many found comfort and help there in their declining years.

Mr. Niddrie never married, but he had a father's heart, for seldom during his ministry was he without a boy companion in his home. These boys he would take when they were quite young, see that they attended the Indian Day School close by, and when they reached the age for advanced education, pay for their board

Roscoe T. Chapin's photo of two canoes working up the foot of rapids in the 1920s gives an idea of the labour involved when missionaries in the north visited their far-flung flock.

and tuition in the distant town or city. Several young men who are doing very well in life can bear grateful testimony to this.

During Niddrie's time at Berens River, the Roman Catholic church was represented by Brother Frederick Leach. Niddrie and Leach had little to do with each other, generally avoiding one another, except when necessity required that they had to work for the good of the community. Percy Berens, a grandson of the first chief, Jacob Berens, recalled at the age of 86 in September 1999, that Niddrie and Leach "got along like cats and dogs" and would walk on opposite sides of the road if they met each other. The following extract shows some of Niddrie's feeling towards the competition. The two consecutive paragraphs are taken from the carbon copy of what appears to be a report or account of his work written in 1934. It is not addressed to anyone and may have been attached to a covering letter. As usual, Niddrie was writing in the third person.

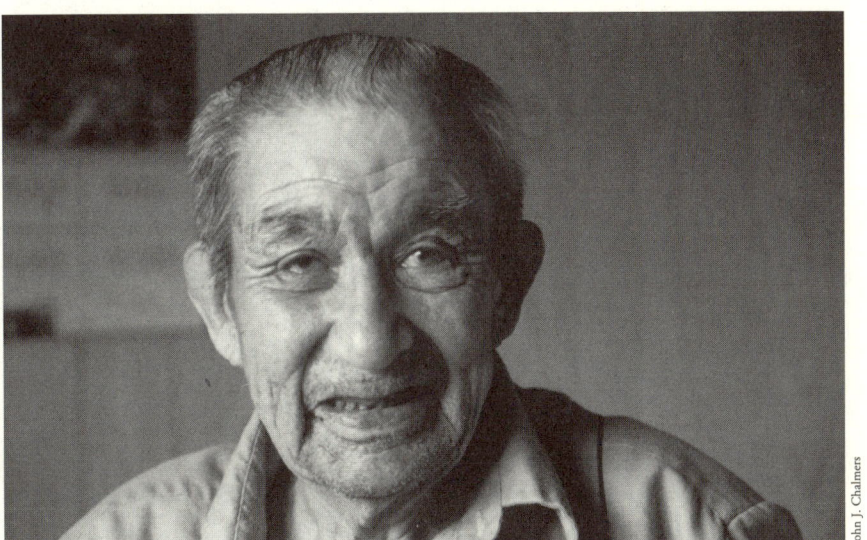

Percy Berens of Berens River, at age 86 in 1999. Mr. Berens grew up knowing John Niddrie and attended his services at the Berens River church. Mr. Berens is a grandson of Chief Jacob Berens, who signed Treaty No. 5 in 1875.

Berens River Mission. United Church Mission.

This is our forty-fifth year in the Indian work. Twenty-one years of that time was spent amongst the Indians in the far west. In 1910 we were appointed by the Methodist Conference to Oxford House, which is situated about four hundred miles north from here. We spent five years at that Mission, then transferred to Island Lake Mission about two hundred or two hundred and fifty miles in an easterly and northern direction. Here we spent another five years and in 1920 we were appointed to Berens River with the superintendency of the inland Missions from this point. These Missions inland are Little Grand Rapids, Pekangecum, Deer Lake and Sandy Lake. We went annually until the Depression came and then funds for travelling expenses were not available. However, the work is still going along very satisfactorily and we are in touch with the men who come from those points each summer for Hudson's Bay freight. The trip we usually made involved a journey by canoe and motor engine of about 1,000 miles and took from twenty-two to twenty-six days according to wind and weather, for we had many lakes to navigate.

Methodist Mission House, Berens River, ca. 1930s.

Now just a few words regarding our home Mission here at Berens River. For a number of years we have been concentrating on the young people. While we have done all we could for the older ones, we have felt that most of our hope lay with the young people. The older people are so imbued with old traditions and customs that it is very hard to make much headway with them. The young people are more easily reached and more readily responsive. We have many very promising boys and girls at this Mission, but are up against a most bitter Roman Catholic opposition, who scruple at nothing at all to get our young people. However, God is good and our confidence unshaken. I must truthfully state that some very shameful things are done by the R.C.'s in the name of religion.

John Niddrie was not one to complain of his rugged life and the conditions in which he lived. However, at the age of seventy-one, still four years away from retirement, now troubled by rheumatism and quite overweight, he would be much less active than in his early days. The following letter was written to his sister Maria, who stayed in Winnipeg where she married Cornelius deWinter. (John, his mother Jane, and his brother William, with wife Hannah and children, had moved on to Morley.)

Here we get an insight to the severe conditions in winter at Berens River and a small glimpse at his domestic life. Niddrie is still interested in the events and news from his home in Scotland and often reflects upon them. As much as he loved the beauty of the foothills in Alberta, he still feels that the highlands of Scotland have no equal. In this letter he identifies the fellow Scot who provided copies of *The Oban Times*, and mentions also Robert and Fanny, a brother and sister who remained in Scotland.

Berens River United Church Mission
Via Selkirk, Manitoba

Rev. J.W. Niddrie
Missionary

March Twenty-third 1934

Mrs. M. deWinter
Winnipeg, Manitoba

My Dear Sister:

For a long time I have meant writing you; but something always seems to have prevented my doing so. Well: at least here goes. I hope this will find you all well and happy. I suppose we have nothing to complain about, although I am much troubled with rheumatism. However, it seems not so bad lately. Only when we are going to have a change in the weather I can always feel it coming.

We have had a terrible winter, one of the worst we have experienced in this north land. At least there must have been 4 feet of snow on the level. The weather has been extremely cold, and even yesterday morning the temperature was 40 below Zero. I expect it is not so severe as this in Winnipeg. I heard you had been west as far as Edmonton. How did you like the west? I would very much prefer it to this north land. We have had a great deal of sickness at Berens River this winter. Whooping Cough with complications has been the epidemic from which our young people have suffered so much. We have had a number of deaths, but should not complain as the people at Cross Lake, Norway House and Poplar River have suffered very much more than we. I had a letter from a young man in charge for the Hudson's Bay Company at Oxford House and he said they had 18 deaths in a year. This is quite serious.

You will be sorry to hear that Willie Hart has lost all of his children but Sonny. Altogether 4 have died, 3 this winter and one before. He must feel very bad. His wife and family have been staying at Norway House and he has been spending the winters now for 3 years at God's Lake trading there. I suppose the poor fellow has been glad to get something wherewith to support his family. I have had some very good reports about him.

Esaias and Tom are at Clear Water Lake, about 150 miles inland from here. They were down about 3 weeks ago for supplies but I did not manage to say much to them. They made a very hurried visit when they came here. On their way back the house was full of people and I could not find much out. I rather think Esaias' wife has had another baby but am not just sure. If such be the case that will be 5 children. I do not see much of them even when they are at home. They live only about half a mile away but I mostly see them on Sundays, only when they come to service.

Annie is keeping fine and is quite cheery. It makes it better for her, Mrs. Street being so near. She walked over to the H.B. Coy's store yesterday afternoon. This is about a mile from here and a good road as it is travelled so much.

We have an old man here, a war pensioner named McKenzie, who used to live in Lismore (an island about five or six miles from Oban). He is a very fine old man comes over here to visit us quite often and gives me *The Oban Times* every mail after he reads them. I search and search and search the columns of that paper but can only very seldom find a name I am familiar with. In one of the second last papers I found an obituary notice of the death of Colin Fletcher. You will remember Johnny Fletcher who worked for Dugald McCalman at Salen. Colin was his younger brother. His father was Sandy Fletcher of Glenaros. I have written a tribute to Colin's memory as he and I used to be at School together and travel home the same way when we lived at Arlo. Colin used to be a nice boy.

There must be many changes in Mull. Very little Gaelic spoken there now. The highlanders are doing a great deal to try to perpetuate the Gaelic language, but am afraid it is doomed. It is surprising to me the wonderful scholarships in the Island of Mull. Lots of boys and girls qualify for B.A. at the age of sixteen. Most certainly they are keen students.

Then the physical features of the island of Mull are so changed that one would hardly know it. So much of the hill country and valleys have been planted for Deer Forests. I do not believe that the high road can be seen any more from Killichronan farm house.

All those hill sides are planted and grown up now. Then they have all kinds of automobile roads everywhere on the island. Salen, Tobermory, Dervaig, Benson and many other villages have grown and are right up to the mark. More especially is this the case with Tobermory and it is now a far famed summer resort. All round that main Street between the sea side and the street has been planted and boulevarded. Two or three churches in Salen and two doctors, and all kinds of stores. Say, wouldn't it be nice to walk over the road through the black rocks again?

The highlands of Scotland have a type of beauty all their own and is the greatest in the world. Just sit down for a minute when you read this and think of Loch-na-keal stretching away out and Ben More, and Eorsa and then again looking across the sound to Morvern from Arla. Where in this world can you find beauty that is as great as this?

Of course you would hear of our brother Robert's death. I wonder if Fanny is still alive? I will try to send you a snap of Bostock Hall sent to me by Will Adam's daughter, Mrs. Carter. Bostock Green is now a wonderful place and has been greatly beautified by the Captain (Hayhurst) Electric light in all the cottages, etc., etc. The old Reading Room turned into a billiard and club room and liquor sold, etc., Sam Stringer being the big push at the Club Room. Will Adams has been retired for many years and lives at Rose Bank. His first wife, Kate Raynor, died some years ago and although they did not tell me, I have heard that he married again.

We have a returned man working here this winter for his board. He is a great worker, but very hard to get on with. I never say a word, but can hear him and Annie chewing the rag all the time in the kitchen. He contradicts every word you say. However, the poor fellow is not getting any pay and so we must not be hard on him. Please give my kind regards to John and his family and also to Con. And with very kind regards and much love to yourself, and may God bless you and fill you with peace and joy is the prayer of your Affectionate Brother J O H N.

John Niddrie's colleague, Rev. Robert Bird Steinhauer, was the son of Rev. Henry Bird Steinhauer, the first native to be admitted to the ministry in Canada. John and Robert had worked together and met each other as missionaries over forty years previously, when Steinhauer worked at Morley,

1895–1903. By this time, Niddrie had lived in Canada for over fifty years and seen a great many changes since 1885, despite living in a remote settlement. He now received letters by air mail, and this letter, postmarked September 4, 1937 was mailed with a three-cent stamp bearing the image of a young King George VI, and was received at Steinhauer's post office on September 6. It travelled by boat to Selkirk, then on to Winnipeg, then by air to Edmonton, and presumably by road to Steinhauer's post office at Ashmont, Alberta, where it was stamped three or four days later. The letter made the trip likely faster than it would at the end of the twentieth century!

In this letter, Niddrie again mentions his niece, Annie, who joined him at Berens River ten years previously, then found herself working among the people there as John Niddrie did himself. It appears that clothing donations are still being received at Berens River from the Woman's Missionary Society (W.M.S.) as they were at Morley forty years earlier. Mention is also made in this letter of Harry Everett, born at Berens River in 1914. Everett himself wrote an account of Annie Niddrie and her work, which begins on page 131.

Robert Steinhauer is addressed as "D.D." in the letter that follows. He had received an honourary Doctor of Divinity degree from Victoria University in Toronto on April 27 of that year. He had graduated with a B.A. from the same institution fifty years earlier.

The United Church Mission
Berens River, Manitoba
August 30th, 1937

Rev. R.B. Steinhauer, B.A., D.D.
Saddle Lake, Alberta

Dear Doctor Steinhauer:

It surely afforded me great pleasure to receive your very kind letter of August twentieth; just to hand today. I hasten to reply, hoping to catch this southbound steamer going out tomorrow evening from here. I was indeed glad to hear that Mrs. Steinhauer, yourself and family were quite well at the time of writing, and trust this will find you all in continued good health and happiness.

I am thankful to say we are quite well, and everything is going along quietly about as usual. I am quite sure you would be kept busy in the east, and the people would enjoy your singing and speaking. They get so little of the real thing in Indian Mission Work. This I can find out from some of the good ladies of the W.M.S. to whom I have written acknowledging receipt of bales of clothing, etc. I wrote our mutual friend Rev. Mr. Ing of Calgary some little time ago in answer to one I had received from him; and I told him how much more tame the Indian work was at Morley than what it is down here. He used to think matters pretty hard in the old days at Morley. Here it is somewhat different.

I am always hearing good words about your deceased brother Egerton from the Fisher River people who come here quite frequently. Egerton did splendid work there, and he is never forgotten by the older people. Matters at that point at the present time are in a desperate condition I fear. However, we must not speak uncharitably of our contemporaries in the work. I try to read and write the Cree a little, but I cannot make much of Rev. Stevens paper, "The Spiritual Light." Perhaps it may be my density, but I cannot find the Indian idiom of the language in his writings. He was going to take one Fisher River man to pieces with an axe and saw (so to speak) when he remonstrated with him about his paper. Then he got out two little books he calls, "The Discipline." Rev. Beaton sent me two at the same time assuring me of what a splendid piece of work it was. I replied, thanking him, and informing him I had one of the old ones bound in morocco and sent me by Dr. Barner and I would continue using that one.

I also informed him I was very glad he was so pleased with what he denominated "a great work." It was only a short time after this that Rev. Mr. Stevens wrote me asking my assistance as Rev. Beaton had threatened at the next Council Meeting of the church, "TO PUT SOME CONTROL ON HIM" for something Stevens had written in "The Spiritual Light" about the Church of Rome. I do not know what Beaton would say if he saw some of the screeds I have written about the church of Rome. Just fancy a half-baked Potentate like Beaton saying, "We must not antagonize the R.C.'s. They are cooperating with us beautifully." He must be a mutt. There, forgive me please, but I have little sympathy with a man who would thus express himself. He knows nothing whatever about the Indian work and has not sense to listen to those who have forgotten more than he will ever know. You will think me uncharitable with Beaton. No, I am not. I could surprise you with some of his actions and speeches at the Indian Conventions at Norway House. However, enuf said.

It would be pleasant for you to meet old friends in Ontario. I am sure you would enjoy it. I am sorry to make such a mess of this letter. I have just put in a new roller in this machine and it seems so stiff that it sticks all the time and I rattle ahead and then have to go back to repair it. I sometimes get letters from Morley. I do not just know how the school is getting along, for I hear so many different tales.

I was supposed to retire last June 30TH, but at the very last the young man from the Maritimes who was to succeed me backed down, so I was asked to stay here indefinitely. It is most likely I shall be here the whole year, but am not yet sure.

Your family must be quite grown up and married as you state. We are very comfortable here. My niece is a splendid woman, and nearly every day out on the Reserve amongst the Indian women. She is much beloved, and a good doctor. I tease her sometimes and tell her she will have to stay at home more, and make pills with the scoop shovel. We have my adopted boy Harry, who put in 3 terms at Wesley, staying with us. He got married two years ago. I have been trying hard to get him into the work as a teacher for he has all kinds of ability, but he wants an outside life. He will be native scout for the Mountie here after October 1ST. $50 a month and a lot of clothing. He is an excellent interpreter. No one here can equal him as he has a proper and grammatical grasp of the English language. He was a great favourite at College, so Dr. Riddell assures me.

How is your brother Augustine? Is he still alive? I always liked that man, he was so genuine. It does one good to meet men of that stamp among the aboriginal people.

This is getting to be a very poor neighbourhood as the forests are all burned up by bush fires and all of the game that is not destroyed has been chased away. Then the fish seem to be becoming depleted at this end of the lake. Very few moose have been killed this summer. Indeed the outlook for this winter is the opposite to cheerful.

Of late, these people have been mortgaging their annuities. That is, they take up from the Department of Indian Affairs two-thirds of their treaty money for the next year. This is taken up in September and the Treaty payments are not made until the following June. I do not think it is a wise policy, but then "mum" has to be the word with me.

We have splendid congregations every Sunday when the people are not away at the commercial fishing. We have a commodious church which is always about filled in the afternoons on the Sabbath. I sometimes tell the people that they would make good "afternoon farmers" for they are like the old settler at Lacombe in the old days who said, "I don't like the smell of coal oil in the mornings."

I sometimes hear from the widow of the late J.A. McLachlan who used to be at this Mission and was drowned in Lake Winnipeg. He was much beloved here as Missionary. Our residential school at Norway House seems to be doing good work; also that at Brandon; but I am not just quite sure that the system is all right. If something were done by the I.D. for the graduating pupils when they leave the school, it would be all right. But ours here just go back to conditions on the Reserve, which are not at all conducive to advancement. It is too bad.

We have an air mail service here, but it is not always quite satisfactory. We have a weekly steamer which arrives on Tuesday evenings and departs south—after making the round of the lake—on Thursday. We have had a great tourist season this summer. Some of them get a stopover privilege for a week at this place at the Log Cabin Inn; but the prices are exorbitant. Our old mutual friend Mr. Butler used to be here ere he went to Morley; and I still hear some amusing anecdotes about him. He was dubbed, "The Fighting Parson."

Well, I must say good-bye for this time. May God very richly bless you and yours. With all kinds of love and kind wishes,

Very sincerely yours,
J.W.N.

The following letter was handwritten by Rev. Dr. Arthur Barner, some five years after his retirement as Superintendent of Indian Work. Barner had travelled with Niddrie during the summer months in northern Manitoba, and this letter showed that the two colleagues kept in contact.

4209 Prince Albert St.
Vancouver B.C.
6TH April 1940

Dear Brother Niddrie,

My correspondence has got a long way behind owing to some developments which have taken place since I received your letter in January. So you will excuse my seeming neglect. You are never neglected in my prayer time.

I was asked by one of the smaller city churches to supply their pulpit for a few weeks until they could secure another minister or make other arrangements so I undertook the work thinking it would be for a short time but it has stretched out till now and they wish me to stay with them until June. This has meant much extra work and during Lent and Easter especially I have been kept busy. I am enjoying the task very much but there are some things I cannot keep up.

You will be interested to know that we had Dr. Riddell in the city this week. He delivered his lecture on the Eldership on Wednesday night, and I enjoyed listening to him very much.

Some of the senior men are passing on—Dr. Ernest Thomas, Dr. T. Albert Moore, Mr. Bradshaw and others. I hope you are keeping well and able to be around, also that Annie is well.

You certainly had a big mail that day, 17 letters would involve time both in reading and answering.

Mr. Black has been quite ill since I wrote you last. He was in the hospital for some time, but is now at home. He kindly loaned me your story of the north to read and it brought back many precious memories. I have just been talking with Mr. Black over the phone. He says that he is improving slowly and he sends kind wishes to you.

I am glad you keep us all on your prayer list. That is a fine piece of work and it helps very much. You will be glad to know that there was another little girl born to Herbert and his wife in England on the 31ST January. They are all well. Maud brought her baby boy, then 8 months old, for a visit with us in January. He was very good and interesting. They were here for a month, then Daddy (Mr. Aufiels) came down for a week and they returned together. They live 200 miles north of here by steamer.

I am very much pleased to read about the recovery of Mr. Ing. How happy Harry and his wife will be to have another daughter. I am glad to know that Will is so useful at Island Lake. It is wonderful the amount of good a faithful layman can do. That is the emphasis Dr. Riddell is giving in his lectures.

Mrs. Barner has been busy this week in the Branch meeting of the W.M.S. and as she has a lady from Victoria staying with us it has meant a very busy week. She joins me in kind wishes to you and Annie.

Fraternally,
Arthur Barner

The following letter in reply to Arthur Barner was likely one of Niddrie's last, as it was written only three weeks before his death. At the top of the first page he had typed a note, "It is just 55 years ago today since we boarded the *S.S. Sarmation* at Liverpool, booked to Winnipeg."

This letter may never have been mailed, as only two pages remain, and at the bottom of the second page Niddrie typed, "I will add to this later." Whether mailed or not, the following extracts from that letter indicate that he kept up with the news of people he knew and took pleasure in the close relationship between Harry Everett's young daughter Sylvia, three years old at the time, and his own niece, Annie. This letter also shows a less formal side of Niddrie's character than what appeared in business letters to church or government officials.

The United Church Mission
Berens River, Manitoba
April 16th, 1940

Rev. A. Barner, D.D.
Vancouver, B.C.

Dear Doctor Barner:

This is to acknowledge with sincere thanks yours of April 6th, safely to hand yesterday. Was glad to hear you were all well at the time of writing; and trust this will find you still in the same state of good health and happiness. I was glad to get your letter for really I was afraid I had in some way given you offence; and even though involuntarily I do not wish to do this. You see how easy it is for a wicked old man like your correspondent to make mistakes. However, please remember that while it is human to err; it is divine to forgive.

    Well, Dr. B., here is the first item of news to you today. The Hudson's Bay Company are going to make Poplar River an independent Post and erect proper buildings; and the young man Allan Nelson (now at Oxford House) is coming down to take charge. He is to be married to Miss Jean McConnell who is the white school teacher here, on June twenty-five. I asked Annie when she came out here yesterday morning what Miss McConnell said about it. Her reply was laconic: "I believe she is tickled pink." I believe he is a very fine young fellow, and helped Mr. Scoates in the Sunday School and am quite sure she is a splendid woman and will — I feel sure — make a very "nifty" housekeeper. So that's that.

I have a little joke to tell you and may as well get it off here. I was sitting here on Election Day either reading or writing, when all at once I saw a dog train arrive and a man tying them up to the post near my door. Then Harry came in and said, "The Mountie sent me over to tell you that he would send you by dog train to Disbrowe's to vote. If you do not like that he will send a horse and sleigh for you. If that does not suit you, he will come with his Patrol Car and take you over."

My reply was, "Harry, please tell Mr. Calcraft I do not want to take a passage in a Police Car." Of course it was kind of Mr. Calcraft, and it is uniform with all his actions to Annie and myself.

We call Annie, "Aunt Ann," as Harry's little girl is so crazy about her, and when Annie comes always wants to come and stay with "Nan Nan." I never in my life saw a little girl like that. She talks perfect English and can say anything at all. Fancy her saying to Annie when she was coming away (running after her to the door) and saying, "I send kisses to Grandpa."

Harry has been stuffing them with Emulsion of Cod Liver Oil, and they surely are little fat chunks. I am sorry they lost the new baby. Ethel (Harry's wife) had to go out to St. Boniface Hospital and the poor baby must have caught cold in the plane. It had first chicken pox, then measles, then double pneumonia. I am sorry for them. You are acquainted I think with Ethel's father. He is old Charlie Mason of Fisher River. There is not one word of native language spoken in Harry's home—all English.

I get some very nice letters from Rev. Mr. Martin at Norway House. I think he is a very fine man and doing excellent work up there (or should I say "down there"). We are told the following fields will need Missionaries next year: Island Lake, God's Lake, Poplar River and perhaps Pekangecum. Mr. Schuetze says Oxford House too, but I rather think not as I have been in correspondence with Mr. Scoates and he said nothing to that effect. Am not really sure that Rushforth is leaving Pekangecum.

Mr. Calcraft, mentioned in the letter, was the Mountie. Harry Everett's young daughter to whom Niddrie referred is Sylvia, born 1937. Another daughter, Annie, was named after Annie Niddrie. Niddrie obviously enjoyed the close relationship between his niece and young Sylvia, and was flattered to be called "Grandpa." The third daughter, mentioned but not named, was Myrtle Augusta, who died in infancy and was named after Augusta Schuetze, wife of Rev. Luther Schuetze, who succeeded Niddrie at Berens River in 1938.

Twenty-five years after his "arduous trip through the wilds" to attend his ordination in Winnipeg, John W. Niddrie died in Berens River. In a publication of the *Sixteenth Annual Manitoba Conference of the United Church of Canada*, the following brief note appeared to summarize the life of a man who worked till he was 75 and died at 76, having spent half a century of service to the church and native people in his adopted country.

REV. J.W. NIDDRIE

The Rev. John W. Niddrie came to us from the Highlands of Scotland, and though the language of the Saultaux Indian became second nature to him, there were still traces of the accent of the Gaelic of his youth. He came to Canada as a young man of twenty, and after spending five years in Winnipeg, was invited by the Rev. John McDougall to become principal of the Indian Residential School at Morley, in Alberta, where he spent seven years. The rest of his life was spent among the Indians in the Lake Winnipeg area, seven years at Island Lake, six years at Oxford House and twenty at Berens River.

He abandoned all other interests to the call of this work and spent his life and his substance with and for his Indians.

Born September 24, 1863. Ordained 1915. Died May 4, 1940.

Rev. John W. Niddrie is buried among the people he served in a small cemetery at Berens River. His headstone is hidden in the overgrowth of the unattended graveyard. It was Rev. Luther Schuetze, who delivered the funeral address, and wrote, "The Indian people have lost a great friend. He had a heart as large as the vast prairie, upon which he loved to ride in his younger days. His spirit showed the handiwork of God even as he oft talked about beloved Foothills, Rocky Mountains with their emerald lakes and streams, rugged and true as the true as the crags of his native Scotland, pointing ever upward through storm, rain and mist to hallowed sky. That was his heart's desire, ever and always pointing his people to the upward way to man's heavenly home."

In June 2000, the small white church at Morley where John W. Niddrie began his service with the church in Canada, celebrated its 125TH Anniversary. Sixty years after the death of John W. Niddrie, the story of this frontier missionary had come full circle with the announcement at the service of the publication of his memoirs.

POSTSCRIPT

Until now, the memoirs of Rev. John W. Niddrie have remained unpublished, some sixty years after his death. They have, for the most part, remained boxed and unshared. Did Niddrie have a sense of his own place in history? Had he ever hoped that his written recollections would be read by others? Did he intend them for publication?

It is easy to believe that he did. Other writing of his as seen in his letters had appeared in print for a wider audience. In his own time he had seen dramatic industrial and social change. His own life spanned the last thirty-seven years of the nineteenth century and the first forty years of the twentieth. Surely he recognized that he had been a man of his times, a pioneer in his work. By tapping out his own manuscript on a manual typewriter at a remote mission post, he has provided for those who follow a written account of life at an adventurous period of time in a young and changing land.

Dorothy Chalmers

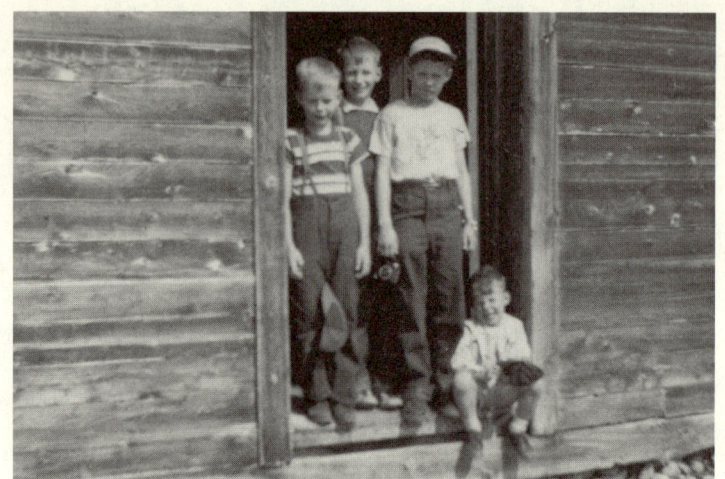

Co-editor John J. Chalmers, at right wearing cap, has had a lifelong interest in the history of the Morley church and area, and the part in it of his great-great-uncle, John W. Niddrie. Chalmers is shown here in the doorway of the church, before its restoration, at age thirteen with his three brothers in 1951.

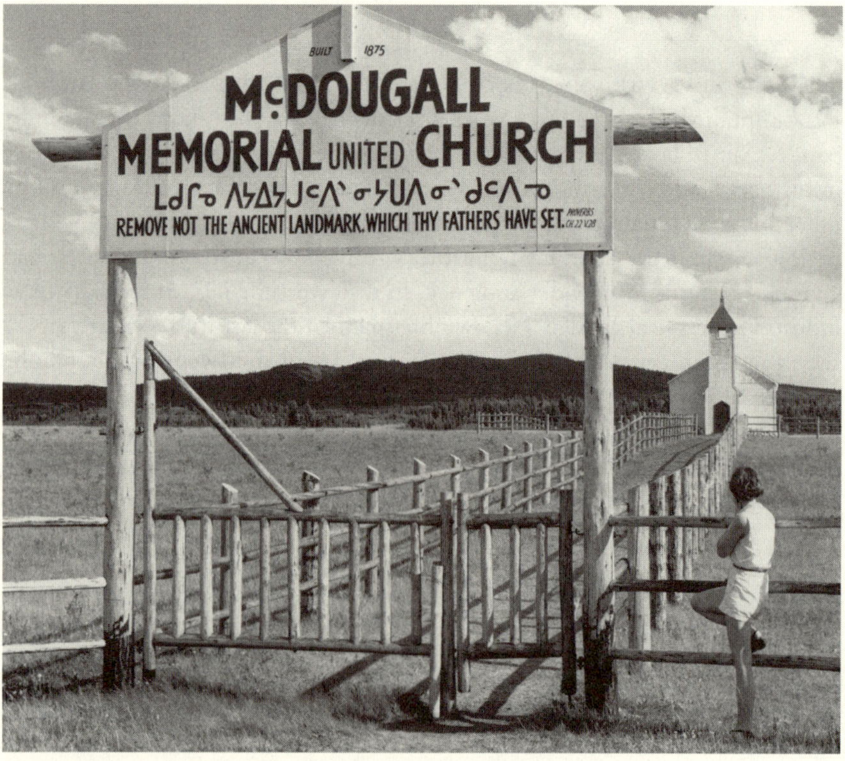

Alberta Government

McDougall Memorial United Church at Morley; view from road.

NOTES

CHAPTER 1 KIRK TO CHAPEL, 1863–1885
Very vivid are the memories (pg 3) "Old Kirk" refers to the Presbyterian Church.
The warning of the prophet Amos (pg 3) "Woe unto them that are at ease in Zion" refers to Amos 6:1.
Here we remained a few days (pg 7) The Allan Line was a Canadian-based shipping line.
One notable feature (pg 8) An exhorter was an itinerant lay preacher.

CHAPTER 2 IMMIGRANT, 1885
Three days out, our ship began (pg 16) "Of all men most miserable" refers to Corinthians 15:19.
Having succeeded in this (pg 16) The Intercolonial Railway was an early Canadian railway line serving points in the Maritimes and Quebec. It became part of the Canadian National Railway in 1919.
Winnipeg in 1885 was quite insignificant (pg 17) Present-day proportions at the time of writing, ca. 1938–40.
He met with his just deserts (pg 18) Riel was hanged in Regina following the Northwest Rebellion.
The Rebellion was now almost over (pg 19) Niddrie had apparently forgotten that the Rebellion was indeed over.
It must be remembered that a hundred years ago (pg 20) That is, from the time of writing, therefore ca. 1840.

215

Right at this point and on the left of the railroad track (pg 22) Sir James Hector explored the Kicking Horse Pass in 1858.

Passing Field and Ottertail Bridge (pg 22) Golden City is now known as Golden, British Columbia.

Humping our swags (pg 25) The term "swags" refer to baggage and tote bags.

Visiting this metropolitan western city today (pg 28) Again, at the time of writing, ca. 1938–40.

CHAPTER 3 MORLEY, 1889–1910

This was the heritage (pg 31) This phrasing provides a vivid example of romantic nineteenth-century attitudes towards nature.

These were the conditions prevailing (pg 31) At the time of writing, ca. 1938–40. Alberta was not established as a province until 1905.

Prior to this, only roving bands (pp. 34–35) "Some passing missionary" might have been Thomas Woolsey or George McDougall.

For seven years more (pg 36) The McDougall Institute was a vocational school for Indians in Morley.

CHAPTER 4 DELAYED VACATION, 1894

Annuity payments to the Indians (pg 39) According to the treaties, Indians were supposed to receive annual payments, usually five dollars per Indian per treaty.

Many times when travelling in the west in the early days (pg 40) What Niddrie calls a buffalo is more correctly, but seldom, called a bison.

Galloping along for two or three miles (pg 43) A stake-and-rider fence was made with posts driven into the ground, whereas a snake fence used no posts.

However, after our arrival in camp (pg 44) Mr. C. refers to Lucius Coleman, a very good neighbour and friend who was held in high regard by the Niddrie family.

CHAPTER 5 NATURE INTERLUDE, 1896

Fifty or sixty years ago (pg 49) That is, from the time of writing, thus ca. 1880–90.

Many men of honest enterprise (pg 50) Agricultural district refers to dirt or grain farming; Niddrie means that the area was better suited to ranching or forestry.

CHAPTER 6 MEN OF MORLEY, 1890–1910

Most of this chapter was first published as part of an article entitled "Memories of Morley" in *Alberta History* (Summer 1992).

The old chief passed away (pg 59) Chief Chiniquay probably died in 1906, at about the age of seventy-two, as he was born ca. 1834.

After the Riel, or North-West, Rebellion (pg 60) The Rebellion ended in 1885.

CHAPTER 7 OXFORD HOUSE, 1910–1915

I must not omit the fact that two of my nieces (pg 71) The nieces who accompanied him were Cora and Martha deWinter, daughters of Niddrie's sister, Maria.

No doubt many of them were anxious (pg 75) The term "Praying Chief" refers to a Protestant clergyman.

I have today many happy memories (pg 80) That is, at the time of writing, about 1937–39.

The changing times, coupled with many fatal maladies (pg 81) Spanish flu refers to a serious strain of influenza, called "Spanish" because it was first emerged as a serious problem in Spain; its effects were later felt in the rest of the world, especially in 1918.

Chapter 8 Island Lake, 1915–1920

It was a dull gray February morning (pg 83) "My Indian boy Willie" is Willie Hart, also mentioned in a newspaper account of Niddrie's trip to Winnipeg for his ordination (see pg. 183) and in Niddrie's letter to his sister, Maria (see pg. 202).

Through the woods, across the back lake (pp. 83–84) John Niddrie's use of "Marse!" was apparently widely used. Some drivers used "Marche!", and today we may hear "Mush!".

Our stay at this point was short (pg 85) The phrase "the king's business required haste" refers to I Samuel 21:8.

Chapter 9 Berens River, 1920–1938

Timothy Bear, a native leader from Norway House (pg 93) E.R. Young is Egerton Ryerson Young.

Then there was our bowsman (pg 94) William Everett was an uncle of Harry Everett, whose memoir of Annie Niddrie appears in Chapter 10.

It was quite dark by the time (pg 95) A mosquito bar is a tent-like cover with mosquito-netting walls and a canvas roof (to keep out the rain), used for protection from biting insects.

Nearly thirty years ago (pg 96) i.e., ca. 1917–19, thirty years prior to the time of writing.

Chapter 10 Annie Niddrie: The Caregiver, 1927–1938

It was right beside the little Methodist church (pg 116) McDougall Church, built in downtown Edmonton, stood at its original location until 1978, when it was moved to Fort Edmonton Park.

He and two of the Indian boys (pg 122) A "cariole" was a toboggan sled pulled by dogs or horses; see photos on pg 68 and pg 123.

The prayer of a righteous man availeth much (pg 129) Here Annie quotes James 5:16.

After my wife died (pg 134) Harry Everett was married to his first wife, Ethel, in 1936. She died in 1944. He married his second wife, Jean (mentioned on pg 137), in 1956. He was left a widower again with Jean's death in June 2000.

There were a lot of babies (pg 136) Harry Everett's second daughter, Annie, was named after Annie Niddrie.

CHAPTER 11 THE LETTERS OF JOHN W. NIDDRIE

The Niddrie correspondence from "The Alberta Years" in this chapter was found in the McDougall Orphanage letterbooks, 1896–1908 (location M1380) at the Glenbow Archives, Calgary. The letter to R.B. Steinhauer, starting on pg 186, was also located at the Glenbow Archives.

ABOUT THE EDITORS

John W. Chalmers and John J. Chalmers, the editors of this publication, are father and son educators and writers.

John W. (Jack) Chalmers, born in Winnipeg in 1910, moved to Alberta in 1931 and spent the rest of his life there. He married Dorothy Niddrie following her graduation from the University of Alberta, then assisted her in raising six children. He worked as a teacher, school principal, school superintendent, high-school inspector, and administrator with Alberta's Department of Education. He retired as a professor at the University of Alberta in 1975. He then taught for another twelve years as professor at Concordia College in Edmonton, from which he retired at age 77. Following his retirement from the University and while teaching at Concordia, he embarked on a graduate program himself, collecting another master's degree from the University of Alberta in 1990 as both the oldest student and oldest graduate at that institution that year. It was his fifth degree, the previous one being a Doctor of Education degree from Stanford

John W. Chalmers   *John J. Chalmers*

University in 1946, following service with the RCAF as a navigation instructor in Edmonton during World War Two. Jack Chalmers had a distinguished career as an educator and writer. He is the author and editor of several books, including history, fiction, biographies, and anthologies of literature used for many years in Alberta schools in junior and senior high school. He wrote many articles, often on historical subjects, and prior to his death in 1998, he donated his personal collection of books to the University of Alberta.

John J. Chalmers was born in Edmonton in 1939. He has worked as a teacher and administrator with educational organizations and has been self-employed as an education consultant. He has B.Ed. and M.Ed. degrees from the University of Alberta. Widely published as a writer of articles and as a photographer, he began work on this book when failing health left his father unable to complete the project. John's little-used fourth name, Niddric, took on a new importance while working on the memoirs and letters of his great-great uncle. John lives in Edmonton with his wife, Linda, also a University of Alberta graduate, in the city which is home to their two daughters, who are the fourth generation in their family to graduate from the University. John's grandfather, John G. Niddrie, mentioned in the book, attended the University of Alberta in 1908, its first year of operation.